READING JEREMIAH

Smyth & Helwys Publishing, Inc.
6316 Peake Road
Macon, Georgia 31210-3960
1-800-747-3016
© 2016 by Corrine Carvalho
All rights reserved.

Library of Congress Cataloging-in-Publication Data

Names: Carvalho, Connie, author.
Title: Reading the Old Testament : Jeremiah / by Connie Carvalho.
Description: Macon : Smyth & Helwys, 2016. | Includes bibliographical
  references.
Identifiers: LCCN 2016044480 | ISBN 9781573129244 (pbk. : alk. paper)
Subjects: LCSH: Bible. Jeremiah--Commentaries.
Classification: LCC BS1525.53 .C37 2016 | DDC 224/.207--dc23
LC record available at https://lccn.loc.gov/2016044480

Disclaimer of Liability: With respect to statements of opinion or fact available in this work of nonfiction, Smyth & Helwys Publishing Inc. nor any of its employees, makes any warranty, express or implied, or assumes any legal liability or responsibility for the accuracy or completeness of any information disclosed, or represents that its use would not infringe privately-owned rights.

Reading Jeremiah
A Literary and Theological Commentary

Corrine Carvalho

Also by Corrine Carvalho

The Book of Ezekiel: Question by Question

Primer on Biblical Methods

Encountering Ancient Voices

Ezekiel, Daniel
(The New Collegeville Bible Commentary, with Paul V. Niskanen)

*To my husband, Keith Yingling,
for all of his love and support*

Contents

Introduction 1
   The Setting of the Book of Jeremiah 1
   The History, Genre, and Structure of the Text 3
      The Book of Jeremiah as a Literary Artifact 9

Jeremiah's Prologue (Jeremiah 1:1-19) 17
   Superscription (1:1-3) 17
   The Odd Call of Jeremiah (1:4-19) 18

Prophetic Oracles of Doom (Jeremiah 2–10) 21
   Israel's Sins (2:1–4:4) 21
   Oracles of Impending Siege (4:5–6:30) 27
      Jeremiah 4 30
      Jeremiah 5 34
      Jeremiah 6 36
   The Prophet at the Temple (7:1–8:3) 39
   Oracles of the Siege (8:4–10:25) 41

The Lamenting Prophet (Jeremiah 11–20) 47
      Opposition from Jeremiah's Circle (11:1–12:6) 49
      Oracles about Judah's Fate (12:7–13:27) 51
      Terror and Silence (14:1–15:9) 55
      Jeremiah's Voice Returns (15:10-21) 56
      Jeremiah Ostracized (16:1-13) 58
      A Collection (16:14–17:27) 59
      God, the Hairy (i.e., Virile) Potter (18:1–19:15) 61
      The Prophet's Final, Futile Protest (20:1-18) 63

Oracles against Judah's Leaders (Jeremiah 21–25) 67
    An Ironic Condemnation of Zedekiah (21:1-10) 68
    A Throne for Executing Justice (21:11–22:9) 69
    The Evil Kings of Judah's Final Years (22:11-30) 70
    Woe to the Shepherds; Hooray for the Branches (23:1-8) 71
    Condemnation of the Prophets (23:9-40) 72
    The Parable of the Figs (24:1-10) 74
    Part I Comes to a Close (25:1-14) 76
    Drunken Nations (25:15-33) 78
    Finale for the Shepherds (25:34-38) 80

The Prophet and the King (Jeremiah 26–29) 81
    An Execution Averted (26:1-24) 82
    Serve Nebuchadnezzar Like a Dumb Ox (27:1-15) 86
    Temple Treasures (27:16-22) 87
    Portrait of a False Prophet (28:1-17) 89
    An Incendiary Letter (29:1-32) 90

Consolation and Restoration (Jeremiah 30–33) 93
    Comfort, Healing, and Restoration (30:1-24) 96
    A Festive Pilgrimage (31:1-14) 98
    A Mother Comforted (31:15-20) 99
    A Compendium of Images of Restoration (31:21-30) 101
    God's New Covenant (31:31-40) 103
    The Symbol of Ancestral Land (32:1-44) 104
    Contours of a Restored Nation (33:1-26) 110

Tales of the Prophet (Jeremiah 34–45) 115
    Free the Slaves (34:1-22) 117
    Models of Obedience (35:1-19) 119
    The Authority of the Written Word (36:1-32) 120
    Jeremiah and Zedekiah (37:1-21) 122
    An Unexpected Ally (38:1-13) 124
    A Secret Meeting with the King (38:14-28) 125
    The Fall of the City of Jerusalem (39:1-18) 126
    The Fate of Gedaliah (40:1–41:18) 127
    Jeremiah Taken to Egypt (42:1–43:7) 128
    Oracles against the Refugees in Egypt (43:8–44:30) 130
    Jeremiah's Scroll Comes to a Close (45:1-5) 132

Contents

Oracles against Foreign Nations (Jeremiah 46–51) 135
    Egypt's Ambiguous Fate (46:1-28) 137
    Oracle against Philistia (47:1-7) 139
    A Long-winded Diatribe against Moab (48:1-47) 140
    Devastation Far and Wide (49:1-39) 142
    Revenge Would Be Sweet (50:1-46) 143
    Pile It On (51:1-58) 145
    Jeremiah's Remote Symbolic Act (51:59-64) 147

A Historical Epilogue (Jeremiah 52) 149

Works Cited 151

Introduction

In the book of Jeremiah, the palace is where books are burned, and the temple is a jail. Reflecting the ways that communal tragedy permeates communal identity, the book of Jeremiah as literary text embodies the confusion, disorientation, and search for meaning that all such tragedy elicits. Just as the fall of Jerusalem fractured the Judean community and undercut every foundation on which it built its identity, so too the book itself (or more properly, the scroll) jumbles images, genres, and perspectives. These images are harsher than is apparent from the book's use in the lectionary.

This study of the book of Jeremiah will engage the text as a collection of literature. To be sure, some of this literature has roots in oral performance, but the fact remains that it comes down to us as a written text. It is a complex collection, however, with little inherent cohesion. In fact, it has been preserved in two different arrangements, one found in the Hebrew version and the other in the Greek. It presumes that the audience hears this material against a particular historical backdrop. This book will flesh out Jeremiah's historical horizon, but it will do so in order to clarify the literature rather than as an end in itself.

The Setting of the Book of Jeremiah

The book of Jeremiah is set in a particular historical period that is presumably familiar to the audience. The historical setting of the material functions as an essential element of the narrative. The events to which the book alludes were moments of national catastrophe for which the book's ideal audience needed no explanation. Clearly the book was written for the survivors and descendants of this collective trauma. For modern readers, however, a brief overview of that history can be helpful.

The book places the commencement of Jeremiah's role as a prophet during the reign of Josiah (634–609 BCE; see 2 Kgs 22:1–23:30; 2 Chr 34–35 for the biblical accounts of his life). Scholars debate whether this period refers to the date of Jeremiah's birth or to the beginning of his active work as a prophet. Since chapter 1 states that Jeremiah is born as a prophet, I would opt for this period as the date of his birth. Josiah reigned at a time when Assyria's power had waned, but Babylonian expansion was commencing. Before the rise of Babylon's imminent threat, Josiah had implemented a sweeping religious reform. The authors of the books of Kings, referred to collectively as the Deuteronomistic Historian, portray this reform as the high point of Judah's history. Many elements of this reform, depicted as the "correct" religious view in the book of Jeremiah, include a narrow definition of what constitutes correct worship practices, a focus on ethical behavior, and the conditional nature of God's covenant with Israel.

LAST KINGS OF JUDAH

Regnal Name	Other name	Years of Reign
Josiah		639–609
Jehoahaz	Shallum	609–608
Jehoiakim	Eliakim	608–598
Jehoiakin	Coniah	597
Zedekiah	Mattaniah	597–587

Josiah died in battle when he allied with the Babylonians against the Egyptians. Ruling a small country situated between two superpowers that were both seeking to build an empire, the leaders of Judah had little hope of remaining fully independent. The only way they could maintain a native king and some autonomy was by becoming a vassal of one of the empires. Josiah chose Babylon. When he died, his son Shallum, who took the throne name of Jehoahaz, reigned for a short three months, only to be removed from the throne and taken to Egypt as an exile (2 Kgs 23:31-33; 2 Chr 36:1-4). The Egyptians put Eliakim (throne name Jehoiakim), another of Josiah's sons, on the throne. His reign lasted longer (608–598; 2 Kgs 23:34–24:7 and 2 Chr 36:5-8) but was no more stable. Although Judah remained a vassal of Egypt for eight years, it became a vassal of Babylon around the year 600. Jehoiakim rebelled against Babylon, however, leading to an attack on Jerusalem (2 Kgs 24:2) and his subsequent exile (2 Chr 36:6). Many of the early oracles in the book of Jeremiah contain warnings about the nation's precarious position on the world stage. Like 2 Kings 24:3, which says that Jehoiakim's death was a punishment from Yahweh for his sins, Jeremiah also casts threats by foreign armies as God's form of punishment for sinful behavior.

Jehoiakim's son, Coniah (throne name Jehoiakin) subsequently took the throne, again for only a short time. After only three months the Babylonians besieged the city of Jerusalem (597; 2 Kgs 24:8-17; 2 Chr 36:9-10). The city did not fall during this siege. Instead, the Babylonians took into captivity the elite members of Jerusalemite society, including the royal family, the priests who controlled the Jerusalem temple, and other high-ranking bureaucrats. They did not kill Jehoiakin, but kept him alive, probably hoping that this would deter those remaining in Judah from rebelling. They placed on the throne Mattaniah, another son of Josiah and thus an uncle of Jehoiakin (597–587; 2 Kgs 24:18–25:21; 2 Chr 36:11-21), and Mattaniah changed his name to Zedekiah. Most biblical texts, including Jeremiah, refer to him as a king (e.g., 2 Kgs 24:18 introduces him as a king), but Jehoiakin is also still called the king, even though he is in exile in Babylon (Seitz 1989a, 121–63).

Although the Babylonians placed Zedekiah on the throne, in the ninth year of his reign he rebelled, presumably expecting Egyptian support. Once again the Babylonians besieged the city, only this time, after eighteen long months, they breached the walls and sacked the city (Faust 2012). Descriptions of the horrors suffered during the siege and battles fill the oracles in Jeremiah that refer to the fall of the city. Some of these oracles focus on the military threat (the stomping horses and sharp swords), others on the famine and disease that wracked the city prior to its fall, and still others on the comprehensive devastation. The harsh language of Jeremiah's oracles serves as testament to these tragic events.

After the city fell, the Babylonians exiled most of the surviving elite. The archaeological record shows that they were settled in Babylon, probably as forced labor to maintain the Babylonian infrastructure while the native workforce was off at war (Pearce 2011). Not all the people living in and around Jerusalem were killed or exiled, however. Those who posed no threat to Babylonian rule, whom the book designates the "poor of the land," were allowed to remain (Lipschits 2003). Some of these went to other parts of Judah left relatively unscathed by the Babylonian advance. The Babylonians themselves set up a local government at Mizpah (2 Kgs 25:22-26), north of Jerusalem. Others fled to Egypt, living out their lives as refugees. The book of Jeremiah contains a few oracles set against this backdrop of the post-fall world of Judah.

The History, Genre, and Structure of the Text

The historical setting of the narrative is not identical to the historical context for the text's production (Fretheim 2002, 4–11, 22–29). The book of Jeremiah as it has been handed down is the result of a long, complex compositional history. Even a cursory reading of the book reveals significant variations in styles, genres, and speakers. The early chapters resemble the prophetic collections of preexilic prophets, but material towards the end of the book consists of prose descriptions of episodes in the life of Jeremiah. Scattered throughout is material stylistically and theologically similar to the material in Deuteronomy and Kings; in fact, the last chapter in the books of Kings is repeated in Jeremiah 52. In the ancient world, at least two distinct versions of the book circulated: one preserved in Hebrew and the other in Greek. These versions have much of the same material (although the Greek version is shorter) but are arranged differently. This is further evidence that the final form of the book is the result of an early text supplemented at a later time by additional material.

Scholars debate the specific dates of these various layers of material. One classic division, advanced by Mowinckel (1914) and building on Duhm (1901), identifies three layers of material: an early layer that contains the oracles of the historical Jeremiah in poetic form, a later Baruch layer (named after Jeremiah's disciple whom Jeremiah told to make a copy of his oracles in Jer 36:4) containing the prose biographical material, and a Deuteronomistic layer evidenced in the characteristic language and diction found in other Deuteronomistic literature at key points in the book (Curtis and Römer 1997). While contemporary scholars no longer have confidence in identifying the authors or dates of each of these sections with such certainty, the consensus remains that the book is the result of at least three different hands. Seitz, for example, who accepts the historical reliability of the first layer, views the book as a site of theological conflict, with new editions representing the community of exiles and, later, the scribal community (1989a). McKane, on the other hand, asserts that the book is far more chaotic than Duhm's schema and uses the model of a "rolling corpus" (1986), while Carroll is skeptical about scholars' ability to reconstruct the date of any early layer of the text (1986).

No matter the origin of individual units within the book, the result is a text with interesting and sometimes jarring juxtapositions of material. Recently, various attempts have been made to read the final text as a meaningful conglomerate. These literary models are not historically naive; they accept the multi-layered nature of the text, but they do not get so bogged down in tracing the history of those layers that they miss the meaning of the final text as a result. Biddle, for example, demonstrates how the layering of material in chapters 2–4, as well as 7–20, reshapes the focus of earlier material; often these later layers create better connections between earlier oracular material and later sermonic and prose sections of the book (1990, 1996; see also Wilson 1999).

Often the identification of various layers depends on a change in genre within the text. Books like Hosea, Amos, and Micah consist primarily of oracular speeches with little discussion of the setting of the speech and little role for a narrator. What is known about those prophets comes primarily from their own speeches. In addition, the arrangement of oracles in those books shows few attempts at organization. They are not necessarily arranged chronologically, nor do they present any implicit narrative. Sometimes similar types of oracles are grouped together (like the visions in Amos 7:1–8:3), but other than that, the structuring devices used by the scribes who produced these books remain subtle at best.

Two further uncertainties adhere to preexilic prophetic collections. First, it is difficult at times to determine the precise boundaries of a single oracle. When oracles were originally performed (and I use this word deliberately; see below), they often began with stock phrases, such as "Thus says the Lord," "Woe" (Hebrew *hoy*), or "Hear this word." When those phrases appear in a prophetic collection, they either indicate the beginning of an oracle or introduce a new section within an oracle. Some oracles are rhetorically stamped as an oracle, with a phrase that the NRSV translates "says the LORD" but is better translated as something like "an oracle of the LORD." Although it would be useful to presume that every time this phrase appears, a particular oracle is finished, that is not always the case. Often the oracle continues or is elaborated in the following verses.

Scholars can reconstruct some of the social settings within which oracles were delivered from clues within the biblical texts. Often prophets speak in or near temples. Amos 7 places Amos in the temple at Bethel. Jeremiah 26 locates Jeremiah in the court of Jerusalem's temple. The visions of both Isaiah and Ezekiel occur inside the sanctuary building of Jerusalem's temple. Other texts place prophets on the street (Isa 20:2), in centers of commerce (Jer 32:11-12), or in some location that allowed them to be consulted (Ezek 20:1). The oracles themselves often included singing (see, for instance, Isa 5:1; Ezek 33:32), symbolic performances of prophetic messages (Jer 27:2; Ezek 4:1-8), frenzied or altered states (1 Sam 10:9-13), or other public acts (see Jeremiah's purchase of ancestral land in chapter 32). Prophets publicly performed their oracles.

Reconstructing the original setting for preexilic oracles is a different task, however, than trying to recover the impetus for their collection within scrolls, something not found within the near eastern culture that surrounded ancient Israel. Why did Jewish scribes start writing these oracles down? Were the words of these prophets proclaimed at regular intervals? Were they consulted by later scholars? We know that sometimes prophets wrote things down as part of their prophetic performance. Writing had a prophetic quality: it made things real. Were the scribes keeping the oracles alive, then, by writing them down (Schaper 2005)? There is nothing in the ancient records that answers these questions. We do know that by the time of Jesus, Jewish scholars knew these texts, which were proclaimed in synagogues (see Jesus' reading of Isaiah in Luke 4:16-21), and scholars debated their meaning, as is exemplified in some of the Dead Sea Scrolls. What we do not know is why they were written down in the first place.

One conjecture is that the first wave of textualization came during the exile when the setting for this public performance irrevocably changed. Fear that oracles of preexilic prophets like Amos might be lost led to scribal activity aimed at preserving these and other traditions. Another model places the scribal activity in the Persian period, after the exile, among the scribal groups resettled in what was then called Yehud (Judah). Ben Zvi, for example, identifies the scribes as *literati* who create texts that become sites for collective memory (2003, 2009a) and can be reread (2009b). Wilson, who provides a helpful summary of previous research, notes that the number of scribes at any given time would have been small (2012b). The fact remains that the organization of the collections of preexilic prophets gives no clues as to their ongoing use or purpose.

The literary organization of the other two Major Prophets in the Hebrew Bible, Isaiah and Ezekiel, is clearer than that of Jeremiah. The material in Isaiah can be divided into three major blocks of material: chapters 1–39, where oracles stemming from the historical Isaiah can be found; 40–55, which contain poems related to the return of the exiles from Babylon; and 56–66, which focus on issues stemming from the rebuilding of the temple. To be sure, chapters 1–39 are the messiest part of the book. The core of the oracles shows the same haphazard arrangement as other preexilic prophets. Later editors added significant material as well, including a historical narrative adapted from 2 Kings, but they maintain at least a general chronological sweep to the book. The book of Ezekiel has a number of rhetorical features that suggest a conscious literary arrangement of the book as a whole. While it certainly contains oracles that presume some type of public performance, these are arranged within an overarching schema of earned judgment and undeserved restoration.

The book of Jeremiah has none of these rhetorical features. There seems to be some organization around literary type (in general the book moves from first- and second-person poetry to third-person prose), but attempts to delineate an outline for the book have failed. The only general consensus is that chapters 1–25 appear to contain an earlier, shorter form of the book, to which editors added the oracles against foreign nations and the prose narratives about Jeremiah's life. Even within this schema, however, the material shifts. There may have been early attempts to record oracles ascribed to a historical Jeremiah (the book suggests this began during his lifetime). The material in chapters 1–10 looks the most like other preexilic prophetic collections. The compiler rarely focuses on the character of the prophet and only rarely attempts to place the oracles within a specific historical or narrative context. This section consists primarily of prophetic poetry. In chapters 11–20, in distinction, the prophet takes center stage, complaining to God about his fate and performing prophetic acts (Friebel 1999, 11–78). Chapters 21–25 have more prose material condemning Judah's kings. A heavier-handed narrator than is found in Isaiah or Ezekiel provided the social context for some of these oracles. Later scribes added to some of the oracles, perhaps to make more explicit how Jeremiah related to later ideologies (Job 2006). Jeremiah 25:13 refers to the fulfillment of all of Jeremiah's oracles, suggesting an original conclusion to the book.

The book does not end at chapter 25, however, but continues into chapters 26–52. It is at this point that the greatest divergences between the Greek and Hebrew versions can be found. There had to exist some kind of Jeremiah traditions, stories about his life, which made their way into the second half of the book, especially chapters 24–29 and 32–45 (Person 1999). Scribes have spliced these prophetic tales, usually found outside of prophetic collections, directly into this collection. The growing corpus developed into two distinct final forms, one found in the Masoretic version of the Hebrew text (the basis for most Protestant and modern Catholic translations of the book) and the other in the Septuagint or ancient Greek tradition (sometimes used as the basis for the translation in older Catholic and some Orthodox Bibles; Smelik 2004). Most scholars view the Greek version, which is about one-seventh shorter and follows a classic prophetic arrangement by placing oracles against foreign nations before oracles promising Judah's restoration (Fretheim 2002, 25–26), as representing the earlier tradition (Jansen; Tov 1981). The Hebrew texts of Jeremiah among the Dead Sea Scrolls, however, have both text types. Clearly, then, the question of which version was the "correct" one was not a concern for the ancient communities that preserved the book. Hill points out that the Hebrew version differs from the Greek version by placing greater stress on the fate of Babylon, the elevation of Jeremiah, and the promise of restoration of both monarchy and temple (2007). I will use the Hebrew version of the text since it is the one that serves as the basis of most modern English translations.

Throughout the book of Jeremiah there is evidence of Deuteronomistic influence (Stulman 2005; Sharp 2003; Römer 2009; Stipp 2010a). For example, stock phrases found in Deuteronomy and the Deuteronomistic (Dtr) History appear at key places, such as Jeremiah 7 and 26. The book of Jeremiah depicts God's covenant with Israel as conditional, dependent on their moral behavior, and tends to depict their paradigmatic sin as idolatry. Scholars debate the nature and source of this influence, however. Some conjecture that Jeremiah himself was part of the Deuteronomistic school (see the review of older scholarship in Childs 1979, 342–45); Friedman goes so far as to suggest that whoever wrote the Deuteronomistic History also wrote the book of Jeremiah (1987, esp. 125–27 and 146–49). I find this conclusion unconvincing, especially since the material that appears to be earliest has the fewest Deuteronomistic reflexes. Others suggest that the Deuteronomists were especially fond of Jeremiah, so they not only preserved his collection but also added to it to make the connections between his work and their ideology even clearer (Thiel 1981). While this would explain the scattering of Dtr language throughout every part of the book, it does not explain why they simply would not have written their own version of the book or made a stronger connection between Jeremiah and Josiah. The most we can say with any confidence is that some additions to the book use language that resonates with Deuteronomistic ideology, perhaps reflecting a scribe or scribal tradition that revered both collections of material. This would explain the use of 2 Kings 24–25 to conclude the book of Jeremiah.

Some scholars also assert that the compiler depicts Jeremiah as a prophet like Moses because of his reluctance to accept God's call, an interpretation that goes back to the rabbinic tradition (Murphy 2014, 729). Römer also notes that the birth narratives of both prophets contain royal elements (2009), while Seitz sees Mosaic parallels throughout the book (Seitz 1989b). There is only one explicit mention of Moses in the book, however, and no reference to Sinai or Horeb. Although there are eleven statements about God bringing Israel out of Egypt (including one reference to the covenant), none of them mention Moses, prophets, or any human leader. The similarities between Jeremiah and Moses may simply reflect a similar view of legitimate prophetic activity shared by the Deuteronomist and the Dtr-like redactor of the final form of Jeremiah (Fretheim 2002, 14–15; Sharp 2003, 147–55).

In both versions of the book, Jeremiah becomes a full character in the second half of the collection, chastising kings, buying property, hiring a scribe, being confined in cells and pits, and eventually being dragged off to Egypt in the sweep of the nameless and faceless refugees that follow social collapse. He exits as he has lived, kicking and screaming. But in these last chapters, his most vitriolic words are reserved for the nations that surrounded Judah, especially its destroyer, Babylon. This second half of the book ends with a historical appendix: the description of the fall of Jerusalem lifted from the end of the books of Kings, as if to remind the audience one final time that the book is a witness to national tragedy and cannot be understood apart from this communal trauma.

The Book of Jeremiah as a Literary Artifact

Although the book of Jeremiah does not cohere as a literary unit according to modern expectations of literary art, the book as a collective whole continues to move audiences with its powerful artistic episodes. In scene after scene, the words and actions pulse with rhetorical force. This interactive layering of voices leads to a text that is more polyphony than monologue (Biddle 1996). The result is a collage or patchwork quilt rather than an epic painting, but it is a collage that invites the audience to linger over each discrete unit.

While the book itself is often jumbled with little inherent structure, all of the material coalesces around the figure of Jeremiah, witness to Jerusalem's fall to the Babylonians (Miller 2001, 560–63; Brueggemann 2006, 3–17). The writer presents Jeremiah's persona so effectively that the audience feels as they have direct access to his life (Bright 1965; Holladay 1986, 1–10). The reality is, however, that even if Jeremiah himself wrote the book (which is clearly not the case in the narratives about his life in chapters 34–45), the way the book presents the prophet is part of the text's overall rhetorical strategy (Carroll 1986, 55–64; Vivano 2002). The character of Jeremiah essentially serves a literary function (Dubbink 2004). Since the figure of Jeremiah provides the most continuous thread in this collective whole, any attempt to read the book should take seriously the rhetorical role played by the various portrayals of the prophet throughout the corpus (Fretheim 2002, 11–16; Patton 2004).

In some ways, this changing role of the prophet corresponds to the different sections of the book outlined above: in the first part, he is a typical Israelite prophet (chs. 2–10) who then becomes the lamenting and at times reluctant prophet in chapters 11–20 (Green 2013). He stands up to kings and other leaders in the narratives (21–45), and then he fades away at the end of the book, swept up by the events of history (46–52). Each of these sections, though, contributes to at least three larger literary features of this characterization: the book depicts Jeremiah as the sole valid prophet. His suffering personifies the suffering of the innocent victims of the city's fall and challenges every human claim to power.

The book depicts Jeremiah as the lone voice speaking God's truth to a community that is not only deaf to this message but also openly hostile (Holt 2007). Scene after scene contrasts Jeremiah's oracles with those delivered by the false prophets (see, for example 14:13-16 and 23:21-22). He himself clashes directly with the prophet Hananiah (ch. 28), and the city's leaders fret over how to deal with a prophet whom they hope is false (ch. 26). Yet over and over again the book punctuates that God has completely controlled his prophetic work. Jeremiah complains in chapter 20 that he tries not to deliver the messages God has given him, but he cannot hold them in. He notes that the prophecies' fulfillment is not up to him (26:12-15). Even his odd call narrative in chapter 1 presents him as a divinely ordained prophet from birth. This theme addresses the question of why God did not warn the people of the city's imminent fall or give them direction so that their fate was lessened. These texts assert that God did warn them, but the people did not believe God's true messenger.

Jeremiah suffers as a result of this unavoidable vocation. The book illustrates his suffering in multiple ways. Probably one of the most distinctive and rhetorically powerful elements of the book are his individual laments, sometimes called his "confessions," in chapters 11–20. These provide a rare glimpse in Israelite literature into a character's inner thoughts, which perhaps make them so compelling. We are not told how to imagine what Isaiah or Ezekiel felt about most of their prophetic work, but readers of the book of Jeremiah come away feeling as if they know the prophet. The laments focus on his work as a prophet, and they elicit empathy from the audience. Here is a man who was never given a chance to lead a happy or "normal" life.

His suffering comes through in other parts of the book as well. For example, the repeated references to his arrest(s) and confinement(s) characterize him as a political prisoner, treated unjustly by the evil political machine that he opposes. The prohibition against him marrying or attending weddings or funerals constitutes a kind of self- (or divinely) imposed social ostracization (Carvalho 2013). In some of the oracles, he gives voice to the weeping city (see, for example 4:19-22 and 8:18-21), linking the figure of Jeremiah with the city's suffering. These laments, which echo poetry found in Lamentations, give voice to the personified city mourning the death of her citizens. The cumulative effect of these images of suffering is that the character of Jeremiah serves as a paradigmatic sufferer in the book (O'Connor 2007 and 2012, 69–91). His portrayal evokes empathy for those who suffered in the fall of the city, even as the words on the surface of the text seem to castigate these victims. The net result is that the fall of the city becomes a catastrophe that, even though it could have been avoided, remains tragic nonetheless.

Part of Jeremiah's marginalization results from his oracles to surrender to the Babylonians. Although some of these oracles are set in the period before the city was besieged, the clearest examples of this message are found in oracles set during the siege. It might be easy for a contemporary audience to miss how politically radical such a message would have been in that context. Jeremiah is depicted as no less than a dangerous revolutionary who would have toppled the government and changed the course of history if his words had garnered followers. This political element appears perhaps most clearly in the final narratives of the book: he is arrested when trying to go to his ancestral lands because the people think he is deserting (37:11-16), and the Babylonians themselves (all the way up to Nebuchadnezzar, so the author notes) assume he acted out of loyalty to Babylon, for which they reward him (39:11-12). This is why the oracles against Babylon in chapters 50–51 have to be so vehement: although throughout the book Jeremiah has protested that he is not acting for the sake of the Babylonians, the oracles against Babylon remind the audience that he hated the Babylonians as much as any other Judean at the time. In a sense, this section portrays him as the ideal hater, in complement to his function as ideal sufferer.

Even though his roles change throughout the book, however, the basic elements of his personality remain consistent. Jeremiah is not a priest concerned with purity regulations, like Ezekiel, or a court prophet capable of composing stunning poetry that exalts the king, like Isaiah. He is prickly, confrontational, and a weaver of horrific images. While readers may empathize with him, most would not wish his fate on any of their own children, and, frankly, I would be worried if one of my children brought him home as a potential spouse. (Jeremiah at the dinner table . . .) He smells. He is a convict. He is a social outcast. He spares no one's feelings. He does odd things. He sings songs full of images of terror, horror, violence, and death. He is the bard of the siege's triple threat: famine, disease, and the sword. He delivers even his brief words of hope with the unwavering recognition of national tragedy.

Jeremiah is not the only character in this book, however. Perhaps one of the most hidden characters is the narrator. So invisible is this narrator that people often assume Jeremiah and the narrator are identical, even though clearly by book's end Jeremiah is gone and only the narrator remains. The narrator interrupts the book only rarely, sometimes to add a date or to sketch a brief outline of a stage. It is clearly an omnipotent narrator: what he or she says about Jeremiah is true and reliable.

In fact, this narrator is more reliable than the other main character in the book: God. First, as with Jeremiah, the portrayal of God is multi-layered and polyvalent (Joo 2006). At times God is the cuckolded husband bent on revenge, but in other parts God weeps for the Judeans; warrior images battle with maternal metaphors (O'Connor 1999). Throughout, the book (through Jeremiah) accuses God of being deceitful, a charge that God never denies. Words for falsehood, treachery, and deceit permeate the book. Much like Jeremiah, God is also not a likable character. In fact, God's willingness and ability to inflict the horrors that the book describes renders the ethical character of God in the book problematic (Kalmanofsky 2008). The ethical issues resemble those found in the book of Lamentations, so it is not a surprise that the tradition has linked these two texts. Both books defend God's sovereignty even if it means sacrificing God's mercy. But contemporary audiences must remember that the fall of the city cannot be denied. Literature that reflects collective trauma, like Jeremiah and Lamentations, attempts to make some theological sense of such devastation. Although Jeremiah seems to be the main character in the book, then, the narrative is actually driven by the authors' theological questions (Biddle 1996, 64–72).

The kings of Judah also make appearances in the book. In many ways, their portrayals are so similar that it is hard to remember whether a given story is set in the reign of Jehoiakin or Zedekiah, for example (Stipp 1996; Roncace 2005). They are all arrogant and complicit in the unjust treatment of God's true prophet. This portrayal is matched by the false prophets, the priests, and the princes or officials who show up in various scenes. These leaders often personify the foolishness of the people as a whole, won over by messages that they want to hear rather than facing the hard truth Jeremiah pronounces. The people become the chorus in the book, responding to Jeremiah's messages (Overholt 1979).

The only exceptions to this sweeping characterization are Baruch along with other scribes, as well as Ebed-Melech. The scribes insert little of their own characters into the story. Baruch is there to copy Jeremiah's words; the audience is given no sense of what he thinks about such a charge, why he was the one who did this, or even if he liked Jeremiah. The other scribes seem to support Jeremiah (see especially ch. 36), but again do little in terms of forming disciples around him. These elements of the scribal characterizations probably stem from the lower social status that scribes might have had. They become true witnesses but not active agents in what they record. The focus on scribes, though, also reflects the growth of writing as a prophetic medium in Israel's history. Here, the scribes replace prophetic disciples (like Elisha as a disciple of Elijah) as those who preserve, carry on, reinterpret, and update the words of the great master prophets of old (Davies 2000; Perdue 2007, 260–83; Thelle 2009).

Ebed-Melech plays an even more fascinating role in the book (T. Parker 2007). The audience learns that he is a foreigner and a eunuch. This dual designation places him outside the patriarchal hierarchy that underpinned Jerusalem society, where only landowning males wielded any true political power. Yet it is Ebed-Melech who saves Jeremiah from a pit, becoming the sole person in the book who pities Jeremiah and takes a risk to help him. Does this make him a true disciple of the prophet? Probably not, but it does contrast with how evil the kings, leaders, and Judean people are when they refuse to treat Jeremiah with any level of compassion or justice.

As with any literary text, physical spaces also serve a rhetorical function. Even though the book of Jeremiah is not a continuous narrative, many of the individual scenes are set within a specific physical space or they engage imaginary spaces. In addition, the book has its own theological geography that codes world powers as players on God's chessboard. The most dominant space in the book is the city itself. Just as the movies *Titanic* and *Das Boot* give the viewer a feeling of claustrophobia as the characters are virtually caught on these sinking vessels, so too does the book of Jeremiah trap the audience in its virtual collapsing metropolis. Even scenes set in a pre-siege landscape echo the approaching death knoll that awaits around the chronological corner. This urban landscape offers no refuge, protection, or blessing. It is personified as a weeping, raped woman. It houses germs and warfare. Even the oracles of restoration, few as they are, offer little exaltation of the capital city itself.

Within that city the focus remains on the public spaces around the temple, with some glances into spaces for the king. The space around the temple, though, is less a place for sacrifice, worship, or praise than the place where Jeremiah is detained. It feels like a busy space: contracts are made, business is conducted, and civic leaders pass through. But it is also the space where, in flash-forwards, dead bodies pile up and walls tumble down. One of the most picturesque spaces in the book is in 36:22-23 where the king sits casually by a fire, burning an expensive scroll, bit by slow bit. The book of Jeremiah is not painted with pastels.

The book also pays attention to spaces outside Jerusalem, not in some vague, "the rest of the land" way, but with clear gazes at other inhabited spaces, some of which avoid Jerusalem's fate. The first of these is Jeremiah's ancestral home, Anathoth, a space that marks Jeremiah as outside the Judean power elite. His attempt to purchase or, probably more accurately, to redeem land in Anathoth from a relative (Domeris 2011) leads to further social isolation when he is arrested as a deserter. Jeremiah 39:10 notes that after the city's fall, some of the land is given to the poorer inhabitants of the area, while the following chapters depict life continuing in nearby Mizpah (Zorn 2003; Becking 2009). This focus on habitable lands outside the city characterizes the capital, seat of government and state religion, as the problem.

Outside the oracles against the nations in chapters 46–51, the depictions of lands other than Judah are mixed. In general, Egypt is a literal dead-end. God promises to destroy Egypt, thus dooming any Judean refugees who have fled there. There are few references to any other foreign place except Babylon. When it comes to the depiction of Babylon, the resulting picture is either intentionally ambiguous or unintentionally conflicted. Some scholars conjecture that the final form of the book represents the perspective of elite exiles in Babylon, or what is called the "golah perspective" (e.g., Seitz 1989a; Carter 2003; Sharp 2003). The prophet tells the exiles to settle into their life in Babylon and support the Babylonian government (29:4-7). This element, however, could be part of the book's rhetorical strategy to depict the exile as the intentional result of Yahweh's decrees. The oracles against Babylon in chapters 50–51 leave no room to view the Babylonians as inherently good. The final form of the book, then, clearly does not depict Babylon as a place of blessing.

The performative nature of prophetic speech also underlies the rhetorical features of many of the texts in Jeremiah. As prophetic material that aims to change people's behavior, it utilizes elements of persuasive speech. For example, it often engages hyperbole in its descriptions of impending events. National calamity is cast as wholesale destruction, while promises of restoration conjure an idyllic future. The book depicts those to blame as completely evil, often using images that elicit the community's disgust as a way to provoke the intended reaction. Prophets use graphic, shocking, and visceral metaphors. The performative element also lies behind the narrative tales; because of his very public presentation of his messages, Jeremiah becomes an enemy of the state.

The most influential analyses of Jeremiah in recent years have been those that read the book through the lens of trauma literature. This field of study arose in literary studies especially reflecting on narratives of the Holocaust, and it represents an intersection of the fields of psychology, sociology, and literature. Trauma is defined as an event that overwhelms a person's ability to comprehend, process, or express one's experience of that event. Trauma studies looks at the way literature reflects these experiences of trauma; it is especially useful in providing an empathetic lens into literature that seems otherwise jumbled, illogical, or graphically disturbing. Initially this approach focused on the activities of an individually traumatized author who gains control over the traumatic event through recovering language, but now it looks at the cross-generational effect of trauma as well as the phenomenon of the collective trauma of a whole group. Jeremiah scholars now view the chaotic structure of the book of Jeremiah as, in part, reflecting the chaotic experience of national disaster (O'Connor 2007). For O'Connor, who has had the most influence with this analysis of Jeremiah, the book testifies to the recovery of language by and for a traumatized individual and community (2012, 29–34, 125–34).

More recently, postcolonial studies have also provided a new way to think about the function of the seemingly contradictory elements of the book of Jeremiah. Postcolonial theory takes seriously the way that a colonized culture must accommodate the ruling, colonizing power, leading the colonized to a new hybrid identity while also negotiating opportunities to express subversive ideas and maintain an indigenous identity. Because contemporary biblical studies arose prominently within the colonizing cultures of Europe and the United States, the dominant paradigm of Jeremiah studies have often not taken seriously Judah's colonized status as an important element of the book's rhetorical context. For example, the book's waffling attitude toward Babylon makes more sense within the context of negotiating colonial rule. As Davidson shows (2011a, 88–129), passages within the book, such as 40:1-12, reveal a subversive character when read as the literature of the colonized.

I have divided the commentary into seven sections with an introduction and epilogue and base my comments on my own translations unless otherwise noted. Jeremiah 1 serves an introduction to the book as whole. The images of planting and uprooting function as a *leitmotif* throughout the book (12:14-15; 24:6; 31:28; 42:10; 45:4). A collection of poetic oracles, whose form most closely resembles other preexilic prophetic collections in chapters 2–10, follows this opening. There are fewer narrative or prose interruptions in this material than in later parts of the book, and the division of the texts into discreet units remains a challenge. Chapters 11–20 also include poetic oracles, but here they are interspersed with laments by Jeremiah bemoaning his own fate. In addition, prose elements increase in frequency. Jeremiah 21–25 collects oracles aimed at specific Judean kings. These oracles have clearer dates, making them easier to delineate. They also contain more of the prophet's symbolic acts than other parts of the book. As a result, in the first half of the book, these chapters contain the most prose. Most scholars conjecture that the book originally ended in chapter 25.

In the second half of the Hebrew version of the book, prose and poetry alternate. The first section of the second part, chapters 26–29, contains episodes from the prophet's life, many of which focus on the question of true and false prophecy. This is followed by the most hopeful section of the book, chapters 30–33, which looks forward, primarily in poetic form, to a restoration of the nation. The book switches back to almost complete prose in chapters 34–45, a collection of tales about the prophet primarily (although not exclusively) set during and after the fall of city. The last section of the book, chapters 46–51, contains oracles against nations other than Judah. In both the Hebrew and Greek versions, the book closes with a historical epilogue that repeats the story of Jerusalem's fall found in 2 Kings 24:18–25:30.

STRUCTURE OF THE BOOK OF JEREMIAH

Jeremiah's Prologue	Chapter 1
Prophetic Oracles of Doom	Chapters 2–10
The Lamenting Prophet	Chapters 11–20
Oracles against Judah's Leaders	Chapters 21–25
The Prophet and the King	Chapters 26–29
Consolation and Restoration	Chapters 30–33
Tales of the Prophet	Chapters 34–45
Oracles against Foreign Nations	Chapters 46–51
An Historical Epilogue	Chapter 52

Jeremiah's Prologue

Jeremiah 1:1-19

Superscription, 1:1-3

Jeremiah opens with a standard prophetic superscription that provides the basic historical and social backdrop against which the book should be read (see, for example, Isa 1:1 and Ezek 1:1-3). While these prophetic superscriptions are often ignored, they serve as important rhetorical lenses for reading Old Testament prophets. Jeremiah's introduction characterizes him in three ways. First, he is a priest, meaning that he has some kind of sacred status. Second, he is not one of the elite priests who controlled the temple of Jerusalem; Jeremiah is from Anathoth, a non-Judean town north of Jerusalem where Solomon had banished the priestly family descending from Abiathar. As a priest from Anathoth living in Jerusalem, he is neither an active sacrificial priest nor among the landed gentry. He is already displaced from his ancestral land, perhaps an unemployed refugee (Patton 2004). Third, he is a Benjaminite, a tribal identity he shares with Israel's failed first king, Saul. The superscription locates him, then, on the fringe of the Davidic royalty and the Solomonic temple personnel, dual power matrixes that controlled Jerusalem during most of his life.

The superscription also locates the prophet temporally, using a conventional length of time: forty years, from 627 BCE (the thirteenth year of Josiah) until 587 (the fall of Jerusalem). It is clear that this is a formulaic number because the book includes events and oracles set in the period after 587. Although the span of forty years may serve to recall the wilderness period, both David and Solomon reigned for forty years (1 Kgs 2:11; 11:42). The superscription does not list all the kings during whose reign Jeremiah prophesied. Instead, three times it mentions Josiah, the king whom 2 Kings 22:2 compares favorably to David, as well as Jehoiakim and Zedekiah (once each), but then oddly omits the two kings who were forced into exile: Jehoahaz, who was exiled to Egypt (2 Kgs 23:33-34), and Jehoiakin, who was exiled to Babylon (2 Kgs 24:12).

When these two elements are brought together, the superscription engages ominous elements of Israel's founding history. Just as the nation had been made secure during the reigns of David and Solomon—through the dual expulsions of Saul's family and the northern priestly family of Abiathar, heralded by the northern prophet, Samuel—so too God's appointment of this particular northern priestly prophet heralds the dethronement of the Judean kings who have not yet been exiled. Jeremiah is depicted as God's chosen one with a forty-year career, while the kings of Judah die young (Josiah), serve briefly (only three months for Jehoiakim), or witness the final unraveling of the Judean twin towers of king and temple (Zedekiah).

The Odd Call of Jeremiah (1:4-19)

The book of Jeremiah is one of only two prophetic books that begin with a description of how that person became a prophet (the other is Ezekiel). While it is traditional to refer to these verses as Jeremiah's call narrative, scholars debate the genre of this material. Clearly the passage refers to two different periods: Jeremiah's "call" in the womb and the dialogue with God that must occur when he is an adult. Does the date of 687, then, refer to Jeremiah's birth or to the date of the dialogue? Many scholars suggest that the date refers to his commissioning as an active prophet; if that is true, then he would be at least a young adult during the reign of Josiah (Lundbom 1995; Fretheim 2002). But the text itself is not clear on this question.

The ways the book fills out Jeremiah's character feel more biographical than those found in most prophetic texts, except maybe Jonah. The superscription has given the audience dates for Jeremiah's career, and some of the texts later in the book have clear historical settings. As a result, one trend in Jeremianic scholarship, especially in the twentieth century, was to date various parts of the book, even within the earliest layer of the material. This attempt, however, resulted in the realization that few, if any, of the oracles in the book can be dated to the earliest period of Jeremiah's career: the years under King Josiah. If his prophetic office started in 627, and if these verses represent the initiation of that role, then why does he not speak prophetically either in favor of or against Josiah's significant religious reforms?

One way of addressing this perceived chronological problem was to suggest that 627 was the year of Jeremiah's birth (since he seemed to be called from birth [1:5]). The dialogue in vv. 4-19, then, would reflect a later conversation between God and Jeremiah. Another way to date the chapter is to place it among the last layers of material added to the book. It would be a fictive beginning to a rolling corpus of oracles and other Jeremianic traditions, written to introduce some of the major themes found in the collection. Whether the text describes an actual event in Jeremiah's life or a later reflection on his prophetic character, details in this exchange build on the ominous notes of the superscription.

Verses 4-19 are cast as a one-sided dialogue between God and Jeremiah (Johnston 2010). It is introduced by a first-person narrator, Jeremiah, who will disappear by v. 19, becoming God's "you" rather than his own "I" (Holt 2007). The course of the dialogue epitomizes this divine-human relationship. Verse 10 introduces a motif that will reoccur throughout the book, with four metaphors of destruction (uproot, destroy, annihilate, tear down) and two of restoration (rebuild and plant). These infinitives appear in various forms in several other places in the book (12:14-17; 18:7, 9; 24:6; 31:28, 40; 42:10; 45:4).

While various structures for the chapter have been offered, a focus on the characterization of this interaction reveals parallels between vv. 4-10 and 17-19, which surround two vision reports that encapsulate the message that Jeremiah will be forced to deliver. The first vision report involves a wordplay in Hebrew. Jeremiah sees an almond sprig (*šāqēd*) and knows Yahweh is watching (*šōqēd*). The word for "watching" is not the kind of gentle oversight to make sure that things will be all right. God is watching to make sure the divine judgments are enacted (1:11-12). The second vision report fleshes out the details of that divine pronouncement (1:13-16). Invading armies will gather on Judah's northern borders and besiege the city as punishment for Judah's sins. Just like God's speech in Isaiah's call narrative (Isa 6:9-13), this decision is inevitable; the prophetic horror in Isaiah comes in his response to the oracle—"How long, O LORD?" (6:11). Here the realization that Jeremiah's work will be a terrible task is captured in the images of vv. 17-19. He will become the fortified city besieged, not by the enemy but by his own community (Carroll 1986; Stulman 2005). The only difference is that he will survive, while the city collapses.

This oracle is surrounded by the account of Jeremiah's so-called call. It is not actually a "call" because he has no real choice. These verses in chapter 1 anticipate later passages in the book where Jeremiah states that he could not keep God's messages silent (20:9). Jeremiah's side of the dialogue evokes empathy in the audience. The passage begins with God's statement that Jeremiah had been personally fashioned by God to be a prophet from before his own birth (Raz 2013). While some scholars read Jeremiah's protest in v. 6 as signifying that he did have a choice, I am not convinced. I suppose he could have run away from God, but that did not seem to work out very well for Jonah. Jeremiah's protest engages a stock response found in a variety of Hebrew texts. He states that he is not fit for the task because he is just a "boy" (NRSV; Heb. *na'ar*), a word that can mean youth but also connotes an underling or person of low status (Strawn 2005). This Hebrew word is used for male servants as well as armor bearers; Solomon says he is just a "boy" in 1 Kings 3:7 when God tells him to ask for a divine blessing (Auld 2009). Here in Jeremiah, the word probably engages both meanings: Jeremiah is young at the start of his career, and he is certainly an underling, not only within his own social setting but also—and especially—before God.

Even so, a focus on what the word means about Jeremiah takes the focus away from the central element of the text: what it says about God's control over Jeremiah's life. Over and over again, the verses repeat that this is not about Jeremiah. It is about God. Jeremiah will speak *God's* words; he will do *God's* bidding. His safety and survival will be the result of God alone. He will have no royal or human patrons. His words will be powerful: through them he can both destroy and reestablish whole nations. But their power comes from God, not the prophet.

The final images of the prophet as a soldier, girded for battle, and a city fortified with metal walls are a most bizarre form of comfort for the prophet (Low 2011). God tells him not to be afraid, a phrase repeated from v. 8. It is a typical response given to a military leader seeking to go into battle (Nissinen 2003). But the image casts Jeremiah as engaging in pitched battle against the whole world. This military metaphor also casts the historical enemy of Jerusalem, Babylon, as a metaphor (Hill 1999a). Jeremiah will be inside Judah, experiencing and serving as witness to the fall that his own prophetic pronouncements will enact, while the mythic foe besieges the city.

These opening verses cast Jeremiah as the ideal survivor, to use an oxymoronic phrase. O'Connor (2012) has especially noted that, throughout the book, his reactions to the fall of the city and his poetic prophecies give voice to the whole community of survivors who collected, preserved, and shaped this literary version of his work. The opening chapter casts Jeremiah as that survivor, a fortified city that will be besieged, torn down, and yet will still, horribly, survive.

Prophetic Oracles of Doom

Jeremiah 2–10

The second chapter of Jeremiah begins a section of the book that most resembles other preexilic prophets. Chapters 1–6, in particular, are similar to the books of Amos and Hosea. It is not clear how to divide these chapters into individual oracles. Some of the poems contain prophetic forms, but these do not always match divisions based on content. The oracles may be organized by theme, catchphrase, metaphoric images, or rhetorical features, but the fact remains that none of these possible organizing features are explicit. Based on content, scholars tend to divide the opening chapters accordingly:

- 1: introduction to the book as a whole;
- 2:1–4:4: oracles describing sins of idolatry;
- 4:5–6:30: punishment for those sins;
- 7:1–8:3: Jeremiah's speech at the temple about the lack of repentance; and
- 8:4–10:25: more oracles describing the punishment.

Even within this schema, further distinctions can be made. For example, Jeremiah 2:1–4:4 does not consist of a single oracle. Many scholars view 2:1-3 and 4:1-2 either as transitional verses that link this section of the text to the material that surrounds it or as framing verses that rhetorically mark off these chapters as a distinct section. Jeremiah 4:2 in particular repeats the theme that the fate of other nations depends on Judah's fate (1:10; Biddle 1990, 159–200), thus tying this section to the first chapter. Similar framing devices can be detected in the other units as well. This suggests some attempt by the final redactor to give shape to the material gathered here (Henderson 2007).

Israel's Sins (2:1–4:4)

The material found within Jeremiah 2:1–4:4 introduces the third main character in the book: the collective population of Judah. These chapters characterize the Judeans as sinners, but a few words of caution are in order, lest modern Christian readers come away with the wrong view of the rhetorical force of the material. It is easy for Christians to read this as a diatribe against "those" sinful Jews, when the material actually reflects the post-exilic Jewish communities' self-reflection on their own role in the fall of the nation. The answer to the question of why Jerusalem fell is not because *they* were so sinful but rather because *we* were sinful (Biddle 1990, 122–58). Since the book is couched in the language of a prophet telling the Judeans how wrong they had been, it is hard to remember that it casts Jeremiah as someone who attempts to change the fundamental ethics of his own community.

Second, while these oracles may have had their source in a historical Jeremiah, the fact that they come down to the modern world in such a complex collection reveals that they had functions beyond the one stemming from their original delivery. The book of Jeremiah as a whole makes clear that there were other prophets in Jerusalem at that time. The Jeremiah traditions were preserved because they continued to speak to and express the thoughts and feelings of subsequent generations (Biddle 1990). They are preserved in a form that reflects that later usage or reappropriation. The scribes who preserved these traditions did so from their own social and theological contexts, which have also left marks on the material. In other words, reading Jeremiah is a lot more like reading Elie Wiesel's *Night*, a later literary production reflecting back on the Holocaust, than reading a record of someone's experiences as they happened, such as *The Diary of Anne Frank*.

The material in this section of Jeremiah seems to castigate all of Judah (and at times Israel as well). This rhetoric of a comprehensive urban sprawl of depravity stems from at least three factors. First, it is part and parcel of the use of hyperbole in prophetic literature mentioned in the introduction. Second, it reflects the way that the trauma of the fall of the nation resulted in a collective memory of that tragedy that became paradigmatic for the whole community, generations later (Smith 2004). Third, it assumes the hierarchical, collective ethics of ancient societies. On a micro-scale, this collective ethics is seen in Hebrew narratives, such as the destruction of Achan's household (Josh 7:24-26), in which the moral behavior of the head of a household represents the ethic of the household as a whole. On a macro-scale, the failures of Judean leaders become the failures of the whole nation. This rhetoric of total depravity masks the fact that the citizens of Judah were the victims—not the perpetrators—of Babylonian aggression. This collective consciousness is found throughout Jeremiah 2:1–4:4, which uses many family-based metaphors in its description of sin. The most prominent of these is the use of female violations of sexual norms as a metaphor for sin

(Kalmonofsky 2011), but the verses also use father and son language as well as slave status to reflect other parts of the household (Watson 1981; Shields 1995).

The material found in 2:5–3:25 is multi-vocal. The most obvious manifestation of this feature, more evident in the original Hebrew, is the variation of pronouns used to address the audience, from second-person singular to third-person common plural forms. The material also seems to switch between poetry and prose. Not to be missed is the use of nature metaphors in chapter 2 (vine, camel, wild ass, lion, etc.) that do not fit the household schema. These details suggest that this is a collection of discreet oracles, each describing an aspect of Judah's sinfulness. Together they do not constitute a manifesto or systematic reflection on sin. Instead they are probably distinct oracles uttered at specific times in Judah's history (unrecoverable now) that have been preserved as part of the Jeremiah traditions. They may have lost some of their specificity as they were preserved in later times or as they were recorded in writing for some later use, but to conclude even that would be an argument from silence.

In this section of material, prophetic formulas occasionally mark shifts in the material. The chapter opens with the first-person notice that Yahweh's word had come to Jeremiah, marking a fresh beginning. The phrase "Thus says the LORD" appears only twice (2:2, 5), but the supposed closing formula, "says the LORD," appears more often without much change in subject, as in 2:9. This section also uses repeated rhetorical forms, such as rhetorical questions and the formula "but you said" (in 2:20b-25, 33-37, translated variously into English; Biddle 1990, 44–55), which suggest some grouping of material but not a wholesale organization of the various statements. There is also a brief reflection on restoration in 3:12-18, which does not match the overall characterization of the audience as terminally sinful.

These oracles are sweeping in their condemnations. In chapter 2, the diatribe is directed at all twelve tribes of Israel (house of Jacob/house of Israel in 2:4) and every leader (priest, king, and prophets in 2:8). Chapter 1 dates Jeremiah to a period after the northern kingdom had fallen, so the language here is clearly hyperbolic. It is important for modern readers of the biblical prophets to recognize this fact; since the colorful metaphors that follow are so rhetorically powerful, they can give the wrong impression that they represent a universal attitude towards women (or animals, for that matter; Holt 2013).

Jeremiah 2:2-9 sets up a metaphorical contrast between Israel's ideal relationship with Yahweh during the wilderness period and its utterly horrible relationship with God at the time of Jeremiah's speech. Again, both sides of the metaphor are hyperbolic. Israel was no more perfect in the wilderness period than it was wholly evil before the fall of Jerusalem. But, then again, subtlety does not make good rhetoric. While 2:2 introduces a metaphor (Israel as Yahweh's wife) that will be picked up later in the chapter, the material first engages metaphors reflecting the male's role within the household. The nation's founding fathers are blamed for turning against God in the wilderness, even though their very survival depended on the LORD's beneficence. God even gives the fathers land that can serve as an inheritance to their sons (v. 7), land that the fathers defiled. Sin clings to later generations. Verse 8 condemns the three elite classes: priests, royalty, and prophets. In v. 9, a transitional verse, God utters a formal accusation against them. In Hebrew, the term used is *rîb*, which is sometimes associated with legal proceedings but can also mean a more general accusation. In one sense the accusation is stated in vv. 2-8 (they rejected Yahweh), but it also points forward to the next set of accusations in vv. 10-19.

Verses 10-19 pile on the accusatory language. They introduce Jeremiah's effective use of rhetorical questions throughout this first section (2:11, 14, 17, 18, 23, 28, 31, 32; 3:1): he seems to ask, "Has anybody ever heard of such a thing?" While Carroll notes that, of course, people had heard of such things (1986), the tone of the rhetoric indicates that the audience should be horrified. Verses 10-13 depict Judah as religiously worse than the pagan nations whom the audience would have viewed as morally inferior. The nation mentioned is "Kittim," or Cyprus, a far-off and foreign nation. If even they would not turn their backs on their gods, how evil must the Judeans be for turning their backs on a God who has done everything for them? The image of turning away from a vibrant spring to drink water from a leaky and dirty cistern captures the insanity of their decisions. That is how bad we were, the book states.

Verses 14-19 develop through a series of rhetorical questions that collectively depict Judah's complicity in its colonization. These verses presume that the audience understands the colonized status of Babylonian Judah. Throughout most of Judah's history, it was essentially a colony of either the Assyrians, the Babylonians, or the Egyptians. From a modern historical perspective, this colonization was the result of the imperial push of these nations to control the whole Fertile Crescent. While the area in and around Jerusalem was not important in and of itself, its fate was tied to a larger effort by these nations to control the land bridge between the vast river valleys in Mesopotamia and along the Nile. Irrigation along the rivers gave these empires the stable economic base needed for military aggression (Green 2012). But from the collective perspective of at least Persian period Yehud, as it was called after the exile, Judah's preexilic attempts to avoid further destruction through treaties and appeasement belied a fundamental lack of faith in God's ability to protect them. According to this section of Jeremiah, what God had wanted was a kind of lone stand against these giant empires, a collective small David staring down a gigantic Goliath of an opponent. The description of Judah's sins in this material is not really about worshiping other gods but rather about condemning Judah's acquiescence to its own colonization.

Verses 14-16 present three metaphors that depict how the punishment for the sin is actually the natural consequence of their own decisions. They have agreed to enter into slavery (v. 14), and not the debt slavery of an equal but the permanent slavery of a prisoner of war. The lions or leaders of other nations roar over them as captured prey (v. 15), while Egypt cracks them open like a helpless clam (v. 16). But they are no victims. Verses 17-19 clearly lay the blame at their own feet. They had abandoned their god, not the other way around (vv. 17, 19), as they pursued the water or wealth of the great river valleys. This section ends by identifying God as the Lord of the armies (NRSV "hosts"), but this is not Judah's army. It is the heavenly armies come to destroy those who have abandoned their divine king.

The chapter then moves to pick up the metaphor first introduced in 2:2, gendering Jerusalem, and by metonymy Judah, as female. The second-person pronouns in 2:20b-25 and 33-37 are all feminine singular. This is not an invention of Jeremiah; it is a tradition that predates the biblical material and is found explicitly in the book of Hosea. It arises in part from the grammatical gender of the word "city" in Hebrew, which was feminine (there is no grammatical neuter in Hebrew), but is fueled by the application of marriage language to describe the ideal relationship between God and people. Israelite marital motifs presume the ancient configuration of marriage, as defined by men (Diamond and O'Connor 1996). Marriages were often arranged at the instigation of the man. They included a contract that was legally and religiously binding. This contract rendered the wife and her children as the property of the husband. While it limited women to one sexual partner, men could have other sexual partners as long as they were not married or betrothed to other men. Husbands had the legal right to beat and divorce disobedient wives. Women who cheated on their husbands brought shame to the household, especially the male head of household, and so adultery was punishable by death (Baumann 2003, 57–81).

Jeremiah 2:2 introduces the metaphor by describing the wilderness as a honeymoon period, with Israel depicted as both a pure and perfect bride and as the first fruits of the harvest that God protects from enemies. In the intervening verses, Israel, first gendered as male, quickly sullies this perfect state by abandoning God. The defiling bride reappears in 2:23-25, 2:33–3:13, and 3:19-20. (Even though Jer 3:6-12 is set as prose, it continues the imagery of the faithless bride. It may be that this was originally a separate oracle, delivered in a more narrative form.) Most English translations do not capture the sexually graphic language of these passages or the way the text slows down by providing detailed metaphors of female sexual impropriety. Most discussions of the text linger over retelling the graphic images, thus reinforcing the assumptions that make the metaphor work: that any female sexuality outside of its function within a patriarchal household is the worst sin imaginable (Shields 1995). Rather than restate what the biblical text says, which is plain enough even in the mild versions contained in most English translations, it is more important to stress how this functions as metaphor.

The message of these verses is that Israel's abandonment of Yahweh is the worst and most senseless betrayal imaginable. That the poet wants to find a visceral image that will communicate how Judah's pursuit of national security apart from reliance on Yahweh would have been seen from God's perspective is not surprising. The power of the metaphor chosen is still felt by audiences today. Although these verses talk about idolatry, Biddle makes a good case that the issue here is the reliance on foreign political powers instead of reliance on God (Biddle 1990, 66–82). Judean alliances with Egypt or Assyria are like underlings rejecting everything their husband, or father, or king, etc. has given them. This betrayal evokes anger on the part of the one betrayed, which Judah should have expected. A cuckolded husband who does not feel anger is as shameful as a wife who cuckolds. The metaphor makes Yahweh's anger, which will be described in disturbingly detailed ways in chapters 4–6, not only justified but perhaps even honorable.

A prose interlude in 3:14-18, which interrupts the feminization of Judah, seems to capture the concerns of later generations. The Masoretic Hebrew text lays out 3:6-12 and 14-18 as prose material, but the distinction between prose and poetry in ancient Hebrew is not as clear as it is in English. In fact, Kugel (1981) believes that there is no such distinction in the ancient language. Instead, he characterizes the difference between them as reflecting a continuum from less to more formal language. The most formal language is marked by extreme brevity, parallel lines, and fluidity with respect to grammar. Clearly, however, certain song types, such as the lament, also had a sense of meter that make them look more like contemporary poetry. The diction of vv. 14-18 differs from the terser language of the verses surrounding them.

All of the previous material also contrasts with the content found in 3:14-18. These latter verses reflect hope in the restoration of all twelve tribes of Israel, with the monarchy and Zion at its center (Yates 2010). This image of restoration uses male familial imagery as well: the return will result in the reestablishment of their own ancestral land (v. 18). Not only are the female metaphors absent here, but so is language of defilement. This is not a nation that needs to be purified; it simply needs to return. Three key elements suggest that these verses come from a later hand. First, 3:14 presumes the audience is already in exile. Second, the phrase "in those days" (vv. 16, 18) is used in post-exilic texts to refer to a glorious future. Third, the vision of the restoration of all twelve tribes resettled around Mount Zion, followed by all the other nations (v. 17), is prominent in post-exilic texts such as Zechariah 14 and Isaiah 66.

The passage focuses not on foreign alliances but on the religious character of the city. Although it calls the city "Zion," thereby affirming its role as religious center, it is not looking for a simple replication of the preexilic temple. In fact, vv. 16-17 state that the restoration will not include the ark of the covenant, which in the preexilic period represented God's presence in the temple. Instead, the whole city will become God's throne, meaning that God's presence will be felt throughout the city, turning the whole of Jerusalem into sacred space. The placement of these verses here introduces a theme that will be seen in other parts of the book as well: that the preexilic temple of Jerusalem gave people a false sense of security.

Oracles of Impending Siege (4:5–6:30)

Chapters 4–6 in Jeremiah more directly reflect the military crisis during the prophet's life. The structure of this section of the book also more clearly resembles the prophetic collections of other premonarchic prophets. The division of oracles is haphazard. There is some repetition of catchphrases, but these do not coalesce into a recognizable structure. The oracles have neither date nor narrative setting. Often scholars disagree about the speaker of each oracle, and the content of the oracles defies cohesion. Instead, this section seems to capture individual prophetic speeches, each with its own irrecoverable historical and physical setting.

The one thing that does seem to unite these oracles is that they reflect the reality of siege warfare, particularly the military strategies utilized by Mesopotamian empires. Although less is known about neo-Babylonian warfare, it seems to have been in continuity with the practices of their predecessors, the neo-Assyrians, who celebrated their military conquests in monumental art projects. Both Assyria and Babylon besieged Jerusalem, as well as other parts of the Levant, but unlike most wars in world history, both the perspective of the victors (in the Assyrian reliefs) and the perspective of the losers (in various Israelite texts) have been preserved in the historical record. This is, frankly, rare. Even if the attestation of the losers comes from later generations, they at least partially preserve the symbolic meaning and emotional traditions of the experiences of loss.

These later generations clearly found it important to preserve the prophetic traditions related to periods of military turmoil. This is as true for the Isaiah oracles that are associated with the attack of the Assyrians in the eighth century as it is for oracles in Jeremiah and Ezekiel that capture the experience of the Babylonian siege. These were certainly not the only prophets who lived and worked through these turbulent times, but they were the ones Israel turned to again and again to express the way those events affected later generations.

Ancient warfare was a slow, painful, and smelly process. The neo-Babylonian army was huge, including foot soldiers with swords, spears, and clubs, bowmen, slingers (meaning those who used slingshots), cavalry, and charioteers. It included servants (and possibly female slaves), priests and other religious functionaries, metalworkers and other artisans, as well as scribes and recorders. The armies also had horses and pack animals such as asses, camels (which could also be ridden), and oxen with carts.

As a result, these armies traveled slowly, only about three to five miles a day. In other words, a city targeted for siege had ample time to prepare. These preparations were no less elaborate. First, they had to prepare the walled city to function as a place of residence for a concentrated population of elite households. In the ancient world, cities were usually administrative centers, not residential hubs. Yet, because the cities were fortified with walls, the residents on the farmland belonging to a city would be gathered inside in case of enemy attack. To prepare for this, food had to be stored since sieges could last months and even years.

Preparations also included attempts to stave off the attack. Three tactics dominated these attempts. First, envoys could be sent to the advancing army to appease or negotiate with the commander. These negotiations could include an offer of either formal subservience (such as becoming a vassal state) and/or tribute in the form of money or goods. There is little evidence that the Judeans tried this tactic during Babylon's second attack on Jerusalem. Second, envoys could be sent to other countries that might be allies against the advancing army. As the saying goes, the enemy of my enemy is my friend. The Babylonians advanced through the Levant in order to reach Egypt, their primary goal. Therefore, Egypt would be a natural ally against Babylon, since they would probably prefer to fight Babylon before they reached Egypt's borders. There is evidence that Pharaoh Psammetichus II approached various kings in the Levant shortly before Zedekiah rebelled against Babylon, leading to the conjecture that Judah was one of the countries in contact with Egypt (Carvalho 2015, 197).

War in the ancient world was a sacred activity (Kelle et al., 2014). Armies did not fight unless they knew through divination that their gods fought with them. The third way ancient peoples prepared for war, then, was through religious activities. These would have included prayers and sacrifices to the warrior gods, divination rituals with prophetic speeches, and appeasement of the gods if the auspices were unfavorable. The biblical record, especially in the prophetic collections, focuses on this third prong of military preparation. The later narratives in the book of Jeremiah depict the Jerusalem of this period as teeming with prophets who were not only predicting victory or defeat but were also advising king and community about how to keep in God's favor.

Jeremiah 4–6 should be read in this light. It contains both predictions based on Jeremiah's prophetic experiences that Judah is not in Yahweh's favor and will suffer defeat, as well as advice on how to appease this angry deity. The texts in Jeremiah that reflect what Judah should have done to prepare for war focus on this last element of preparation: their relationship with Yahweh. These oracles castigate the monarchy for seeking mortal allies (characterized as the city's lovers in 4:30) while ignoring the anger of their own God, who is the source of the impending disaster. The speeches more often, though, focus on Judah's internal behavior. Judah is condemned for a variety of nondescript charges: wickedness (4:14), acting unjustly (5:1), swearing falsely (5:2), ignoring God's commands (5:4-5, although few specific commands are referenced), worshiping other gods (5:6-7, although the identity of these gods is also not specified), speaking incorrectly about Yahweh (5:12), and generally disrespecting God's power. Perhaps the original oracles were more specific in their condemnation, and those specifics have dropped out as the traditions were handed down to and reused by later generations, or perhaps prophetic oracles were themselves ambiguous so that a diviner was needed to interpret them properly. Either way the collection builds up a portrait of Jerusalem as irredeemably sinful.

Naturally, this characterization then justifies Yahweh's response and mitigates the audience's potential horror at a God who would wreak such cruel havoc on God's own people. It is remarkable that the most detailed parts of this section of the book are the descriptions of attack and siege that the author clearly attributes to Yahweh. Yet even contemporary readers come away from the text feeling that Judah deserved it and that God's violence is justified. In other words, the rhetoric of the book is highly effective.

The poems do provide a kind of verbal iconography of siege warfare from the perspective of the besieged, a portrait that counters the imperial depiction of such war from the conqueror's viewpoint, as found in the Assyrian reliefs. To be sure, the passages here are poetic reflections, and so they do not present a chronological or even historical description of the events. Instead they provide flashes of images that symbolize the emotional reality of defeat. They are more like *Saving Private Ryan* than war documentaries. The reality of the war itself lies behind these images.

Siege warfare entailed the slow and painful death of a city. It was a kind of urban torture whose aim was either the acquiescence of the victim or a demise so shameful it became an object lesson to motivate the obeisance of other potential rebels. Siege warfare employed multiple strategies in its quest to subdue a city. First and foremost, the attacking army wanted some kind of "peaceful" resolution, since actually attacking the city with weapons would be more costly both in terms of people and equipment than would the nonviolent surrender of that city. Starvation was one way to convince the city that they should yield to a superior enemy. The attackers also used psychological warfare to get the residents to rebel against the leadership who resisted. This evoked internal dissension among those caged up in the city: should they surrender or should they resist?

As this was going on over the course of months, the attacking army continued to assault the city walls, capture those who tried to escape, and kill whatever citizens they could. When the city walls were eventually breached, as was the case with Jerusalem after an eighteen-month siege, the sack of the city was accomplished by hand-to-hand combat that resulted not only in the physical devastation of this built space but also the repopulation of that space with corpses, blood, and body parts. Killing was not accomplished remotely; it was an assault on all the senses. Survivors were no less victims, either by having experienced or witnessed the ensuing physical and/or sexual assaults. The oracles in Jeremiah 4–6 reflect the collective legacy of victimized survivors. These oracles use powerful metaphors to capture the emotional impact of the slow progress of siege and fall.

Jeremiah 4

Although there is some disagreement about how to divide the individual oracles in this section, a brief overview that is sensitive to form-critical cues in the extant text is helpful. The most common prophetic form in this section is the closing statement, "An oracle of Yahweh" (translated in the NRSV as "says the LORD"). This formula can be used as one option in dividing the text. Based on this, then, the first oracle, 4:5-9a, reflects the city's reaction to an advancing army. The trumpet or *shofar* in v. 5 was used to call people to battle. An appeal to gather within the city walls follows this trumpet blast (v. 5). They prepare for battle through prayer and lamentations in order to appease God (v. 8). This appeasement, however, has little hope ("the hot anger of Yahweh will not retreat from us"). The approaching enemy, depicted as a lion arising from its lair for the hunt (v. 7), comes along the major highways in the area, that is, it approaches from the north (v. 6).

The material in 4:9-18 is more difficult to divide. There are clear changes in speaker, which may or may not indicate different statements. The Masoretic text seems to place the break at the end of vv. 8 and 18, while the statement "an oracle of Yahweh" would place the break halfway through v. 9. Ignoring both of these cues, the NRSV places the break at the end of v. 9. In terms of the content, there is not a huge difference: does the reference to Jerusalem's leaders signal their reaction to the advancing Babylonian army, or is it an introduction to God's speech in v. 11? Perhaps it is best to see it as a transitional verse that connects the two sections.

What is clear is that Jeremiah's voice breaks in at v. 10. Reading vv. 9 and 10 in tandem contrasts Jeremiah with other Judean leaders. They are paralyzed by this impending attack. The king does not enter into negotiations, the princes do not prepare for battle, the priests do not initiate negotiations with God, and, worst of all, the prophets are completely baffled. Clearly the text depicts the Babylonian encroachment as wholly unexpected. Jeremiah's shock is also recorded in v. 10, but his shock is directed at God. How could Yahweh have suddenly turned from a God who guaranteed peace to one who leads the charge against the city?

Jeremiah's short statement, which is clearly not an oracle but rather is meant to add to the text's characterization of him, is only the second time in the book that he has voiced a nonprophetic speech. The first time was his objection to his prophetic call (1:6). Here he accuses God of deception. The tension over truth and falsehood, introduced explicitly at this point in the text, permeates this whole section of oracles. The statement accuses God of deception, while 5:12-13 blames the people and their prophets. The text accuses these prophets of deception a second time in 5:30-31 and a third time in 6:13. On the one hand, this interplay contributes to the overall portrayal of Jeremiah as a prophet at odds with the rest of his community. He is the one formally charged with false prophecy, a charge that eventually leads to his arrest (first recorded in 20:2). On the other hand, this theme also reveals the hopeless situation faced by people in national crisis. While later verses will suggest that the people should have acknowledged their sinfulness, Jeremiah's outcry reveals that God had duped them into a false sense of security.

Jeremiah is not the only biblical text that attributes deception to God. In 1 Kings 22, the prophet Micaiah ben Imlah states that God sent a lying spirit into the northern prophets in order to ensure that the king of Israel would meet his death on the battlefield. In Isaiah 6, Yahweh commands that the prophet make sure the people do not understand that they have been sinful so that they fail to repent, justifying God's destruction of them. In Ezekiel 20, God gives the Israelites laws that are "not good" so that when they follow them, they will actually be sinning, again justifying God's destruction of them. Here, Jeremiah attests to the fact that the oracles leading up to this crisis moment have all been positive ("Peace will come to you" [4:10]), even while God planned their destruction.

Jeremiah 4:11-18 represents either God's response to Jeremiah's question ("where is my master, Yahweh?") or a separate oracle unrelated to the preceding verses. Again the verses refer to the advance of the attacking army. Metaphoric language in v. 13 captures their path of destruction (they are like a tornado) and the speed of their advance (likened to swift horses and eagles). In this section, the author places blame for the attack squarely on Jerusalem's shoulders. This attack is a divine judgment (v. 12) for their evil deeds (v. 14). Although there is a brief reference to "rebellion" (which can simply mean not following God's commands) in v. 17, the language of sin here is generic, spoken as if the audience knows what it has done wrong. In fact, according to vv. 15-16, it seems to be obvious to any onlookers, from the northern tribes of Israel to other nations who note Jerusalem's fate. This is a powerful rhetorical device that seems to answer Jeremiah's objection: there was no deception. Even foreign nations can see that Judah deserves its fate. Verse 18 summarizes God's response: "Your ways, your deeds have done this to you; your fate is so bitter that it extends into your very heart."

The next section, 4:19-22, contains another change in speaker, although scholars debate this speaker's identity. Like the previous verses, these verses are also first-person speech. This might suggest that the speaker is God, but the content identifies the speaker as a victim of the violence that God has unleashed. The speaker likens the anguish to a woman in labor, a powerful metaphor in a world where many women died in childbirth (Bauer 1999b; Brummitt 2013). This female voice does not preclude the speaker being God, but the fact that other parts of Jeremiah identify the city as a lone female raises the probability that this is the voice of the personified city. A common literary genre in the ancient Near East encompasses poems that lament the destruction of cities and their temples. In many of these laments, the city's patron goddess laments the loss of her people in much the same way that v. 22 does. The female voice in these verses could be either a female manifestation of Yahweh as a weeping goddess or the city personified as female, taking the role of the goddess found in Babylonian literature.

Many scholars identify the speaker as Jeremiah. Other parts of the book certainly portray him as anguished over the city's fall, to the point of weeping. A reference to feeling like a woman in labor does not necessitate that the speaker is female; the same metaphor is used in 6:24 to refer to a probably mixed-gender audience. However, attributing this to Jeremiah does not fit the references to urban structures in the poem. The speaker first refers to her heart as having fortified walls (v. 19). In the following verse she talks of tents or curtains, which could refer to the hangings in the temple or to the military tents set up in the context of war. Last, 4:31 explicitly calls Zion a woman in labor (Claassens 2013). While this is a separate oracle, it raises the likelihood that this image has a standard referent for Jeremiah's audience.

Even if the speaker is the city, however, the reader of the text has to imagine a male prophet named Jeremiah performing this speech as the oracle was delivered (Bauer 1999a, 63–66). What should a contemporary audience imagine? While Lee reconstructs an actual female dialogue partner (2002, 47–73, and 2007), there is no evidence of such dialogic performance of prophetic oracles. Did Jeremiah act out this oracle, writhing like a woman giving birth? Did he speak in a different voice, wear different clothing, or simply rely on the words to convey the gendered nature of this oracle? Although these questions are not answered in the text, evidence from Mesopotamia does reveal that some of Ishtar's religious functionaries would dress up as half men and half women in certain processions, so the idea of a prophetic enactment of gender transferal was not unheard of (Nissinen 1998, 19–36).

The gendered voice captures the pathos of the city's fall. Rhetorically, the language elicits sympathy for this dying mother. The text conjures the screaming of a woman in labor at the point of death. The clipped language in v. 20 conveys panic, while the images of military standards, the bleating of the *shofar*, and the total destruction paint an impressionistic scene of urban collapse. As a result, Jeremiah identifies himself with the voices of powerless women (Baumann 2003, 105–34).

Verse 22 is another transitional verse, perhaps originally a separate oracle, but here it serves as a bridge between the image of the woman in labor and the following description of the unraveling of the created world. This verse is also in the first person, referring to "my people," a phrase used by the goddess in city laments to refer to the citizens of the destroyed city (Jindo 2010, 55–70), but here the speaker again seems to be Yahweh, who complains that the people do not know their god. The passage calls the people fools, who pursue wisdom only to commit evil deeds, erasing the empathy elicited in vv. 19-21.

Jeremiah 4:23-26 depicts the fall of the city as a reverse creation (Brueggemann 2006, 41–55) in a tightly structured poem. The destroyed land has become "formless and void," a phrase echoing descriptions of the cosmos before God imposes order on it in Genesis 1:2 (Jindo 2010, 71–150). Just as Genesis 1 proceeds from there to describe a sequential order of creation, so too this passage follows the notice of chaos with an ordered undoing of God's creation. The heavens grow dark; the mountains dissolve; humans, animals, and plants all disappear. Verse 22's reference to wisdom elicits the connection between wisdom and creation found in other biblical literature, such as Proverbs 8. In the proverbial literature, the wise person acts in accordance with God's created order, thereby eliciting God's blessings in the form of fertility, social stability, and economic prosperity. Jeremiah 4:22-26 plays with this paradigm, connecting "wisdom to do evil" (translated as "skilled" in the NRSV) with the return of creation to its primal chaotic state. The ending of the oracle does not leave this power in the hands of the people, however. It squarely attributes it to God. An unspoken question asks, "Why does the world unravel?" Because of Yahweh's "fierce anger" is the firm reply. Echoing a standard parental threat, it is as if God says, "I brought you into this world, and I can take you out."

The most detailed description of the fall of the city in this section comes in 4:27-31. It is couched as a speech by Yahweh pronouncing judgment over the city. Flashes of battle play across the surface of this poem. Chariots skitter across the scene, bowmen shout offstage. The army descends like a tornado, people fleeing willy-nilly before it. The poet captures the inanity of the leaders' attempts to resist the onslaught: they dressed up in finery (perhaps referring to some sort of diplomatic envoy) for their own demise. "You have adorned yourselves for nothing!" (4:30). The ending of this poem reengages the female personification of the city as a woman whose lovers have turned against her. Panting through the labor pains that will kill her, she screams, "Woe is me," as she collapses at her killers' feet.

Jeremiah 5

The opening verses of chapter 5 upbraid the people of Jerusalem for their sins. In vv. 1-5, Yahweh has Jeremiah search for someone worthy enough to save. In the book of Genesis, Abraham argues with God about the destruction of Sodom and Gomorrah: "Will you indeed sweep away the righteous with the wicked?" (Gen 18:23 NRSV). In the first chapter of Job, God sends Satan to search for sinners and saints, while in Ezekiel 9:4, God commissions divine emissaries to mark the righteous before the city is destroyed. Patrolling, apparently, is not God's job. Jeremiah, incredulous at his unsuccessful search, first attributes the outcome to the voices of the lower classes (5:4), but even when he turns to the educated elite (the "great ones" of 5:5) he finds no one.

Verse 6 briefly refers to the ensuing destruction, now cast clearly as punishment. It depicts the Babylonian army as a lion, a wolf, and a leopard—all wild, predatory stalkers—waiting for an opportunity to pounce. As a result, God offers them one more chance in vv. 1-6. At the start of the oracle, all is not yet lost; God calls on them to repent. The people of the city should have included in their preparations for battle formal lamentations and sin offerings, coupled with an acknowledgment that they had brought this on themselves. Because they failed to do this, the punishment ensues.

Yahweh speaks in 5:7-9, perhaps signaling a new oracle. The theme of this section replicates 5:1-3: although God has continually forgiven them, they still sinned. The metaphors are different in this section, however. The author once again uses sexual metaphors. The oracle depicts the men of Jerusalem (v. 8), sons of the female city (v. 7), as insatiable horses neighing after sexual partners. God defends the destruction of them, noting that the same fate would befall any nation, a jab that insinuates that Judah was more sinful than the conquering Babylonians.

Verses 10-11 elaborate on the punishment but with another change of speaker. While the passage does not explicitly state who speaks or is addressed, the content suggests it is God's commission of the Babylonian army to carry out the destruction. Verse 10 includes the cryptic note, "do not execute a full end." While scholars debate what this verse meant in its original context, its placement within the current book renders it multivalent. It refers to the first siege of Jerusalem in 597 that subdued the city but did not destroy it, but it also refers to the Babylonians' leaving Judah less than totally annihilated in 587, as attested by the archaeological record. The Babylonians did devastate Jerusalem, but many parts of Judah suffered only minor losses. In addition, the passage alludes to exiles and refugees who survived the onslaught (S. Parker 2003), probably as a later addition to the oracle that foreshadows the restoration oracles in later parts of the book. As a kind of rhetorical teaser, which piques the readers' curiosity, all of these meanings and perhaps more are at play in this short phrase.

Jeremiah 5:12-15, along with vv. 16-18, focuses on the emptiness and deceit of the speech of the people. They lie (v. 12) and heed the prophets who are literally airbags (v. 13). They deny that Yahweh will hold them accountable. The punishment fits the crime: a divine word will be put in Jeremiah's mouth that is not just hot air but a literal fire that will incinerate them

(v. 14). This leads into vv. 15-17, perhaps originally a separate oracle but now statements that complement the metaphor of the fire, as it describes the Babylonian army devouring the nation as it advances.

This section ends with what appears to be a prose addition in 5:18-19, which returns to the idea that the nation did not experience a "full end" (NRSV). Rather than depicting this as a hopeful remnant who will become the seeds for a restored nation, here the remnant fails to understand what has happened: "Why did Yahweh, our god, do all of this to us?" (v. 19). Again, the punishment fits the crime: because they "served" foreign gods, they will become servants in a foreign land (NRSV). These verses remind the reader that these very survivors wrote and preserved this whole book, which asks why God let this happen. In answering this question, they cast themselves as the responsible party, while using the figure of Jeremiah as the voice internal to their own community that they should have heeded. When the text implies that "they" should have known better, it is really the later community saying "we" should have acted differently.

Dividing the remaining verses in chapter 5 becomes increasingly difficult. Content alone seems to guide the reader. Verses 20-25 continue the focus on the obstinate sinfulness of the people. They not only fail to recognize their own sin but also ignore God's power. The passage invokes the image of a beach as a barrier God has established for the sea, which Israel's neighbors personified as a god. How could anyone be foolish enough to feel complacent about a deity who can keep the sea at bay? Verses 26-29a admit that the whole nation was not equally responsible for these sins. These verses condemn the elite for their greed and fraudulent profit at the expense of the lower classes: the poor and those who are not among the landowning class. The passage gives voice to God's rhetorical question, "Should I not punish this?" (v. 29). The chapter ends with a summation of the previous oracles. God notes that a foreign nation would have been treated in the same way (see 5:9). Yahweh promises that the land will be publicly devastated (v. 30; see 4:27 and 5:16-17) because the people have listened to false prophets and corrupt priests (v. 31; see 4:9; Huffmon 2012).

Jeremiah 6

The oracles in chapter 6 continue to focus on the advancing army and the resultant siege, but they are not arranged in any sequential order. The oracles at the beginning reflect the siege, while later verses return to the army's initial advance and Judah's failed attempts at appeasing Yahweh. The opening oracle utilizes the personification of the city as female (6:1-8), but these poems use metaphors less often than in the previous chapter. The images in the first oracle, for instance, stem directly from the stages of battle: the oracle advises the Benjaminites to flee Jerusalem (v. 1; a detail corroborated by archaeological evidence that the land of Benjamin experienced little destruction in the Babylonian period; Faust 2012) while outlying cities send signals of the army's advance. Images of siege pile up: the blare of the *shofar* (v. 1), the city surrounded by a military camp (v. 3), the rituals of battle (hidden in NRSV's "prepare war" in v. 4), followed by assaults night and day (vv. 4-5), the construction of siege works (v. 6), and the constant sounds of people dying (v. 7). While these verses speak from the perspective of those inside the city, the end of the oracle undercuts any pity that the reader might have for them. Verses 6b and 8 mark the attack as God's punishment for the city's sins. When read in concert with God's command to the Benjaminites to flee (6:1), the poem pinpoints the evil to this particular group of people.

Verses 9-12 allude to the result of the siege. The people have ears that are metaphorically uncircumcised (v. 10), meaning they are shut. The passage suggests that if they would have listened, they could have avoided Yahweh's anger (v. 11). The speaker in this section seems to shift. It is introduced as divine speech, but vv. 10b-11a speak of Yahweh in the third person. The speaker, presumably Jeremiah, tries in vain to refrain from delivering Yahweh's decree that unleashes God's anger against the city. The image projects prophetic speech as the catalyst that initiates the ensuing violence. Once Jeremiah speaks the oracle, the events inevitably unfurl. Verses 11b-12 spell out that horrible end: God's anger sweeps away all the inhabitants, young and old, male and female, with every man's property, which includes fields, daughters, and wives, "turned over to others."

Verses 13-15 provide some explanation for Jerusalem's recalcitrance: its religious leaders have deceived them. These verses state that *all* the priests and prophets delivered false oracles that assured the people the city would not fall. In contrast to 4:10 where Jeremiah accuses God of deceiving the people, this passage, echoed in 8:11, places the false promise of peace in the mouths of Judah's religious leaders. In other words, these priests and prophets did not view the attack as orchestrated by Yahweh: all of them, that is, except Jeremiah. Behind this passage is the question of why, if Jeremiah was a true prophet, was he unable to save the city (on Jeremiah's role as a prophet, see DeJong 2011)? Behind that question is their cultural memory of the prophet Isaiah, who, in a similar circumstance, was able to save the city from falling to the Assyrians (see, especially, 2 Kgs 19). The difference is that King Hezekiah heeded what Isaiah said, while here the false prophets deceive the people, who ignore Jeremiah.

Verses 16-21 allude to prophets and priests as well, first with the metaphor of the sentinel in v. 17. Ezekiel 3:16-21 and 33:1-9 provide a fuller depiction of the trope: God makes Ezekiel a "sentinel" sent to warn the people of impending disaster unless they change their behavior. In neither the case of Jeremiah nor Ezekiel do people heed the warnings of the prophetic sentinels. Here in Jeremiah, the prophet warns them to return to an "old" and "good" way of living, which v. 19 equates with God's *torah*. This verse and the following one allude to priests, since it was the job of priests to teach *torah* and to administer the sacrificial rituals. Verse 20 shows them conducting these sacrifices, but without attention to their other duties to teach the correct way to live, God rejects the sacrifices. They will not appease the divine wrath; everyone will perish (v. 21).

The chapter ends with a long poem describing the fall of the city. In staccato phrases, the passage depicts the three stages of battle: the advance against, the attack on, and the sack of the city. The enemy comes from the ends of the earth, armed to the teeth, merciless; the detail of the noise of this armed mass likens them to a tsunami (v. 23), a horrible force that cannot be held back. It also hearkens back to the depiction of God who alone sets the sand as the boundary for the sea in 5:22, who now removes that barrier so that the land returns to chaos. The poem identifies two victims: the inhabitants of the city, and the city itself, personified as a female. In this particular interchange, the city takes on the role of the patron goddess mourning the fall of her city, as outlined above. These voices play back and forth: the people at first speaking for themselves, but quickly silenced as the city takes up the lament. The appeal in the poem to aural images evokes sympathy in the audience. The clanging of an advancing army gives way to the cries of the dying inhabitants, wailing like "women giving birth" (v. 24). Their cries of anguish elicit Zion's lamentations (v. 26). Verses 27-30 replace those sounds with the noises of the burning city. Fire, the final stage of the sack of a city, rages through Jerusalem—a fire hot enough to melt precious metal. This section depicts Jeremiah as the metalworker come to "test" the people with a fire used to purify metal of any impurities, but the result in this case will be a pile of dross that can only be thrown away.

The opening chapters of the book of Jeremiah come to a close with this image of worthless ash. The book portrays the prophet, created by God to deliver the oracles that would enact the fall of the city, in sharp contrast to the people who have failed to properly prepare for war. Although they have prepared the city for siege, they have not recognized Yahweh's control of every aspect of their fate. While Jeremiah rarely appears in these chapters, the brief references lead the reader through the oracles in a way that causes them to identify with the prophet. Like the reader, he is at first reluctant to accept the events as orchestrated by God. He accuses God of deception (4:10), and depicts this as a sudden and unexpected change in God's character. He identifies with the fate of the people, taking no joy in their destruction. He tries to resist uttering the prophetic oracle; unspoken, the oracle cannot take effect. But this resistance is untenable (6:11-12). God's speech to Jeremiah closes the section, returning to the divine charge that opened the book about which he has no choice. Only here, there is no planting and rebuilding: he is the forger sent to unleash a fire that will rage through the city, destroying everything in its path.

The Prophet at the Temple (7:1–8:3)

The literary style changes noticeably at chapter 7. While chapters 2–6 read as a collection of poetic oracles, chapter 7 switches to narrative prose that describes Jeremiah's interactions with both God and the people. Jeremiah is not presented as the author of this material. The text does not preserve the pronouncements in poetic form with the clipped language found in previous chapters. Instead, the speeches list the people's sins, defending the punishment that other chapters describe. The voicing in the text is complex, with no narrator speaking. Instead, God's voice takes the lead, telling Jeremiah what to say even though the people will not listen. This results in a complex layering of voices within the section: God speaking to Jeremiah about both the people and Jeremiah himself, interlaced with Jeremiah speaking to the people who have no response because they ignore him.

The section transitions into prose oracles that read more as sermons than poems. Moral arguments replace staccato images. The sermons do not assault the senses but rather invite Jeremiah's audience to consider their view of God (Stulman 1986). Some of the language in this section resonates with the sermonic language in other parts of the Bible that are attributed to the Deuteronomistic writers. For example, the description of Israel's idolatry parallels similar descriptions in, e.g., Deuteronomy 12:2-3; 13:11-13; 17:2-3; 1 Kings 11:9-10; 22:43; and 2 Kings 23:10. The list of sins in 7:9 summarizes some of the commandments in Deuteronomy 5:6-21. The passage not only refers to events narrated in 1 Samuel 1–4 but also contains parallels to 1 Kings 8 (Römer 2009). This change in literary style, coupled with the use of theological language found outside of Jeremiah, has led scholars to view the material as stemming from a different and perhaps later hand than the previous oracles. At the very least, it attests to a varied and lively preservation of traditions associated with Jeremiah that constitutes the final form of the book.

The content focuses on the ritual activities of the citizens of Jerusalem. The chapter opens with Jeremiah standing inside a massive gate through which the people would process on their way to participate in the sacrifices at the temple. While the text does not describe those rituals in full detail, the allusions to various ritual elements reflect the author's confidence that the ancient audience would know the reference, even if today not all of those allusions are clear.

What is certain is that both the beginning of the passage and its ending engage the ritual activities of the Jerusalemites, first referencing their worship of Yahweh (7:1-30) and then describing rituals directed to other gods (7:31–8:3). The resulting picture depicts a people who, while certainly acting in a pious way, are blind to the real purpose of ritual. The theme of delusion also traces its way through the section. They are deluded to think that their participation in the sacrifices to Yahweh at the temple will save them. The passage lays bare their misconceptions that their prayers are efficacious, as it goes on to describe them replicating the same pious actions in their appeasements of other gods (Domeris 1999).

Jeremiah 7:12-15 couches the idiocy of their delusion in the references to Shiloh. Shiloh had been an Israelite city north of Jerusalem that was razed, probably by the Philistines (1 Sam 4) before David became king. Before its destruction, however, the ark had been housed at Shiloh (Clements 1996). In the ancient Near East, it was believed that a city's patron deity would protect the city from enemy assaults. In both 2 Kings 19:32-35 and Isaiah 37:33-36, the fact that Jerusalem had survived an earlier siege by the Assyrian army reinforced the Judean belief that Yahweh truly resided in Jerusalem and would effectively defend the city. When cities did fall, it would be explained with the assertion that the god had abandoned the city. Ezekiel 1 and 8–11, for example, describe God's abandonment of the temple before the Babylonian siege, effectively rendering the city bereft of divine protection.

Jeremiah explains the fall of the city differently; God is present, actively punishing the city for its sins. This speech paints Jeremiah's opponents as trusting that the city will once again survive a siege as long as they continue rituals directed to Yahweh. It is a reasonable conclusion; when the Assyrians attacked, Hezekiah's prayers at the temple saved the city. Jeremiah dashes all hopes that such a strategy would work again, however. He points out that the appropriate historical parallel is not the miraculous rescue of Jerusalem from the Assyrians but rather the devastating fall of Shiloh to the Philistines.

The next verses negate the Judeans' second hope for divine rescue: intercession by the prophet. In ancient Israel, prophets not only delivered messages from gods to the human community but also interceded on behalf of the community, pleading for mercy even when it deserved none. Exodus 32:10-14 provides perhaps the paradigmatic example of this role when God wanted to destroy all the Hebrews who had been delivered from slavery in Egypt because they had worshiped a golden calf. Moses' intercession alone saved them. In contrast, God forbids Jeremiah to intercede on behalf of the citizens of Jerusalem in Jeremiah 7:16-19, thus assuring their destruction (Biddle 1996, 55–64). The verses that follow paint a picture of practices that elicited such a divine response, contrasting their deliverance from Egyptian slavery with allusions to abhorrent ritual practices (7:30–8:3). These include child sacrifice (7:31-32), something involving an idol or ritual object that the author views as illegitimate (7:30), and worship of foreign deities, such as the queen of heaven (7:18, a practice taken up again in Jer 44), along with various other astral deities (8:2).

Scattered throughout this section are more allusions to the destruction resulting from siege. The reference to the fall of Shiloh sets the context for the allusions that follow. The author compares the destruction of Jerusalem to a ravaging fire that devours not just the city but the surrounding lands as well (7:20). The sacred areas of the city will be renamed "Murder Valley" (7:32; NRSV: "valley of slaughter"), while the corpses littering the ground after the siege will become fodder for carrion birds (7:33).

Oracles of the Siege (8:4–10:25)

Chapters 8 through 10 contain various oracles related to the fall of the city, most in poetic form. Many aspects of these poems are ambiguous, including how to divide these texts. Even the Hebrew text seems confused, placing verse numbers in the middle of lines that have been divided using a different schema. In addition, the identity of the speakers in each poem is not always clear, as the pronouns shift from first to third person. The poetic ambiguity results in images that convey impressions of the events and evoke an emotional response. While some of the language is quite disturbing, the poems effectively communicate some of the horrors of siege warfare. Many contemporary readers of these texts, however, are bothered by the way the poems blame the victims for their fate. These passages characterize the Judeans as sinful idolaters, thus distancing the reader from an empathetic engagement with the victims. Instead, casual readers often wonder why the Judeans were so stubbornly evil in not changing their ways, a dangerous conclusion when the reader is a Christian who then concludes that Jews, even the ancient Jews, were uniquely obstinate or evil.

A second dangerous but too common conclusion made by Christian audiences is that God in Jeremiah is so much more violent and judgmental than Christ is, as if God and Christ are two different beings. It is hard for a contemporary reader to remember that this literature was written by those who would have considered themselves part of the group that they are critiquing, like an American who criticizes American consumerism. The perspective in Jeremiah is that certain members of Jerusalemite society, especially those in elite positions, led the rest of the people astray with their promises that they had the crisis under control. Some verses echo the way the book of Deuteronomy projects idolatry as the paradigmatic national sin, carrying forward a theme found in Jeremiah 7. The poems castigate both rituals that the elites used to appease the Babylonians as well as native Israelite practices that these authors opposed. In both cases, those in power with whom Jeremiah disagreed were not necessarily evil, although they may have been more concerned with national security than theological debates. They had a different interpretation of what was best for the city. The book of Jeremiah reflects the community's conclusion after the event that they had been wrong.

The sins mentioned in the oracle in 8:4-12 focus on deception, resuming the theme found in chapter 6. Many prophetic texts presume that once people know what they are doing is wrong and that God will punish them, they will repent. In Isaiah 6:9-10, God forbids the prophet to tell the Israelites to repent because they have been doomed for destruction. The poem here claims that, since the need for repentance is obvious, the Judeans are even more to blame for not responding properly to the impending disaster. Verses 7-9, in particular, measure the supposed "wisdom" of Judean elites against what the most untrainable animals know on their own. The comparison is not flattering; the wise ones in Jerusalem act dumber than a silly bird (v. 7), while priests and prophets deliver false oracles (v. 10). At heart, then, this deception is really a form of self-delusion.

The second half of the oracle (8:10, 13-17) focuses on the divine punishment for such willful blindness. The assumption that the oracle's audience consists of elite males is revealed in the details of the punishment: loss of possessions defined as wives and arable land. The poem captures the moments just prior to the city's fall, when the food and water supplies are contaminated, when those from outlying areas gather in the city, vainly hoping its fortifications will protect them, and when predatory animals invade urban spaces. As the horses of the invading army snort at the gates, those inside the city at last recognize that they are doomed (v. 15). All that is left is to wait for the fatal "bite" (v. 17).

Jeremiah 8:18 begins with a striking change in speaker. While vv. 4-17 alternate between the words of Yahweh and the reported speech of some of the people, the first-person speaker of vv. 18-23 clearly represents neither group. Scholars debate who the speaker is. While many assert that Jeremiah grieves over the fall of the city, the imagery is better explained by viewing this speech as the words of the personified city. As in Jeremiah 4:19-22, this type of lament often focuses on the fate of women and children, evoking empathy in the audience (Pilarski 2014). Israelite texts such as the book of Lamentations, for example, explicitly name this vocal personification "Daughter Zion." The poems here and in 10:19-25 serve the same function. The redactor sandwiches between these poems references to the actual women who served as public mourners in ancient Israel (9:17-22 [9:16-21 Hebrew]; Brenner and van Dijk-Hemmes 1993, 83–90), again suggesting that the voice in 8:18–9:1 (Heb., 8:23) is a female voice.

These poems raise to the surface the tragedy of the fall, with little focus on whether or not it was deserved. Most trauma literature, i.e., literature that recounts traumatic events in the life of a community, strives to elicit empathy in the audience. Studies of trauma literature, which have grown in the post-Holocaust era, show how the empathy that the texts elicit calls for an ethical response in the audience that now becomes the virtual witness to the tragedy. Although most Israelite prophetic texts, including many of those in Jeremiah, utilize a rhetoric of blame rather than empathy, the poems here and in chapter 10 serve as a striking contrast because of the power of that pleading, empathetic female voice.

Like Lamentations 1, the speaker seeks a comforter who does not arise. The "comforter" was someone who would ease the suffering of the one mourning, either by suffering with them or by removing some of the pain. The plea for comfort and healing frames the poem. Similar to Ezekiel, God's departure is prompted by their worship of other gods, but this note of Judean sin is muffled compared to the way the poem highlights the horror and terror that this supposed "punishment" entailed.

In chapter 9, starting in v. 2 of the English translation, the poem reverts to giving voice to God's perspective. Verses 2-16, although probably including pieces originally composed at different times, contain God's explanation for the fall of the city. A variety of explanations are given: the people are unfaithful to God (vv. 2, 14); they lie (vv. 3-5, 8); and they have rejected the Torah (v. 13). God weeps, but not for the people. Divine mourning is reserved for cultivated land and domesticated animals (v. 10). Rather than pathos for the fate of the people, these texts project a God who feels justified for the slaughter that ensues. "Will I not punish them for what they have done?" Yahweh asks rhetorically in v. 9. This rhetorical context distances the audience from the horror of the punishment that is described in these same verses. The poems belie the fact that the devastation is so thorough that even the birds have fled (v. 10) and, once God violently removes the people (v. 16), the city becomes a haunt for wild animals (v. 11).

God schedules the city's funeral in vv. 17-21. Weeping has been passed from the city (9:1) to God (9:10) and on to the mourning women (9:17-21). As Bauer notes, this is the only place in the Hebrew Bible where God directly addresses a group of women; their mourning is designated as "teaching" because, through this act, they make some sense of the disaster (2002). Jeremiah 9:16 also ties their mourning to wisdom (Baumann 2002). The women lament for their own deaths as well as the deaths of others in their community. Strong images permeate the text: streams of water flow from their eyes (v. 18) while a personified Death creeps in through the windows, permeating every nook and cranny in the city (v. 21).

The viewpoint changes once more in 9:22, as the chapter turns its focus to those being mourned, now reduced to corpses littering an open field, engaging the same image found in 7:33. While Lamentations 3:45 depicts the bodies that God has torn to shreds as pieces of garbage, here they are likened to shit spread across the surface of the fields. Although these images are often hard to appreciate, O'Connor has shown that this rhetorical move reflects the need for survivors of trauma to recover language adequate to express their experiences. To a non-traumatized audience removed from the horror, this language may feel hyperbolic or distasteful while to the traumatized audience, witnessing their experience honestly is a necessary step for any type of integration of the traumatic memory (O'Connor 2012, 47–58).

The final three verses do not fit as well into the flow of the chapter. Jeremiah 9:23-24 returns to the irony that those who claim to be wise are actually fools, while v. 25 promises divine retribution on Judah's enemies. The three verses shift the image of God in the chapter. While the previous section focuses on God's role as the agent of their violent destruction, v. 24 insists on God's justice and loyalty to the covenant, which lays the foundation for the treatment of foreign nations in v. 25. Apparently it is not just contemporary audiences who are uncomfortable with God's portrayal in 9:2-22; even ancient scribes wanted to temper the divine violence with a reminder of God's other attributes.

These verses smooth the transition to the main focus of chapter 10: the foolishness of worshiping other gods. Similar to Isaiah 44, these verses describe how the Babylonians made the statues that represented their gods. The passage's focus on the material composition of these cult objects (wood and precious metals) casts these idols as mute, no better than "scarecrows in a cucumber field" (10:5 NRSV). The poems hint at the fact that Judeans turned to the worship of these Babylonian deities because of their fear (10:2, 5, 7). The sheer size and terror produced by the Babylonian army justified the conclusion that their gods were better, more powerful, and therefore more deserving to be feared than the relatively unknown God of the Judeans, who had been rather ineffective in protecting them.

The poems in this section of the book build to the refutation of this prevailing perspective. To be sure, these verses that cast other gods as nothing but wood and metal address the problem most directly, but this diatribe invites the reader to rethink the function of the language of God's violence in the preceding chapter. When the poems assert that God has scattered the corpses of the Judeans across the open fields, they actually counter the claims by the Babylonians that their deities had won a great victory and that the Judeans' God was powerless before the twin forces of Marduk and Ishtar. These poems refuse to acknowledge such a conclusion (Lundberg 2007) and prefer to depict God as violently vengeful rather than benevolent but defeated. To reinforce the connection between these two poetic pieces, this section on the worthlessness of idols closes with a return to the depiction of God as the Babylonian army exiling, capturing, and slaying the inhabitants of Jerusalem (vv. 17-18).

This section of the book closes with a return to the voice of the personified city (10:19-25). Once again, her voice evokes empathy. She calls the inhabitants of the city her "children," accepting responsibility for sin while still begging that the punishment fit the crime. These verses raise the difficult issue that, no matter how sinful the people may have been, what they endured at the hands of their enemy was far worse than anything they deserved. This same ethical conundrum is found in the book of Lamentations. They reveal the difficulty of explaining truly tragic events while preserving the character of Yahweh.

The Lamenting Prophet

Jeremiah 11–20

Each section within the book of Jeremiah is marked off not so much by formal features as by subtle changes in rhetorical style, focus, and, at times, ideology. While the first ten chapters more closely resemble the prophetic collections of preexilic prophets, with little attention to the life or thinking of the prophet as an individual, this second section of the book presents Jeremiah as a tragic figure. This section has had the greatest influence on readers' ability to empathize with Jeremiah.

The rhetoric of this section seems to present an autobiography of the prophet, a kind of direct window into his life and thoughts, although a closer read reveals it is a highly stylized literary arrangement. The section contains dialogic poems between the two main characters, God and Jeremiah, with an occasional chorus of unrepentant sinners gradually facing their horrible fate (Diamond 1987). By depicting Jeremiah in such a sympathetic light, the writer takes the focus off the tragedy that the city faces and places it on the figure of Jeremiah, who is presented as someone treated unjustly by those closest to him, yet unable to escape his fate.

Chapters 11–20 contain poems voiced by Jeremiah, lamenting his prophetic role. These poems, often called Jeremiah's "confessions," resemble individual laments found in the book of Psalms. The speaker bemoans his fate, seeking relief from God. Unlike in the lament psalms, however, here God responds to all but the final poem. Jeremiah laments the rejection he faces from his kin, his social ostracism, and the fact that he has even been born. These last complaints echo the book's opening, which presents Jeremiah as a prophet formed in the womb (1:5), the same womb Jeremiah wishes had been his grave (20:17; Stulman 2004b). Because of this framing device, many scholars suggest that chapters 1–20 were meant to be read as a coherent whole.

These laments cast Jeremiah as an ideal sufferer. His laments evoke empathy in the audience, and through his prayers the text explores issues of theodicy (Stulman 2004a). The language of the laments remains so vibrant, even for contemporary audiences, that it is difficult not to read the whole book through their lens. Yet one can ask how the characterization of Jeremiah within the book would be experienced differently if these laments were absent. He might be a less vibrant figure as well as less sympathetic. By looking at them from this direction, the literary function of the laments becomes clearer.

Standard oracles condemning various communities to the fate of exile along with scenes introducing some of Jeremiah's symbolic acts connect the poems in chapters 11–20. A symbolic act records instances when prophets acted out their oracular messages (Friebel 1999, 11–78). These symbolic acts remind modern audiences that prophetic speech was a public performance, designed to be noticed, to engage an audience, and to provoke a response. In fact, Overholt points out that prophetic legitimation depended not on the prophet but on the community (1989). Symbolic acts were much like modern performance art where the actions are meant to symbolize a larger message. For example, Isaiah walks around the city of Jerusalem naked (Isa 20:1-6) to symbolize that the Egyptians will be left with nothing when the Assyrians defeat them. In this section, Jeremiah acts out three oracles (13:1-11; 18:1-11; 19:1-15), all expressing God's deteriorating relationship with the nation. As prophetic performance, however, these oracles would have the force of any prophetic utterance (Uehlinger 2015).

This section of the book stresses the very public nature of Jeremiah's work (O'Connor 1988, 85–92). While the description of these symbolic acts is the most obvious case, there are other indications of a public backdrop as well. For instance, God's command in chapter 16 that Jeremiah refrain from marriage and avoid weddings and funerals would have placed him outside the bounds of acceptable public behavior (Carvalho 2013). His laments would have been set to music, suggesting that they too constitute public performances (Nissinen 2010a). God's repeated prohibition of his intercessory role (11:14; 14:11-12; 15:1), which is replaced with oracles of unmitigated disaster, would have also had a public impact. This is borne out by the opposition Jeremiah faces throughout this section, starting with his own family's rejection of him in chapter 11 and continuing to his very public arrest in chapter 20.

At the heart of this section is the question of the legitimacy of Jeremiah's prophetic call, a theme that permeates the entire book (Diamond 1987). Jeremiah 14:13-16 contrasts Jeremiah's message of inescapable doom with the prevailing message of the prophets prior to Jerusalem's fall—that God would save them. Israelite prophets had two roles: to deliver messages from the divine realm and to intercede on behalf of the people to God. The destruction of the city simultaneously substantiates Jeremiah's message even while it undercuts his legitimacy since he failed to save the city. This section of the book addresses the dissonance in two ways. First, it presents Jeremiah as attempting to intercede while depicting God as not only rejecting the intercession but also refusing to let Jeremiah take on that prophetic role. Second, as a consequence, when Jeremiah eventually laments, he does not and cannot lament the fate of the city, as seen in the poetic laments voiced by the personified city in other parts of the book, such as 4:19-22 and 8:18-22; that would amount to intercession. Instead, he can only lament his own fate, a lament to which God responds by promising him some form of survival (15:20-21). The rhetorical mastery of this section is that it continues to convince readers that Jeremiah was a true prophet, falsely accused of treason by a wicked populace.

Opposition from Jeremiah's Circle (11:1–12:6)

This section of the book returns to prose narrative that again contains language reminiscent of Deuteronomistic texts (Stulman 2004b). It castigates the people for worshiping other gods, breaking their exclusive covenant with Yahweh. God, who has sent ample warning, curses those who will not repent (11:3-5), a curse that cannot be revoked. Jeremiah's assent to the divine pronouncement in 11:5 is only the third time in the book that the prophet has spoken directly to God (see the dialogue in chapter 1, especially 1:6 as well as 4:10), marking a turning point. Jeremiah's great "Amen" in 11:5 signals the inevitably of divine judgment.

In this chapter, the divine speeches focus on Judah's breach of its exclusive covenant with Yahweh. In fact, the word "covenant" appears five times in vv. 1-13, the highest concentration in the oracles of doom. Here the covenant is tied to the Israelites' delivery from Egypt and their entry into the land of "milk and honey," thus designating the covenant usually associated with Sinai in the Pentateuch. While the pentateuchal accounts enumerate laws covering a variety of social, ritual, and moral situations, this passage focuses primarily on the laws' demand that the Israelites worship Yahweh alone. It is this violation of the covenant that warrants God's unstoppable curse (11:11-13).

Jeremiah 11:1-17 seems to follow a pattern found already in the wilderness narratives. The book of Exodus pairs the revelation of God's laws on Sinai or Horeb with the account of the Israelites worshiping a golden calf, which Exodus presents as a form of apostasy. When their actions come to light, God plans to annihilate them completely (Exod 32:10) until Moses intercedes on their behalf, so that God relents (32:14). In Jeremiah, however, God's curse is followed by Jeremiah's prohibition to intercede (11:14-17). Judah's fate is sealed.

This interchange leads to Jeremiah's first lament in which he bemoans the fact that the prophetic word he must convey sets him at odds with his own community. Thus chapter 11 introduces the twin themes of chapters 11–20: the irrevocability of God's pronouncement and the public opposition to Jeremiah. Each theme will intensify over the course of subsequent chapters. In this opening chapter, Jeremiah's opposition comes from his own clan, the people of Anathoth. Israelite males functioned within a web of interlocking patriarchal hierarchies, and a male's honor was dependent on both his own actions within that web as well as the approbation of those more elite than he. The book presents Jeremiah as someone on the lower end of that social scale. He is neither an elder nor a head of household (level of the clan), neither from an elite family (he is not exiled with other elites) nor a member of an elite priestly group (not a priest serving at the temple of Jerusalem). His vulnerable social position plays out over the course of these chapters as males in his clan (ch. 11), Jerusalemite society (ch. 16), and the ruling priests (ch. 20) oppose him.

Scholars disagree over the exact shape of the first lament. Clearly 11:18 switches to the voice of the prophet speaking in the first person, although whether it is originally poetry is unclear. This prophetic voice petitions God to destroy the speaker's enemies, a plea found often in lament psalms. Using imagery of fruit and sacrifice, the speech suggests that they seek to kill him before he has children. Yahweh responds to this initial plea, identifying the enemy as the people from Anathoth, named as Jeremiah's hometown in 1:1 and as his kin in 12:6. Although God has stated that they will be utterly destroyed (11:22-23), Jeremiah engages legal language, wishing the same fate for them as they had devised for him (12:1-4). God responds once more, promising their destruction (12:5-6) while warning the prophet that his own plight will only get worse (O'Connor 1988, 21–22). If you cannot withstand the pressure now ("run with horses"), God says, then how will you fare as opposition to your messages increases (as it will over the course of the next eight chapters)?

Whether or not 11:1–12:6 contains a record of a historical encounter between Jeremiah and God, the account has clearly been crafted to resonate in interesting ways within its larger literary context (Callaway 2004). The interchange introduces the major themes of this section of the book and anticipates their development over the next nine chapters. It also engages other parts of the book, echoing God's "knowledge" of Jeremiah (see 1:5) as well as Jeremiah's social location (1:1) and foreshadowing the restoration of the covenant, especially in chapter 31. It engages traditions found in other biblical books as well, such as the wilderness tradition, with its stories of effective prophetic intercession, and the lamenting traditions found primarily in the Psalms. These allusions result in a text that richly resonates with a broad swath of Israelite cultural identity.

Oracles about Judah's Fate (12:7–13:27)

When I was in high school, I bought a copy of *Norton's Anthology of Modern Poetry*. I still have that dog-eared volume, pages crinkled by my overuse. I used to thumb through its pages almost every day, finding little poetic treasures here and there. When I found myself going back to one over and over again, I would copy it into what I called my "poetry journal," my own collection of poems I savored repeatedly throughout the years. *Norton's Anthology* was never meant to be read straight through, with the reader acting like a general on a mission that needed to be completed. Each poetic unit is meant to roll around the tongue over and over, releasing its complex flavors over time.

Many of the books in the Old Testament should be approached in the same way. While the editors certainly used a rhetorical framework to arrange the poems in *Norton's Anthology*, that framework is not a reading plan. The same is true for much of Jeremiah: while scholars have shown that the book offers evidence of conscious arrangement, this does not mean the book is intended to be read straight through.

I bring this up now because, once again, this section of material is made up of discreet units. Jeremiah's lamentations that are strung together throughout chapters 11–20 connect to oracles tracing the continuing buildup of tensions in Judah before the fall of the city. The figure of Jeremiah ebbs and flows in this section, but the spotlight stays on Yahweh's un-appealable sentence on Judah. The preceding chapters have prepared the reader to accept the city's fate as thoroughly justified. When even those closest to Jeremiah, who should be his natural allies, turn against him, this demonstrates that the whole land is corrupt. The book then moves to a series of oracles that the reader is meant to imagine delivered by Jeremiah, oracles that describe the fate of the city. On the one hand, Jeremiah continues to intone Yahweh's messages of destruction, while on the other, the people continue to ignore these warnings. Yet, even within this sequence, each unit has its own integrity, its own terrible beauty.

The oracle in 12:7-13 is one such unit. For the readers who plow through the book of Jeremiah, this poem may sound like just one more oracle of destruction: Judah is evil; they are all going to die. For the readers who are resistant to or repelled by the violence of these pronouncements, it becomes one more set of verses to hurry through. But for the readers who take time to savor the language and the intricacies of the use of metaphor, the way that the passage transforms from one metaphoric realm to another exhibits a deliberate interweaving of Israelite traditions that result in a horrifying picture of exile. It opens a collection of oracles linking the lament in 11:18–12:6 to the next one in 15:10-21. This collection includes an oracle against Judah's neighbors (12:14-18) that Jeremiah acts out (a sign-act; 13:1-11), followed by at least six separate oracles in 13:12–14:22. Jeremiah 15:1-9 provides the hinge from the discussion of false prophets in this material (14:11-16) to Jeremiah's second lament (15:10-21).

The poem that starts this collection utilizes many metaphors from nature, especially the animal kingdom. The animals mentioned are predators: the lion who hunts living prey and the hyenas with carrion birds who feed off dead bodies. In both cases, though, the poet of these verses turns the metaphors on their heads. Both animals appear in Mesopotamian iconography, in particular in Assyrian monumental reliefs that glorify Assyria's violent acquisition of empire. Kings often likened themselves to lions: the Assyrian kings depicted themselves as lion hunters, while Judean kings used the lion as a royal symbol on their seals. In Jeremiah 12:8, however, God attacks Judah because she has dared to turn on Yahweh. Recalling a common motif found in Assyrian battle scenes that depict vultures flocking to pick up the body parts of dead soldiers, in 12:9 God summons these corpse-cleansing animals to feed off the presumed dead body of "his beloved" (12:7; Foreman 2011, 197–245). The poem then shifts to metaphors of land. The beloved is a fertile, cultivated, ancestral field (vv. 10 and 13) that includes a vineyard (v. 10). Although originally a "treasure," it will soon witness its own horrible destruction and desolation, with no one mourning its loss or even noticing it (v. 11; Hayes 2006). The destruction extends to the wilderness, that is, to the places city-dwellers try to escape to in order to avoid death (12:12a).

Verses 12b-13 disrupt the flow of the poem. The speaker in v. 12b is no longer Yahweh. There is another shift in v. 13, where the subject becomes the actions of the people. While vv. 12-13 seem to come from a later hand, they do not stand on their own, and so should be read with the verses that precede them. They focus on Yahweh's agency in this destruction: God's own sword will devour the people of Jerusalem (12:12). The futility of Judah's efforts is the direct result of Yahweh's anger (12:13). Read together, then, Jeremiah 12:7-13 is a poem with two additions, describing the fall of the city using metaphors from nature, that focuses not on the identity of Judah's historic enemy but rather on God as the agent of the horrors the city experiences.

The addressee in Jeremiah 12:14-18 is lexically ambiguous. The word often translated as "neighbor" in v. 14 (NRSV) has the more common meaning of "inhabitant," suggesting that the oracle is addressed once again to Judah. But the oracle characterizes these people as having taught Judah to worship Baal. Translating the term as "neighbor" may reflect contemporary assumptions that Baal worship was a foreign practice. However, archaeological evidence suggests polytheism was prevalent throughout Israel's monarchic history. These "neighbors" then could simply be those within the community who did not accept the practice of worshiping Yahweh alone.

What is interesting about the passage is that it focuses primarily on the period after the exile. While God says that the people will be exiled, the oracle also promises a return (12:15). The passage repeats the infinitives of Jeremiah 1:10, especially uprooting and rebuilding, suggesting that this material may have been added at the same time as the first chapter, i.e., at a later stage in the book's development. No matter when the material was added, however, this promised restoration should not be understood as entailing eternal security in the land. If those whom God returns fail to worship Yahweh alone (12:16), the same fate awaits them (12:17). This oracle, then, is a discreet literary unit, separated from the surrounding material by formal speech markers at the beginning of v. 14 and end of v. 18, as well as by the presumption of a post-exilic context.

Chapter 13 opens with the first of Jeremiah's sign-acts, a sign that centers on the symbol of dirty underwear. God commands Jeremiah to ruin his loincloth, first by not washing it even after a long journey to the Euphrates, about 400 miles (Brummitt 2006), and then by burying it among the rocks next to a river for "many days" (13:6). Naturally, when Jeremiah went back and recovered the loincloth, it was "good for nothing" (13:7 NRSV). The divine speech clarifies that the dirty underwear represents the full nation of Israel. This is not about just the elite in the city or even just the tribe of Judah. The whole nation is like dirty, useless boxers. And in case the audience misses the insult, God continues talking about how that underwear clings to the "loins," reminding them of their lowly function (Brummitt 2011). Oddly, though, this is depicted as a place of honor. The oracle insinuates that if they had fulfilled their function (remained clean, clinging to God's privates), they would have enjoyed the benefits of being intimately close to God. The oracle ends, though, with the reality check: "but they did not listen" (13:11). They have become a useless, dirty piece of underwear, easily thrown away.

The image is a powerful one, even for a contemporary audience, but the story, along with the short oracle that follows it, also invites the contemporary reader to try to imagine what this oracle would have looked like in its original setting (Friebel 1999, 99–115). Surely, Jeremiah did not have a crowd following him around, trailing him to the Euphrates, lingering for days on end until he dug up that underwear and then announced God's judgment (Brummitt 2006). Is this text a record of a tale Jeremiah told about himself? Is it a tradition with origins in some public act he performed with a loincloth? Was it a later tale about this legendary prophet, perhaps always circulating in written form? Such questions reveal that the author expects the audience to know the answer. The same is true for the short oracle that follows in 13:12-14. Here the passage likens Israel's fate to wine sloshing about in a jar or pitcher. The people are drunk, i.e., senseless and indiscriminately destroyed. In vv. 12-13, the passage notes the presence of an audience that interacts with Jeremiah, suggesting a similar performative act for all the oracles in this section. This, though, is the challenge of reading the book of Jeremiah in a contemporary context; although the meaning of a given passage may be clear, its genre may not (e.g., biographical detail about Jeremiah, a record of a public speech, or a prophetic tale that developed over time).

This oracle is followed by a longer poem that returns to the fate of the city (13:15-27). Because the metaphors and speakers change, this may be a collection of shorter poems, but the result is the same: the construction of images of destruction that build to create a picture of utter devastation. The concrete images in vv. 15-21a come from everyday life: pride (v. 15), light and darkness (v. 16), and shepherding (vv. 17 and 20). Verses 18-20 have flashes of the city's fall: the dethroning of the king, the approach of the army, the city's depopulation.

All this seems to serve as prelude to the longer metaphor that structures the second part of this poetic section: the return to the city as woman. The siege is likened to labor pains (13:21), which to our ears may sound like a hopeful image, but, given the high rate of death in childbirth in the ancient world, it actually intones an ominous note. This image is quickly replaced, however, in vv. 22-27 where the city's feminized body is once again victim of sexual assault. The meaning of the text is clear enough in most English translations, but the full force of the images are even starker in their Hebrew original. The reference in v. 22 to the city's rape, an all-too-common reality for women in war contexts, is echoed by God's actions in v. 26. It is presented as a sort of just deserts here; since the worship of other gods is likened to sexual promiscuity, so the punishment for this violation of the covenant is also described in sexual terms (Niessen 2004).

Two things add to the shock value of this oracle. First, the poem slows down considerably here, lingering over images of rape, here a legitimate method of punishment. Second, the rhetorical question in v. 23 (can persons or animals change the way they look?) suggests that Jerusalem is innately evil. While punishing Jerusalem for something it cannot avoid seems unfair, the author's point is that it is futile to expect the city to repent or change its ways; its condition is hopeless. This assertion should remind a contemporary audience that poems such as these are not meant to be read as philosophical or theological treatises on sin. They are poems meant to evoke a response. This poem is surely still effective in its ability to do so.

Terror and Silence, 14:1–15:9

Chapters 14 and 15 have two interlocking pieces: laments over the tragedies that the city sustains (14:1-10 and 14:17-22) and God's refusal to listen to any prophetic intercession (14:11-16 and 15:1-9). This interweaving structure reveals that those experiencing drought would feel shame (14:3) because communal devastation was a sign of divine disfavor. In other words, God is angry.

The section opens with a communal lament for widespread drought. The poem lingers over three images that capture the extent of the calamity. The first is an image of the city: people of all economic stations returning from dry wells, their vessels empty (14:3). The second moves out to the cultivated fields that surround the city: the cracked ground that should be bristling with produce (14:4). The third moves into the steppe: even the wild animals pant for water (14:6). The poem immediately attributes the drought to God as a response to communal sin (14:7). But even with the confession of sin, the people plead for relief (14:8-9).

The focus on drought picks up again in 14:19-22, where the communal voice of the people returns. Again these verses acknowledge that the drought was punishment for their sinfulness, and again the people pray for the punishment to cease (Boda 2001). In both places, they appeal to God's own self-interest (14:9 and 21). The final verse, which suggests that their sin had been that of worshiping other gods, reads as their repentance. "Can any idols of the nations bring rain? . . . Is it not you, O LORD our God?" (NRSV). In many ways this poem about drought reads like a standard communal lament over a natural disaster (or, more properly, a penitential psalm since it contains a confession of sin; see Boda [2001, 193–94]).

The divine judgment inserted into this lament raises the stakes. The images of the lamenting elements, especially in 14:17-19 and 15:5-9, derive from the violent deaths of siege warfare. Thirsty tongues are replaced by heaps of unburied corpses. Once again the poem couples urban images with agricultural ones. The bodies in the fields that have met a violent death and those in the city streets felled by starvation (14:18) evoke the twin towers of siege: decimation and slaughter. As a divine response to the lament about the drought, it is devastating. It is as if God says, "If I won't respond to your puny drought, how much more will I ignore your pleas when I finally kill you off?" Apology not accepted.

Just in case the audience does not follow the argument, the passage includes prose accounts in which the divine speaker refuses to let Jeremiah intercede (14:11-16; 15:1-4). At the heart of this passage lies the question of whether Jeremiah was a false prophet: either because his message differed from other prophets at the time (14:13-16) or because he actually saw the disaster but failed to intervene (15:1). God responds that the other prophets are the false ones who will suffer the same fate as the nation as a whole (14:14-16), and that even if Israel's paradigmatic prophets, Moses and Samuel, interceded for them, God would refuse to listen (15:1). The choice of these two prophets is significant: both had not only successfully interceded with God (see Exod 32:11-14; 1 Sam 12:17-18) but also dialogued with Yahweh. Throughout the book, elements in Jeremiah's portrayal link him to these prophets, such as his objection to becoming a prophet (Moses; see Jer 1:6-7), and his focus on Shiloh (Samuel; see Jer 7:12-14; 26:6). While other parts of the book allude subtly to these prophets, the fact that the prophets are named here makes the point of this oracle explicit: the fault for the fall of the city is not Jeremiah's failure to intercede. It resulted from God's unshakable decision to proceed.

In the midst of the communal voices crying for relief for themselves and their children, the divine voice responds with the sentencing. God rejects their plea to relieve the drought (14:10) and sentences the whole community to further punishment by sword and famine (14:15-16). Even those who try to flee from the punishment will face a divinely decreed violent and shameful death (15:3). While the lament about the drought refers to male shame, probably stemming from the elite's inability to provide for their families (14:3), the heightened punishment makes sure to include images of women and children widowed, violated, starved, slain, and unburied (14:16; 15:8-9). These are the literal "terrors" (14:19 and 15:8) that God has decreed.

Jeremiah's Voice Returns, 15:10-21

The oracles in 14:1–15:9 culminate in depictions of the fate of the women of the city. Stacked up at the end of the passage are depictions of the growing numbers of widows deprived of husbands and mothers bereft of children

(15:7-8). Even those women formerly blessed with fertility become rape victims, with no men left to defend their honor (15:9). This focus on women hammers home the horror that the city experiences, and its placement here serves as a hinge to Jeremiah's next lament in 15:10-21, which opens with his address to his mother. It is not an organic connection; nowhere in this poem does he lament his mother's fate, which had been the focus of what preceded. In fact, one of the most striking things about all of his laments is how self-centered they actually are.

The lament seems to be interrupted in vv. 11-14 with an oracle of God to the city, but the text in this section is unfortunately corrupt, at places nongrammatical. It could be that the "mother" whom Jeremiah addresses is the personified city, but the pronouns referring to the city in these verses are masculine, which cuts against such a conclusion.

With these verses set aside, the lament in vv. 10 and 15-21 focuses once again on Jeremiah's opposition. The poem opens with a legal metaphor: Jeremiah has had to pronounce God's verdict on Judah's behavior (15:10). He states that he did the job swiftly (v. 15), joyfully (v. 16), and diligently (v. 17), but the result of his dedication is rage (v. 17), pain, and incurable damage (v. 18). Jeremiah's speech culminates in his accusation that Yahweh has deceived him (v. 18; Johnston 2010): seeming to promise him blessings (flowing fresh water) only to leave him high and dry (but a brook that deceives; Boda 2014, 94–99).

God's response offers little comfort. The conditional statement with which it opens ("If you turn back" or "repent") asserts that Jeremiah's accusations are blasphemy (15:19). The Lord allows him to recant but makes it clear that his fate will remain the same. He will still be attacked for being God's mouthpiece. God only promises that his opponents will not prevail over him; Jeremiah will be made into a metal wall that will survive these attacks (v. 20). The reality of this offer is cold comfort. If Jeremiah does not repent of what he has said, he will share the fate of the city (whose punishment is itself the result of failure to repent). If he does repent, then what he is complaining about will only get worse, although he will at least "survive." But what is "survival" when your whole nation collapses? As the book progresses, it becomes clear that it merely means he will neither be killed nor exiled. But he will still be a witness to the horrors of the city's fate and become a refugee. His world will be torn asunder, and he will have no joy or peace.

Chapters 14–15 reinforce this fate through their rich vocabulary of horror and terror. English translations mask the tragic variety of terms that Hebrew has for describing horror: pure terror in 14:19; sudden terror in 15:8; horror that shakes a person (15:4); as well as trembling in fear (15:21; translated as "ruthless" in NRSV). Each of these verses uses a different word in Hebrew. This language of terror will be picked up again in chapter 20, which will add another Hebrew term, one conveying a sense of overwhelming dread (20:3, 10). Jeremiah, then, has two choices: either be a victim in the horror or be a witness to it.

Jeremiah Ostracized, 16:1-13

Chapter 16 further dashes Jeremiah's hopes for a happy ending when God commands the prophet neither to marry nor participate in any of the social activities that would have given him a sense of community or family. To a modern ear, these social prohibitions may not sound too severe, but in the ancient world, Jeremiah's absence at weddings and funerals along with his own failure to marry would have resulted in his complete alienation from the community.

Israelite society did not view celibacy as honorable. Jeremiah 32 depicts Jeremiah as a landowner, eligible to buy or redeem another person's field (Domeris 2011). Land was supposed to be handed down through the family, so men had an obligation to have heirs. While it was certainly true that sometimes men had to adopt an heir, they still had a duty to marry, thus also providing male protection for women whose sons would eventually take care of them (Macwilliam 2013). In Jeremiah 16:2, the meager hope contained in God's promise to Jeremiah that he will survive (15:20-21) comes to light when it becomes clear that this promise extends to Jeremiah alone and not to a whole household. He will have no wife or children who will survive with him. Verses 3-4 try to cast this as a divine blessing since Judean parents will only have to watch their children die horrible deaths; the details devoted to the children's fate might cause the audience to scream, "No, anything but that!" This divine speech reveals that the future that Jeremiah's prays for is impossible. It is like boarding the *Titanic*, expecting that this time it will reach New York safely.

God forbids Jeremiah to participate in any social gatherings. No matter what the exact contours of the celebrations may have been, his shunning of weddings and funerals constitutes social suicide (Maier and Dörfuss 1999; Stavrakopoulou 2010). The text invites the audience to imagine the community's reaction as he refuses, time and again, to attend the funerals that must have proliferated at this time (16:5-7). He will not intone a dirge, feast (van der Toorn 1988), or offer comfort, a formal role in the mourning process (Pham 1999). God also forbids him to take part in social celebrations such as weddings (16:8-9). Instead, he is supposed to tell his friends, family, and social circle what sinners they are and how God will punish them for being so evil. It is not surprising that, as a result, the book depicts a growing opposition to this odd and cheerless prophet.

The people's reaction in v. 10 demonstrates how important these social activities were to them. The cessation of weddings and funerals evokes an almost stronger reaction than the predictions of famine and sword. What sin could have been so great, they ask, that it warrants such a horrible punishment? The response once again focuses on worshiping other gods, but this is not just a religious issue. Such idolatry also involves following other laws that would have governed their view of a civil society (v. 11). The language in this section recalls language in Deuteronomy, as does the punishment: expulsion from the land (see, e.g., Deut 28:63-64).

A Collection, 16:14–17:27

The texts linking Jeremiah's social restrictions in 16:1-13 and his next prophetic sign-act in chapter 18 do not form a cohesive whole. At best, they make up a collection of primarily (but not exclusively) oracles of doom, written in a variety of styles. Each passage seems to address a different audience or topic. Some of the passages do not fit well within the major themes of the book and may stem from later hands. Overall, they add to the depiction of the city as evil, God as justified, and Jeremiah as the sole righteous Judean.

Jeremiah 16:14-21 vacillates between hope and condemnation. Verses 14-15 contain a brief oracle of hope or salvation. God promises to return those who had been exiled back to the land. This includes the northern citizens of Israel, exiled by the Assyrians in 722. Because these verses seem out of context within the overall sweep of this section of the book, they may be a later addition triggered by God's decree of exile at the end of the previous section. Hope does not last long. The book immediately returns to chastising the people of Judah for idolatry (16:16-18), countered by an oracle that predicts the eventual conversion of all the nations of the earth (vv. 19-21). It ends with a phrase more characteristic of the book of Ezekiel than Jeremiah: "they shall know that my name is Yahweh" (16:21).

One of the most popular passages in Jeremiah is 32:39, where God promises to give Israel "one heart," an image of the renewal of the covenant. What is often missed is how this promise responds to the problem outlined in passages such as 17:1-4, where the sin of the people is literally engraved on their hearts. The image of engraving with an iron pen or diamond-tipped stylus connotes a stony heart that is stubborn and unmalleable. The people have been tattooed, if you will, with their own sinfulness, and, like a tattoo, this branding results from their own choices. Again the paradigmatic sin in this passage is illegitimate worship practices for which they will be conquered and exiled.

Jeremiah 17:5-8 uses the pattern of blessings and curses to contrast the fate of the wicked with that of the righteous. Blessings and curses were attached to treaties and other agreements. The book of Deuteronomy follows this pattern by placing blessings and curses at the end of the ceremony ratifying Israel's covenant with God (ch. 28). The same language is used here, but the order is flipped, with the curse before the blessing. Both halves of the contrast use plant imagery: a shrub shriveling in the desert (curse) as opposed to a tree in full bloom thriving at the edge of a stream (blessing).

The poetic verses in 17:9-13 can be read as a collection of short sayings attributed to Jeremiah. Verses 9-11 attest to God's ability to discern undetected sin, with the final verse echoing the language of the proverbs. Scholars conjecture that 17:12-13 is a fragment of a hymn of some sort. The throne refers to the way that the Israelites represented God's presence in their temples. While the Egyptians, for instance, placed a statue of their deity in their temples, the Israelites used an empty throne, above which God was invisibly present. Biblical texts identify the ark and cherubim as forming this throne in the temple of Jerusalem (see Ezek 43:7), from which pours fresh water (Ezek 47:1). This hymnic fragment in Jeremiah projects a royal deity who issues decrees that cannot be deflected.

A short individual lament follows. Many scholars conclude that the first-person speaker of these verses is Jeremiah, but the speaker again could as easily be the personified city (see the discussions at 4:19 and 8:18). Once again, these verses, following immediately on a notice of Yahweh's punishments, would fit the pattern of a female mourner, like the city's patron goddess, attempting to provoke empathy in the attacking male deity. The referents in these verses are ambiguous, however; are the persecutors in v. 18 those in Jerusalem opposing Jeremiah, or the Babylonians attacking the city? It is likely that the poetic language is deliberately ambiguous in order to evoke both readings.

Jeremiah 17:19-27 forms a coherent whole that attributes Judah's sin to forsaking the laws of the Sabbath. In addition to the commandment that the Israelites should refrain from work on the Sabbath (Exod 20:8-11; Deut 5:12-15), Sabbath prohibitions also appear in Exodus 31:12-17 (repeated in 35:2-3) and Leviticus 23:3. In all of these, Israelites (and their land) observe the Sabbath by refraining from work, although Numbers 28:9-10 makes it clear that sacrifices were offered on the Sabbath. While the Decalogue in Exodus 20 ties Sabbath rest to God's rest at the end of creation, Deuteronomy 5 makes it an explicit labor law noting that, as slaves in Egypt, they could not rest. The implication is that Sabbath rest is a time to reflect on God as the one who delivered them from such oppressive working conditions. Jeremiah 17 seems to reflect this latter association. God will reward proper behavior on the Sabbath with the reestablishment of Jerusalem as the central sacred site for a wholly restored nation of Israel. The piece plays with a kind of positive irony: if the elite cease from their working practices on the Sabbath, then the reward will be people streaming into the city through the very gates where the passage places Jeremiah, bearing burdens themselves, but this time in the form of offerings destined for the temple's Sabbath rituals.

God, the Hairy (i.e., *Virile*) Potter, 18:1–19:15

Pottery was ubiquitous in the ancient world; it was their version of Tupperware, totes, and plastic storage bins. Two thousand years from now, an archaeologist armed with the appropriate Tupperware catalogs could date the occupation levels of the twenty-first-century American city by the Tupperware found at the site. We do not pay much heed to Tupperware, however (or at least not the lids, which seem to disappear with the same alacrity as socks in my house). In ancient Jerusalem, pottery would have served the same function. It was everywhere: small jars, large urns, platters, cups, goblets, and bowls. When a pot broke, people used the shards as scratch paper. It became part of fill dirt and even served as a back-scratcher for an itchy Job (Job 2:8).

In Jeremiah 18 and 19, the prophet turns this ancient household good into a prophetic symbol of God's impending disaster. Jeremiah 18:1-12 casts God as the potter who has the right to fashion clay in any way God chooses. While a contemporary reader may feel unease at the idea that God's creative work may be imperfect, the image as it plays out in these verses is not far from the creation of humanity in Genesis 2:7-8, 18-25. In Genesis, God, who has formed the human person out of mud, eventually realizes a flaw in this creation (he should have made more than one of these creatures). The metaphor of pottery focuses on the dynamic element of creation and depicts it as a kind of artistry, where the potter plays with the material until settling on a final form that should be fired and rendered permanent. In Jeremiah 19, however, it will be clear that even fired pots can be destroyed. This image undercuts any assumption by the ideal audience that they are safe because God has formed them.

Jeremiah 18:7 echoes the language of Jeremiah 1:10. Once again, God promises to destroy as well as to build, but here these alternating acts of devastation and support depend on the activity of the nation under scrutiny. The word for "nation" used in this passage usually refers to foreign lands. By the end of the passage, it is clear that the prophet applies this image to Judah:

its fate rests in its own behavior. But by using the term for any nation, the passage also insinuates that God can reward Babylon as easily as Israel. In fact, the word normally translated as "kingdom" (vv. 7 and 9) can also mean "empire," further recalling Judah's mortal enemy. This text then casts Judah as more wicked than the enemy it despises.

Jeremiah 18:13-17 builds on this indictment with yet another oracle promising sweeping destruction to the nation. Using the structure of a formal dirge or lament, the poem sings the death knoll on the nation. The voice of God through the prophet promises them no respite from the impending disaster. As these songs of destruction pile up in what is to be imagined as public performance after public performance during a time when the Babylonian army is literally knocking on the city gates, it is no wonder that the opposition to a lone voice sowing despair through the city grows with each verse.

At last it cannot be held in. The book places the plots to arrest and even assassinate the prophet immediately after this funeral song (18:18). While prophets in general hope to change people's behavior toward the will of God, Jeremiah's words have only resulted in them steeling their resolve to ignore everything he has to say. Jeremiah's next lament responds to this heightened threat to his life (vv. 19-23), weaving together images of death and burial. Jeremiah's opposition seeks to treat him like a wild animal that falls into a pit or is ensnared in a net. Verse 21 lingers over the catastrophic scope of the impending disaster, while the poem ends with Jeremiah's appeal to God to kill his opponents' children (see Ps 137:9 for a similar plea for vengeance). While the text reads as a glimpse into the personal life of this famous prophet, its preservation reflects the frustrations of those survivors caught up in a disaster they could not avert.

Chapter 19 contains another prophetic act involving a fired clay jug, a potter's finished project. The reader pictures Jeremiah standing at the public entrance of the "Potsherd Gate," perhaps referring to the entrance to the city dump (Fretheim 2002, 282), jug in hand, delivering a horrifying oracle of destruction. At the end of the speech, he smashes the jug into fragments so small the jug cannot be repaired. When read in concert with the symbolic acts in chapter 18, the section depicts Judah as evil from its inception (moldable clay) until its bitter end (a fired jug). God can destroy any and all forms of the nation.

The description of the destruction that Jeremiah intones weaves together images of death with references to idolatry. The Valley of Beth-Hinnom and Topheth (19:2, 6, 11–14) probably refer to burial places adjacent to Jerusalem where child sacrifice may have also been performed. The passage also mentions incense offerings to gods other than Yahweh (vv. 4 and 13), as well as the establishment of shrines or "high places" dedicated to Baal and other gods (vv. 5 and 13). In most prophetic texts, child sacrifice is associated with the worship of Canaanite gods, but Ezekiel 20:25-26 presumes people were sacrificing their children to Yahweh. God's strong protest in Jeremiah 19:5 ("it did not [even] enter my mind") should be read against this backdrop.

The passage ironically twists this motif since the punishment does include God's slaying of children (v. 9), but as punishment rather than sacrifice. Verse 7 initiates the death scenes, first by relegating the corpses of warriors as fodder for carrion birds and wild animals. Verse 9 turns to the fate of noncombatants within the city walls, piling up images of cannibalism: fathers eating dead sons, mothers munching on daughters, neighbors filleting neighbors. The text invites readers to view the tableau like tourists perusing the horrible images, clucking their tongues and shaking their heads (vv. 3 and 8), like tourists at the Holocaust Museum. "Terrible, terrible," they mutter as they parade past horror after horror.

The Prophet's Final, Futile Protest, 20:1-18

At the end of chapter 19, Jeremiah returns to the court of the temple, spewing his oracles of utter destruction, but chapter 20 opens with the confrontation that ensues between him and Pashur, a priest who had some sort of high office. The priests had the right to defend the sanctity of the temple area and, in certain instances, to adjudicate legal matters. One area under their control was the treatment of false prophets. According to Deuteronomy 18:20, false prophets received the death penalty. Deuteronomy 18:9-22 characterizes false prophets either as those who are channeling a deity other than Yahweh or those who claim to have received a message from the divine realm but have not. First Kings 22:22 suggests that prophets can also be possessed by "lying spirits," not knowing that what they proclaim is false. Deuteronomy 18:21-22 goes on to say that the veracity of a prophet's oracle can only be determined after the fact. As a result, people accused of false prophecy could be detained in some way until the events they described had evolved (1 Kgs 22:26-28). The exact meaning of the Hebrew term (*hammahpeket*, v. 2) used to describe how Pashur restricts Jeremiah is not clear.

While this treatment of false prophets suggests that the prophet's job was to predict the future, this conclusion is incomplete. They conveyed messages from the divine to the human world, often with the purpose of changing people's behavior and averting the threatened punishment. Therefore, not everything a prophet predicts comes true; sometimes they successfully change the course of events, such as Isaiah's ability to convince Hezekiah to pray (2 Kgs 19:3-7, 14-20). Pashur confines Jeremiah, however, for too short a duration to determine if he is a false prophet. What he predicts would not have occurred overnight, the apparent length of his sentence. It is not clear what Jeremiah's violation was, then, except that his message was unwelcome; after all, there was no notion of the right to free speech in the ancient world. The high priest of the temple at Bethel similarly tries to silence Amos when his message predicts a dire fate for the northern kingdom (Amos 7:12-14).

Assuming then, that Pashur used the confinement to silence the prophet, Jeremiah's speech to Pashur as he leaves is hilarious. Pashur, whose name means "fruitfulness on every side" (Holladay 1976), not only fails in silencing the prophet but also elicits a diatribe deliberately aimed at him. It starts with Jeremiah renaming the priest ("Terror-all-around"), followed by the description of the terrible events that will ensue as the result of his decision to discredit Jeremiah. The prophet thereby recasts the predictions of utter destruction so that they are now seen through the eyes of this high official. *Pashur* shall witness the invasion of the city by Babylonian troops, the exile of the people, and the widespread death. *He* will watch the city stripped of its wealth, the houses plundered, and the temple itself raided. *He* will survive so that he can see his household exiled, so that all that will be left to him is an ignoble, shameful death in a foreign land. Jeremiah punctuates the prediction by charging Pashur as the false prophet (v. 6).

Jeremiah intones his final lament in 20:7-18, the longest of all of the laments. It remains stubbornly focused on the prophet's own fate. He rails against God for putting him in this situation. He never doubts the veracity of the messages he has been delivering. Not once does he feel pity for the fate of the city. In fact, he has repeatedly begged God to enact vengeance against his opponents. Jeremiah's reaction, far from being a compassionate plea to spare the city and the households whose fate he has described, consists in an impatient cry for the destruction to commence.

This lament opens with Jeremiah charging God with seduction. Other forms of this Hebrew word can be translated as "rape" (Bauer 1999a, 113–17), but the form used here connotes trickery of some sort, including seduction, a kind of sexual deception. It is a rich word, suggesting that there is something attractive about being close to God, perhaps reflecting a complex matrix of dominance and submission (Stone 2007). The passage's allusions cast Jeremiah as a willing participant at first who eventually realizes the gravity of what he must do. This idea is not too far from the depiction of Isaiah's call to be a prophet in Isaiah 6; there the prophet willingly volunteers to deliver God's message (v. 8) before he realizes that this commits him to participating in the utter destruction of the kingdom (vv. 9-13). While Isaiah reacts to his fate with the cry, "How long, O LORD?" Jeremiah's lament describes the pain of trying to hold in the message that the prophet is supposed to deliver. It is a rare glimpse into Israelite assumptions about the prophetic experience. The text creates a picture of Jeremiah unable to control his compulsion to speak the frightening images that swirl within him.

This depiction subverts any inclination to view true prophets as acting out of self-interest (O'Connor 1988, 75–80). This was the charge that Amaziah laid against Amos, who countered by stating that he was overcome with the prophetic message he was sent to deliver (Amos 7:14-15). Jeremiah's lament suggests that the prophets know that what they say not only evokes opposition but also puts them in real danger. The poem repeats the verb of seduction but in the mouths of Jeremiah's enemies, including the renamed Pashur; using the same word found in v. 7, they hope to seduce Jeremiah so they can finally silence and rebuke him (v. 10). Jeremiah calls on divine aid for his revenge, and, in a form true to individual laments in the book of Psalms, he asserts confidence that his plea will be heard (20:13).

The tone quickly changes in vv. 14-18, however, away from self-righteousness to despair. This prophetic character voices a lengthy curse on the day he was born and on those who celebrated his birth as a blessing. These verses invert the standard view in antiquity of pregnancy and childbirth. Here instead of images of fertility, prosperity, and virility, the poem makes the pregnant womb an image of death. It recalls the skeletons archaeologists have uncovered of women with their infant children's skeletons still within them, births that never saw the sun.

Woven through the passage are references to honor and shame. Ancient Israelite society functioned within an honor-shame code. For elite, landowning males in particular, honor was accrued by enacting the gendered expectations of society: marriage, children, an honorable household, success in business, interactions with other males in the society based on varying degrees of status, etc. Loss of family, prestige, or control conferred shame. Jeremiah's inability to marry or to attend weddings and funerals brought shame to him. The defeat of the city, the inability of males to defend their households, and their own subordination to a foreign invader brought communal shame to them as well. This lament ends with the prophet characterizing his status as one of shame, which stands in parallel to the suffering and sorrow that accompanied the city's siege and fall. While to a modern ear, shame seems to be the least of Jeremiah's problems, the poem speaks to the prevailing traumatic effect of the city's fall. This was not just about political allegiances. Its impact could not be measured by a count of the dead, wounded, or exiled. Its effect is best conveyed through the utterly thorough way it changed the community's relationships to each other, to other nations, and to its God. Children of the promise no more, they now saw themselves as unworthy, helpless heirs of pain and sorrow.

In this honest expression of how communal tragedy elicits a fundamental questioning of group identity and meaning, the poem also brings into focus the book's theological agenda. Communal tragedy at its heart leads to questions about everything that previously gave life meaning (Wilson 2012a). It is no wonder that such an experience would cause the people to rethink the nature of God. The same questioning is found in the book of Ezekiel, which staunchly refuses to attribute love as motivating any of God's treatment of Israel throughout its history. Unlike Ezekiel's self-absorbed, fully controlled deity, however, Jeremiah's God is deeply passionate; but, like any divine attribute, such passion is dangerous, terrible, awe-full. Jeremiah's God has loved Judah but is also enraged. This God will forgive but will also fully exact any punishment due. This God can dupe, deceive, and trick. Yahweh will fight, seek vengeance, and wipe out entire households. In this section of the book, the authors engage a rich vocabulary of terror and horror as they craft a God capable of being the agent of the destruction that this community experienced.

Oracles against Judah's Leaders

Jeremiah 21–25

Chapters 21–25 in the book of Jeremiah serve as a transition between the oracles focusing on the response of the prophet to the oracles he has been forced to deliver (chs. 11–20) and the prose accounts of his confrontations with various leaders in Jerusalem (chs. 26–29; 32–45). Like the material that precedes them, chapters 21–25 consist primarily of prophetic oracles, but like the material that follows, they are framed by references to specific historical contexts and often named audiences. In addition, they address the same leaders with whom Jeremiah interacts in the subsequent prose narratives. As with any division within the book of Jeremiah, however, these stylistic differences are subtle and often variable, so it is more a matter of emphasis than a clear and sharp line between sections of the book.

All oracles in this section target leaders in Jerusalem (Boadt 2007), especially kings but also prophets (27:9-18) along with the priests (23:33-40). These references do not appear in chronological order (Seitz 1989a, 226–28). In this section it becomes clear that the author of the book did not believe that everyone who was killed, maimed, or exiled by the Babylonians deserved this violence. Many of the victims were simply collateral damage (see especially 23:1-8). The descriptions of the fall of the city contained in the oracles, however, are no less horrific than in the first two sections of the book.

The oracles turn a sharp focus on the Davidic monarchy. The kings who ruled Jerusalem traced their lineage back to David, an amazingly long dynastic succession in the ancient world. The book of Jeremiah as a whole mentions David or the Davidic monarchy seventeen times, five of which appear in these chapters. These chapters contain two prominent metaphors for the Davidic line: branch (23:5) and shepherd (22:22; 23:2, 4). "Branch" is used in Isaiah, Zechariah, and Malachi to refer to a future king who will be a sign of God's blessing to Israel. While poetic texts sometimes liken the nation of Israel to a tree or bush that God plants, the branch is a shoot or family that grows out of that main plant to become the royal family. The king as shepherd is more common in the prophetic books, and even weaves its way through the narratives about David in the books of Samuel. In the ancient world, shepherds were not owners of the sheep they tended; they worked for rich owners to whom they were held accountable (Mein 2007). This is a fitting metaphor for Israelite kings as well, since they ruled in place of God, who remained the true king of Israel. Jeremiah's use of the metaphor, then, reinforces this idea that the human king simply acts on God's behalf. Just as an owner can fire a shepherd who does not recognize divine ownership of the flock, so God has the right to dispose of Judah's human kings when they act against the divine owner's wishes (Foreman 2011, 35–106).

The book of Jeremiah contains even more references to thrones than it does to shepherds or branches. In fact, this focus on varying thrones permeates the book. Taken in isolation, the references to thrones do not appear to be particularly metaphoric, but when read together, it is clear that a "throne" represented the ruling function of the one sitting on it, much like a bishop's *cathedra* or seat stands for his authority in Catholic ecclesiology. The whole book of Jeremiah refers to thrones fifteen times, nine of these to David's throne (13:13; 17:25; 22:2, 4, 30; 29:16; 33:17, 21; 36:30), four to Yahweh's (3:17; 14:21; 17:12; 49:38), once to Nebuchadnezzar's (43:10), and once to other kings in general (1:15). The three in these chapters are paired with the king's duty to enact justice. The combination of metaphors usually used to exalt a king (branch, shepherd, throne) with oracles condemning kings for their failure to maintain a civil society results in a bitterly ironic diatribe against Judah's divinely appointed leaders (Varughese 2004).

An Ironic Condemnation of Zedekiah, 21:1-10

Nebuchadnezzar of Babylon first besieged Jerusalem in 597. At that time, although the city remained standing, the Babylonians exiled its reigning king, Jehoiakin (formerly called Coniah), along with his family and officials and placed a different member of the Davidic house, Zedekiah (formerly named Mattaniah), on the throne in Jehoiakin's place. It is possible that many people felt that Jehoiakin remained the legitimate king and that Zedekiah was merely a temporary regent while the true king was in exile. Probably this was the purpose of this original exile: if the loyalists believed Jehoiakin was the true king, then they would be less likely to rebel against the Babylonians who could execute him at any time. Zedekiah followed this script until he rebelled against the Babylonians, thus provoking a renewed and eventually fatal siege of the city.

Jeremiah 21:1-10 is set against this backdrop. Envoys come to Jeremiah from Zedekiah, seeking relief from the Babylonian attack, a practice that has precedent. According to Isaiah 37:9 (and 2 Kgs 19:2), King Hezekiah sought the prophet Isaiah's advice when the Assyrians attacked Jerusalem. He heeded Isaiah's instructions to pray, and the city was miraculously saved. The story does not play out in quite the same way for Zedekiah. Jeremiah's infamous priestly enemy, Pashur, along with another priest, Zephaniah, approach Jeremiah, seeking a favorable oracle to help the city avert the disaster so imminently threatened. In short, they expect a miracle. What Jeremiah delivers, however, is a sweeping condemnation of the king that borders on treason (Maier 2013).

The oracle begins with images of reversal: God promises to turn Judah's own weapons against them (v. 4a). Not only will God not turn the Babylonians away; the divine warrior will also lead this enemy into the very heart of the city (v. 4b). Citing the image of God's outstretched hand and strong arm that signaled God's deliverance of the Hebrews from slavery during the exodus, Yahweh declares that, with these symbols of heavenly power, "I myself will fight against you" (v. 5). God's slaughter will be a full ban or *ḥerem*, a term used in Deuteronomy 20:15-18 to refer to the wholesale destruction of Israel's enemies. But Yahweh will carry out this ban against Judah instead, destroying both humans and animals (v. 6). Death will come via disease, violence, and famine, and if any survive, Nebuchadnezzar will show no pity (v. 7).

The prophet then turns to the people who will suffer this fate, appearing to offer them two choices: one will lead to "life" and another to "death" (v. 8). This verse is not really about the people's ability to make a choice, however. Its primary purpose is to justify God's decree against the city. Zedekiah had a choice and he made the wrong one. The disasters described in these verses are merely the unfolding of the "road to death" that he chose. Again the prophetic speech emphasizes the comprehensive quality of the destruction: even if someone escapes the city, Nebuchadnezzar will hunt him down (v. 9). The final verse of this section summarizes the oracle: there really is no choice. God has already decreed that Jerusalem will meet a horrible fate at the hands of the Babylonians (v. 10).

A Throne for Executing Justice, 21:11–22:9

Three short oracles against unspecified members of the Davidic line follow the diatribe against Zedekiah. The first two condemn a king from the house of David for failure to maintain justice (21:11-14; 22:1-5), while the last one describes the judgment that will ensue for this failure (22:6-10). Within Israelite traditions, one of the main duties of the king was to ensure that justice was practiced throughout the land. The book of Judges, for example, attributes the snowballing cycle of injustice to the lack of a king. Nathan tricks David into condemning himself for his treatment of Uriah by asking him to judge a case of a poor man who was exploited by a rich one (2 Sam 12). When Solomon asks for wisdom in 1 Kings 3:9 and 12, the narrative illustrates his gift by his just judgment in favor of a poor woman. While landowners maintained a system of justice at city gates, the king ensured that justice was extended to all those living in the kingdom.

Jeremiah's condemnation of these kings plays with the assumption that kings ensure justice. These oracles do not condemn them for idolatry or ritual violations. They do not entail sexual sins. They focus specifically on unfair practices and travesties of justice. Jeremiah 21:12 attributes the fall of the city to the king's ineffectiveness in protecting the "oppressed" from those who would plunder them; v. 14 promises that this situation will be reversed, implying that Judah will be plundered by someone else. Jeremiah 22:1-5 contains a similar message but with more detail. There, God speaks up on behalf of those who do not have the same legal protections as landowners, those who are more vulnerable to exploitation and unfair practices (v. 3). This includes those who are not landowners (often translated as "resident aliens"), women who are not attached to a landowning male ("widows"), and minor children who have no landowning father or are not recognized heirs ("orphans"). The fate of the nation depends on the king's treatment of these lowest members of Judean society.

The final oracle of the three (vv. 6-10) describes the fate of the royal household, once again using contrasting images. On the one hand, this family could have been as great as the rich forests of Lebanon or the healing properties of Gilead, but because they broke their covenant with Yahweh (v. 9), God has decreed their utter destruction. Sacrificial language is used in v. 7: Jerusalem's dedication to destruction ("prepare destroyers" in the NRSV) invokes a phrase used to describe the animal burned in a sacrificial fire as an offering. This destruction has witnesses (v. 8), presumably non-Israelites, who will remark on the city's ruins as they pass by on their way to someplace else. The oracle ends by stating that rather than mourning those who died, the real lament should be directed towards those living in exile who will never see their homeland again.

The Evil Kings of Judah's Final Years, 22:11-30

The book of Jeremiah now turns to the condemnation of Judah's last three legitimate kings: Jehoahaz (also named Shallum; vv. 10-12), Jehoiakim (vv. 13-23), and Jehoiakin (also called Coniah; vv. 24-30). As discussed in the introduction, along with Zedekiah who is condemned in Jeremiah 24, these are the final kings of the nation of Judah. They reigned during the turbulent decades leading up to the city's fall. These oracles place the blame for the fall squarely on their shoulders.

The condemnation of Shallum is as brief as his three-month reign (22:10-12). It alludes to his exile to Egypt and his death in a foreign land. The prophet asserts that Shallum's death should not be mourned, insinuating that his fate was punishment from God. The poetic oracle against Jehoiakim that ensues after this brief condemnation focuses on economic justice (vv. 13-17). It contrasts the opulence of building a rich house with the treatment of the poor. The poem undermines the potentially positive image of the king's large house with cedar paneling and expensive fabric (22:13-14) by connecting these achievements to his economic exploitation and use of force (v. 17). This passage also contains one of the only clear references to Josiah in the book; vv. 15-16 depict Josiah as a righteous king who prospered as a result of his ethical behavior.

The ultimate fate of Jehoiakim is unclear in the historical books. Second Kings suggest he was killed when Babylon and its allies attacked the city, while 2 Chronicles asserts he was exiled to Babylon and died there. This passage attests to a shameful death and dishonorable burial, a notice contradicted in 2 Kings 24:6 (Grabbe 2006), but does not specify where it occurs. Jeremiah 36:30 contains a second equally ambiguous reference to Jehoiakim's death and lack of burial. Both passages assume that his shameful death played out on the world stage (v. 19).

The oracle in chapter 22 ends with a return to images of opulence in vv. 21-23 coupled with their ironic unraveling in vv. 24-30. The king who would not heed God's warnings as long as he lived in luxury will no longer live in a cedar-lined palace but rather in a foreign land (represented by the cedar forests of Lebanon in v. 23). These final verses of the chapter focus on the fate of Jehoiakin, formerly Coniah, whom the Babylonians exiled in 597. The passage begins with a reference to his formerly elevated status as Yahweh's "signet ring" (v. 24), now torn off God's right hand and flung to the Babylonians, the very enemy whom Jehoiakim most feared. His fate involves three horrors: death and burial outside of the land of Israel, shame and loss of status (a broken pot), and ultimately the end of the Davidic dynasty.

Woe to the Shepherds; Hooray for the Branches, 23:1-8

These verses present another set of contrasting images representing the fate of the royal family, but this time vv. 1-4 contrast their dire fate at the hands of the Babylonians with their glorious restoration in vv. 5-8. Both halves of the poem engage the prevailing metaphors for the Davidic dynasty. The condemnation depicts the kings as ineffective shepherds who have failed to keep their flocks herded and safe (Foreman 2011, 44–58), placing the blame for the exile clearly on the shoulders of the kings (Plant 2008). This serves as a reminder that the sweeping condemnations of all Judeans in other parts of the book are rhetorical hyperbole. The image of God's restoration of the "flock" in vv. 3-4 explicitly addresses the injustice of their fate. Without the addition of vv. 5-8, God's promise to provide a new shepherd can be read as the ultimate punishment of the Davidic monarchy: the replacement of that dynasty with another. This would accord well with the end of chapter 22. God will preserve the flock, but the line of shepherds will pass to another family.

Jeremiah 23:5-8 presents a different view. Once again God promises restoration, but from the outset it is clearly a restoration of the Davidic monarchy. These verses use another common metaphor for the royal family: that of the branch. Several elements in these verses suggest that they are a late addition to the text. First, the branch metaphor appears primarily in postexilic prophetic literature. Second, the phrase "the days are surely coming" (v. 7), which occurs throughout Jeremiah but also in other prophetic texts, introduces oracles of restoration that often expect a significant change in world order. Most prominently, however, is the fact that these verses are quite at odds with their surrounding material. The oracles both preceding and following this one give no inkling that any of these kings deserves restoration or divine favor. The immediately preceding verses poignantly note the helplessness of those who suffered the tragic fate of their nation brought on by evil and incompetent leaders. It is not a stretch to imagine someone in later years adding these verses, perhaps at a time when the restoration of a Davidic line seemed to be possible (see, for example, Zech 4:6-14).

Condemnation of the Prophets, 23:9-40

This section of Jeremiah not only blames Judah's kings for Jerusalem's destruction; it also condemns the false prophets. It is not entirely clear where one oracle stops and another begins. For example, this material commences with a first-person speaker who is not God (v. 9), yet by v. 11, the first-person speaker is clearly Yahweh. The phrase "says the LORD" (NRSV; more properly translated "a statement of Yahweh"), which is sometimes but not always used to close off an oracle, punctuates the passage. In the Hebrew manuscript on which English translations are based, the passage also fluctuates between poetry and prose. These variations suggest that at some point, oracles against prophets were gathered to this section of the book either without attention to structuring those oracles or in a deliberate attempt to create a passage that literally piles up the condemnations against the prophets.

These oracles also occasionally include the priests (vv. 11, 33, 34). Together, prophets and priests represented the religious leaders of the Israelite city (Nissinen 2010b). Both served as intermediaries between the human and divine realms, the priests through the rituals that took place at the temple and the prophets through various forms of communication with the divine. While some prophets operated outside the temple system, others were connected with the temple. Samuel, for example, grows up in a temple and, as an adult, blesses a sacrifice (1 Sam 3:1; 9:13). Isaiah's vision in chapter 6 takes place in the temple. Ezekiel is from a priestly family (Ezek 1:3). The references to prophets and priests together in these oracles function to condemn the whole religious system.

The compiler of this final text places these oracles in the middle of oracles condemning Judah's kings. In the historical books, prophets were supposed to keep kings in line because they could critique kings with impunity. Although kings did not always follow the advice of the prophets (or at least not the advice of the correct prophets), prophets were to blame if they failed to serve as conduits for God's messages to the king. The condemnation of king, priest, and prophet serve to condemn the totality of Judean leadership, especially those leaders who had been appointed by God to guide the people as a whole. Once again the oracles lift part of the blame off the common citizens, who had little autonomy in such a social system, and place it where it more properly belongs.

The language in these oracles is vibrant. The first oracle (vv. 9-12) begins with the voice of the victim, perhaps the personified city, becoming "like a drunkard" as Yahweh's punishments overtake them, probably a reference to being powerless and overcome. All of nature responds to God's anger; it mourns and shrivels up. Since the evil of both the prophets and the priests has reached into the temple itself, their behavior will lead them into deep darkness, a metaphor indicating lack of divine knowledge. The next section (vv. 13-15) likens the prophets of Jerusalem to the inhabitants of three cities that represented wickedness to the Jerusalemite audience—Samaria, Sodom, and Gomorrah—justifying God's punishment. A prose interlude (vv. 16-18) sums up the message: the prophets who claim that the city will not fall are all false prophets, a message reiterated in vv. 21-22. The rhetorical questions in v. 18 ask who has sat in Yahweh's divine council where the fate of Israel is decided. According to Isaiah 6, Isaiah had been transported to this divine council to bear witness to Yahweh's impending disaster. The insinuation here in Jeremiah 23:18 is that Jeremiah alone sees the parallel comprehensive disaster descending on the nation. Verses 19-20 liken the disaster to the approach of a storm, complete with tornadoes. As anyone who lives in Tornado Alley (or has seen the movie *Twister*) can attest, the approach of a wall cloud is a scary thing: a symbol of overpowering, unavoidable disaster. Just as a person cannot hide from the force of a tornado, so too Judah cannot escape the approaching force of God's anger as it sweeps out of the heavens and over the earth (vv. 23-24).

The text next turns to those prophets who claim to have had a prophetic dream or other vision (vv. 25-32). Dream divination was rather common in the ancient Near East, but it usually entailed a prophet interpreting someone else's dream, much like Joseph in Genesis 40–41. In this passage, the false prophets exclaim that they have had a dream, and then they proceed to interpret it for the community. The oracle likens their dreams to empty straw as opposed to nutritious wheat. But while wheat seems to be a positive image for God's message, this pericope returns to metaphors of destruction: God's utterance is a fire that incinerates everything in its path or a hammer strong enough to shatter rocks. This fire, this hammer, will be turned against the false prophets (vv. 30-32).

The final section in the oracles against the prophets presents a scene of people coming to official prophets, probably working at the temple given the inclusion of the priests in vv. 33 and 34, to seek an oracle from Yahweh. The NRSV translates the noun here as "burden," certainly a possibility, but translating it as "oracle" makes better sense given the context. The passage plays with the contrast between something a prophet falsely claims is an oracle and a message that is truly divine. Verse 36, for example, distinguishes the true oracle from human speech. In v. 37, the supplicant asks for an oracle, and by beginning his answer with "an oracle of Yahweh," the prophet lies, claiming to be delivering a genuine oracle. The punishment for such an offense is expulsion from the land, distance from God (who will "forget" them), and perennial public shame because their ruse has been exposed.

The Parable of the Figs, 24:1-10

Jeremiah 24 contains a classic vision report. The prophet sees something rather ordinary, but uses that item as a metaphor for an oracular pronouncement. Here, Jeremiah sees baskets of figs, probably in a marketplace near the temple. One basket, the choice basket, contains figs for eating, while the other one has inedible figs, perhaps gathered for disposal. Jeremiah uses these props to deliver an oracle that distinguishes between various social groups following the fall of the city: exiles, refugees, and those remaining in the land (Rom-Shiloni 2013, esp. 198–252).

The pronouncement is set in the period between Jehoiakin's deportation in 597 and the final fall of the city in 587. It also recognizes a community of Jews living in Egypt. In this interim period in Jerusalem, the prophet declares those who had been exiled (the former Jerusalem elite) to be the righteous group, and those living in Egypt and Judah to be sinful communities. It is an odd pronouncement in the context of the book as a whole. Nowhere else is Coniah spared from the condemnation on the post-Josiah kings. In fact, 22:24-25 states that even if he had been God's favored king, an idea presented as something contrary to fact, God would still have hurled him out of the land.

The passage actually reflects the situation after the fall of Jerusalem in 587, when the three groups were more clearly delineated along the lines suggested here: those exiled to Babylon (in both 597 and 587), those who fled as refugees to Egypt (see, for example, Jer 41:16-18), and those who remained in the land after the Babylonian takeover. Given these three substantial post-fall communities, it would not be surprising that conflicts would arise over which one should be identified as the true remnant of Israel. This question became more acute in the late exilic and early restoration periods, when the nation of Judah was being reconstituted and the question of leadership was a burning question. Was the exile of the Davidic kings a clear sign from God that this particular dynasty had been rejected? Was theirs a temporary time of punishment that cleansed them of their offenses, making them suitable to serve again, or was it a permanent rejection?

The text clearly sides with the former view, that the exile of the elite leaders in no way negated God's permanent covenant with the Davidic monarchy (as outlined in 2 Sam 7). But by setting the oracle in the interim period before the final fall, the passage also serves as a clear statement that Zedekiah was not a legitimate Davidic king. In addition, it also condemns not just the refugees who fled to Egypt but also those already living there. Archaeological evidence shows that there had been a sizable Jewish population in Egypt already in the period of the Divided Monarchy. By condemning this community before the fall of the city, the text lays the foundation for Jeremiah's resistance to going to Egypt later in the book.

The condemnation of the people left in the land seems most surprising (v. 8). The book does not characterize Jeremiah as a member of the elite classes. His family, although priestly, is not part of the priests serving in Jerusalem. He does come from a landowning family, but he does not live on that land, so he is a kind of internal refugee who has left his native land to dwell in the city. He is not exiled in either 597 or 587, which means whatever status he had in no way threatened Babylonian hegemony. Although some scholars view discrepancies such as this condemnation of the people of the land as reflecting the chaos that ensued on the fall of Jerusalem (O'Connor 2011a), it seems odd that this part of the book would depict this same social group as more evil than the royal elite with whom Jeremiah contends in the rest of the book. It is also at odds with the immediately preceding chapters, which lay the blame on the leaders rather than the general populace. These discrepancies imply that the material here has been added later by those wanting to see a restoration of the Davidic monarchy. This later date also makes better sense of the references to planting and uprooting in v. 6, which, echoing the language of Jeremiah 1:10, are generally viewed as part of the last layer of this section of the book. In addition, the notice of a new heart in v. 7, which anticipates the reference to a singular heart in 32:37-41, may also be a late concept (see Ezek 11:19; 18:31; 36:26; Patton 1999, 212–14).

The placement of this material in this part of the book counters the harsh presentation of the Davidic line in the material that surrounds it (Brueggemann 2006, 99–115). Without it, Jeremiah would sound like someone opposed to the Davidic monarchy. After the nation fell, perhaps the need for something to hope for and the desire to maintain some kind of continuity with the preexilic traditions led to the addition of this material at this point in the book. As will be clear in the discussion of chapter 25, chapter 24 is the penultimate chapter of the first part of the book, perhaps of a first edition of the book of Jeremiah. When read in that context, the brief note of hope connects the material of pervasive judgment that dominates the bulk of chapters 1–25 with a community trying to survive in a post-fall world.

Part I Comes to a Close, 25:1-14

Chapter 25 in Jeremiah serves a pivotal function in the overall structure of the book (Kessler 1997 and 1999). The book is preserved in two distinct traditions: one extant in the Hebrew versions of the book (seen most explicitly in the Masoretic text, or MT, on which most English translations are based) and the other preserved as a whole in the ancient Greek versions (the Septuagint, or LXX, with some fragmentary Hebrew witnesses). The most obvious difference between these two versions occurs at Jeremiah 25:13a, where the LXX inserts the oracles against foreign nations (OAN; Aejmelaeus 2002) and which the MT locates in chapters 46–51. While the placement of the OAN does affect how they function within the book as a whole, the simple fact that significantly different arrangements of the book start at this point suggests that Jeremiah 1:1–25:13a may have reached a more stable form earlier than the material that follows.

In addition to the different arrangements of the versions, the style of writing also continues to change in chapters 26–45. These chapters are dominated by historical-like prose narratives of the prophet's life, punctuated by a brief musical interlude in chapters 30–31, which contain the most hopeful texts in the book. The stylistic differences between the two halves of the book are so stark that either could almost function as a separate collection of Jeremianic traditions. In fact, it could be that the final edition of the book represents a collection of various traditions: poetic oracles ascribed to the prophet, laments presented as his inner musings, stories about his confrontations with kings and other elites, and a collection of oracles against foreign nations. This model of the text's final production would allow for the completion of various sections at different moments in Israel's history and would account for some elements appearing at different spots in the arrangements of the collections.

My hesitation to endorse such a model wholesale is that (1) it tends to view the sections of the book as discreet units that have little impact on their surrounding material and (2) it disregards the fact that many of the prophetic collections that precede Jeremiah contain oracles against foreign nations, which makes a model of their secondary addition at odds with other similar prophetic material. As result I would suggest that the development of the *books* of Jeremiah were the result of very complex processes of transmission that demonstrate the scribes' license to arrange material in different ways, add material to preexisting cycles of traditions, and edit existing material in ways that fit within a new larger corpus of Jeremiah traditions. In sum, scribes not only added material but also edited the older material that they had received.

The opening verses in this chapter contain clear resonances with the first chapter in the book, signaling a rounding off of the material up to this point. First, the prophet refers to the commencement of his prophetic activity in the thirteenth year of Josiah, the same date given in Jeremiah 1:2. In addition, the reference to Nebuchadnezzar's first year sounds an ominous tone. The book presents the oracle that follows, which briefly describes the fall of the city to this enemy who functions as Yahweh's servant (vv. 9-11), as a prediction by Jeremiah before the first deportation of the elite in 597 (Hill 1999b). Later in the book, this will be designated as the same year that Jeremiah commands Baruch to write down all of the messages God had sent to him (36:4). In the ancient world, writing itself had a prophetic force: the act of writing out a curse was part of what made that curse come true (Boer 2013). The reference to writing in Jeremiah 25:13 foreshadows the textualization of his oracles narrated in chapter 36.

The message or "word" contained in these verses summarizes many of the main themes of the book up to this point. First, it characterizes Judah's sin as idolatry (v. 6), a theme already seen in numerous places throughout this first half of the book. Second, the punishment for such sin is both violent devastation and exile (especially v. 9). Third, God claims that prophets had been sent to warn them (v. 4); this statement is a bit at odds with the earlier part of the book that depicts Jeremiah as the sole legitimate prophet, but the reference could be to earlier prophets such as Moses, Samuel, or Isaiah. Fourth, the oracle reuses the inability to attend weddings and other festive gatherings as a symbol for a life not worth living (v. 10).

One of the most influential verses in the whole book of Jeremiah is the reference to the seventy-year exile in 25:11-12. The length of the exile was a matter of concern to post-587 audiences. The book of Ezekiel repeatedly asserts that each generation is punished for its own sin and not for the sins of their ancestors (see especially Ezek 18:1-4), but a seventy-year time span encompasses roughly three generations of exiles. Jeremiah 31:29-30 similarly asserts that each generation is punished for its own sin. The prediction of a seventy-year exile casts the length of the exile as a matter of divine decree, unchangeable once penned. Its narrative function here, however, is to serve as a message of hope, even as destruction is announced. Verse 12 adds the image of God punishing Babylon itself as illustrative of that hope. The same prediction of disaster followed by a shorter message of hope is found in Jeremiah 1:10 with its four verbs of destruction (uproot, destroy, annihilate, tear down) followed immediately by two verbs of restoration (build, plant).

Jeremiah 25:1-14 is crafted then from the perspective of those who knew how Judah's history would play out: they would be destroyed, as part of Yahweh's plan, and exiled for a long time, but eventually restored. In the Hebrew version of this chapter, this section ends by defending God's righteousness in bringing disaster to the nation. The Judeans have brought this on themselves "according to their deeds and the works of their hands" (v. 14 NRSV).

Drunken Nations, 25:15-33

While the LXX inserts the full swath of oracles against Judah's enemies at this point in the book, the MT version contains a briefer overview of Yahweh's destruction of these nations. The metaphor that dominates this overview is that of forced drunkenness: God will force alcohol down their throats until they die (Dubach 2009). The comparison of death in battle to intoxication may form a startling image, but it is one found in other prophetic texts. God's "cup" that judges the guilty appears in a number of texts, such as Isaiah 51:17-23; Ezekiel 23:31-34; Obadiah 16; Habakkuk 2:15-16; and even Psalm 75:8 (E). Van der Toorn reconstructs an ordeal ritual as the background for these texts (1988b 435–40). In this reconstructed ritual, a person swears an oath of innocence at the temple, drinks a cup of wine, perhaps laced with potentially poisonous herbs, and is deemed innocent if he or she survives until the morning.

While such a reconstruction is plausible, it is more applicable to Jeremiah 8:14 and 9:15 (E), which reference a poisoned cup that God makes the nation drink (McKane 1980). The specific language in this passage, however, seems to engage how a violent death resembles overdose. Similar to the image of drunkenness in Isaiah 28:7-8, the drunkard staggers and vomits (see also Isa 19:14). Here, however, vomit is connected to the sword or a violent death, making the metaphoric connection clearer. This is not the only place in Jeremiah that links intoxication with death on the battlefield. The image is also applied to Judah, especially in 13:12-14, and reappears in the oracles against Moab (48:26, which also mentions vomit), Edom (49:12), and Babylon (51:39-40; see also 51:7).

In this passage, all victims of the metaphoric overdose appear together, starting with Judah. This beginning may seem odd if the assumption is that the passage is about God's judgment on Judah's enemies, but it makes perfect sense as a passage designed to show God's control over the whole world. By paralleling God's punishment of other nations with the punishment of Judah, the passage claims God's sovereignty over nations that had more power than Judah and whose gods therefore seemed more powerful than Yahweh. In some ways, this passage echoes the oracles against foreign nations in Amos 1–2, which end with condemnations of Judah and Israel. The purpose in Amos is to highlight that Israel was more wicked and therefore more deserving of God's punishment than any of its neighbors. Here the purpose is to set Judah's defeat within the context of global disaster and undercut the idea that Judah was more evil than Babylon (called Sheshach in this passage).

The word used to describe the wine, translated as "wrath" in the NRSV, is deliberately ambiguous. The word is associated with heat, which seems to lead to its figurative use for the heat of venom in Deuteronomy 32:24 and 33 (the sting of spiders and snakes); Psalms 58:4-5 (E) and 140:3 (E). The root meaning of the word, however, is anger, the same word used to describe the flaring of God's anger in twelve other passages in Jeremiah (4:4; 6:11; 7:20; 18:20; 21:5; 21:12; 32:31; 32:37; 33:5; 36:7; 42:18; 44:6). The book also applies the lexeme to the metaphoric tornado that will destroy Judah (23:19 and 30:23). The only other use of the word is in Jeremiah 10:25 where the prophet asks God to "pour out" divine wrath on Israel's enemies, perhaps engaging the metaphor of a tainted cup. The cup in 25:15, then, symbolizes the heat of God's anger that will destroy them as surely as venom (Holt 2011).

This venomous heat that cannot be avoided is poured out on the whole global village in 25:15-33. The ordering of the nations is in part geographical, starting in the audience's center of Jerusalem and then fanning out, first to the southwest, starting with Judah's biggest ally prior to its fall, Egypt. Egypt would have also been a place where many refugees from Jerusalem's fall would have settled. Next come Judah's immediate neighbors (Philistia, Edom, Moab, Ammon, and Phoenicia). It then moves east into the Arabian Peninsula and then north and east beyond Mesopotamia, with the penultimate statement that this includes "all the kingdoms of the earth" (v. 26). Only then does it turn back on Babylon/Sheshach, making it the ultimate object of God's fury. This order is almost identical to the order of nations condemned in chapters 46–51 (Egypt, Philistia, Moab, Ammon, Edom, Damascus, Arabia, Elam/Persia, and then Babylon). Whether or not these two places in the book that condemn other nations were written by the same hand or were somehow dependent on each other, both provide a place in the book that expresses the desire for revenge on those who had destroyed Jerusalem. But it is a revenge that costs dearly, as the prose conclusion notes, resulting in piles of unburied corpses strewn across the face of the whole earth (v. 33).

Finale for the Shepherds, 25:34-38

The final passage in this section of Jeremiah links back to the oracles against Judah's kings by focusing on the metaphor of the shepherd. The passage never explicitly states that it applies only to Judah's kings; in fact, its placement after the worldwide order of mass destruction could connote that the "shepherds" are all kings throughout the world. The passage is differentiated from the previous verse, which states that no one will mourn the dead, by starting with the image of shepherds lamenting. The unit is tied together with pastoral images: the flock now slaughtered, the bleating of the lambs replaced with the wailing of the shepherds, the devastation of the pastures (vv. 36-37). Even the destruction participates in this metaphor: God is an enraged lion devouring the flock.

The Prophet and the King

Jeremiah 26–29

In chapter 26, the book of Jeremiah transitions into primarily prose narrative stories about the prophet. As has been shown, this switch is not an abrupt one; chapters 21–25 contained a mixture of prose and poetry as they wended their way through condemnations of Judah's final kings, culminating in God's judgment of the whole world. In chapters 26–45, while prose will dominate, poetic oracles reappear prominently in chapters 30–31. The oracles against foreign nations in 46–51, which parallel the ending of chapter 25 in expanded form, are also primarily poetic.

Accompanying the transition from prose to poetry here is the metamorphosis of the narrative function of the prophet Jeremiah, who goes primarily from the first-person speaker of the oracles at the beginning of the book to a third-person character in the narratives about his life. This particular set of four scenes from a prophetic life (chs. 26–29) shows the reader concrete illustrations of the scope of Jeremiah's opposition. To be sure, the prophet's laments in chapters 11–20 alluded to formidable resistance to his message, but these four scenes provide paradigmatic, hostile encounters with every element of Judean society: priests, prophets, elders, and royal leaders, as well as those already exiled to Babylon.

Not that this opposition was unprovoked. Jeremiah, the ever-cranky prophet, spares no one. While the material in this part of the book shows signs that it was either composed by a different group than chapters 1–20 or perhaps added later, the picture of Jeremiah remains that of a social agitator unwilling to soften his message. Although chapter 26 attributes this to God's command, the Jeremiah traditions clearly maintain it as a defining element of his character.

While some scholars conjecture that the stories in this part of the book reflect actual events in the historical Jeremiah's life, such a conclusion is based more on assertion than any corroborating evidence. In point of fact, the historical prophet clearly did not write the book of Jeremiah (unless he liked to refer to himself in the third person), as the references to Baruch in Jeremiah 36 demonstrate. There is no way to know if the scenes presented here go back to historical events or are later creations meant to capture larger themes in the book. In some ways it does not matter, because even if they contain traces of historical events, they have been preserved, edited, and collected in this form to serve a specific literary purpose within the current larger text. Read in this way, it is clear that these stories have at least three functions: to present God's punishment as justified, to demonstrate that the people had ample opportunity to repent, and to vindicate Jeremiah as a heroic prophet.

An Execution Averted, 26:1-24

Jeremiah 26 ostensibly retells the story of Jeremiah's delivery of the oracle found in Jeremiah 7 at the temple of Jerusalem, in which the prophet reminds the narrative audience that their trust in the temple's ability to save them is unfounded. Both accounts of this oracle are set in the exact same place, and in both the prophet reminds the audience of the fate of Shiloh in order to undercut their misplaced confidence.

The two passages have significant differences as well. First, the oracle in chapter 7, which focuses on Jeremiah's characterization of the people, is much longer than the one in chapter 26, which instead focuses on the audience's reaction to the oracle. It may be that chapter 26 only means to summarize or briefly refer to the longer oracle so that it can turn to the larger issue of Jeremiah's survival. Or it could be that there were variant traditions about a speech so closely associated with the prophet. No matter which alternative is chosen, both versions set Jeremiah at odds with the ruling elite's insistence that support of the national temple was piety enough to appease Yahweh. By delivering this message on temple property, the prophet challenges a central institution of Judean government, economy, identity, and society. The speech is treasonous.

He does not call for the cessation of temple worship, although that is hinted at in the divine speech found earlier in 7:21, which prioritizes obedience to God's "voice" over temple sacrifice. Given that God's "voice" is manifested in the prophets, this oracle asserts prophetic authority over priestly control. Jeremiah 26:4-6 similarly places obedience to God's law and prophets above ritual observance. Even if Jeremiah was not being accused of false prophecy, I find it likely that in a city experiencing so much external pressure, those whose ideas threatened national security would be considered dangerous. Both the opening and closing elements of the chapter attest to the reality of mob violence, which the officials attempt to control through a formal judicial proceeding.

The redactor gives this particular scene a relatively clear date compared to other texts in the book: the beginning of the reign of Jehoiakim (Yates 2005), soon after the death of Josiah, who was killed in battle at Megiddo in 609 BCE. Jehoiakim, the second of Josiah's sons to reign after his death, was a vassal of Egypt, at least at the beginning of his reign. This story, then, is not supposed to be read against the backdrop of the siege of the city by the Babylonians, but rather in the years prior to Babylon's renewed campaign into the Levant as tensions between Egypt and Babylon were mounting.

In the accounts of Judah's history in 2 Kings, Josiah's religious reform had been successful and marked a period of "obedience" to God's law that was found in the temple (see 2 Kgs 22). The beginning of Jehoiakim's reign came approximately three months after the death of his father. The oracle's depiction of the people as stubbornly refusing to follow God's commands, then, would seem to depict God as relatively quick to turn against them if, in fact, Jehoiakim's reign represented a distancing from Josiah's reforms. On the other hand, from the perspective of the final form of the book, the destruction of the temple that the oracle threatens does not occur until more than twenty years later. The dating of the oracle, therefore, depicts God as providing ample time for Judah's repentance.

Within an ancient city, there were three spheres of judicial process: elders who officiated when an offense involved landowners, priests who acted when the offense was a cultic one or when the process involved an ordeal that tested whether or not the person was telling the truth, and the royalty who decided cases for non-landowners (traditionally designated as "widows, orphans, and resident aliens"). This passage engages all three platforms of judgment. The narrative is interesting for the way that it designates these different social groups: priests and prophets who represent the religious professionals; officers or princes who insist on a formal judicial proceeding for Jeremiah; and elders who weigh in with social memories, to which it adds "all the people," a fickle lot who seem to follow whichever group takes center stage at a given time. Although the movement of the passage may be hard to follow for a contemporary audience, the passage simply collapses the legal reactions to Jeremiah's ministry across all three spheres.

The story begins with the reaction of the temple court. Jeremiah delivers an oracle against the temple while on temple grounds, a little like condemning the Vatican in St. Peter's Square. Just as the Swiss Guard would presumably remove such a person from the square, especially if he or she were attracting a large audience, so too do the religious personnel of the temple try to silence the prophet. Priests were charged with protecting the sanctity of the temple area; some of the priests served as guards who could remove and even execute anyone entering into spaces where they were not allowed (see 2 Kgs 11). The temple offered sanctuary to those unjustly accused of a crime, which meant some temple personnel were armed to fight those trying to exact revenge (Deut 19). Both Exodus 32:25-28 and 1 Kings 18:39 (v. 40 Hebrew) depict priests and prophets killing those accused of idolatry. The priest in charge of the temple at Bethel confronted Amos when he prophesied there (Amos 7:10-13). In sum, the reaction of the priests and prophets to Jeremiah's predictions that the temple would be destroyed was expected, as the support of the people in v. 8 attests.

The temple's authority competed with royal authority in the ancient world. The "officials" (NRSV) of v. 10 represent the interests of the palace. The word used here is one reserved for those closest to the king, including the princes. They would have the interests of the whole land in mind. After all, the destruction that Jeremiah predicts here would not happen without the collapse of the whole city. Formal trials outside of Jerusalem occurred in city gates, large complexes that could accommodate such a gathering. The officials taking their seats in the temple gate designates the commencement of a formal procedure, one that requires a degree of due process (Westbrook 2007).

Part of that due process is the testimony of the accused, found here in vv. 12-15. Jeremiah asserts that it is Yahweh who has sent him, a claim that makes the royal officials hesitant to carry out the execution. His speech sums up what is at stake: if Jeremiah's claim is true, then they incur God's ire if they do not believe him. Deuteronomy 18:21-22 deals with the question of true and false prophecy by stating that the only way to distinguish the two is to see if what the prophet predicts comes true. In 1 Kings 22:26-27 the king detains Micaiah, a prophet who predicts that the king will die in battle, so that he can execute him as a false prophet when he returns safely. In Jeremiah 26, the officials decree that, as a prophet, Jeremiah should not (yet) be executed, since in this case delaying the execution would be in order. From their vested interests, if they execute a true prophet of God, the nation as a whole would incur bloodguilt.

At this point the elders of the city weigh in. It could be that they are asserting their right to make this judicial decision because Jeremiah is in the class of landowning males. The elders in that society preserved institutional and communal memory. They did not decide the cases by consulting written law codes, but rather on precedent handed down in oral tradition. Here the elders recount how Hezekiah had not executed the prophet Micah when the Assyrians had attacked Jerusalem around the year 701. In a rare instance of one biblical book quoting another, the elders find the exact parallel to

Jeremiah's situation: Micah had also predicted the fall of the city but was not executed. This precedent supports the view of the officials that Jeremiah should not be executed.

Most translations of this passage, following scholarly consensus, view the elders' speech as ending at v. 19. Ending their speech at this point, however, makes little sense of what follows: the story of a different prophet and the rescue of Jeremiah from execution, neither of which would be necessary if there had just been a stay of execution decreed. If, however, vv. 20-23 represent the continuation of the elders' speech, the flow of the passage makes better sense. (There are no quotation marks in ancient Hebrew, so translators must determine the exact contours of direct speech.) If these verses continue the elders' deliberations, then they give a counter-example, a different precedent for what should happen to Jeremiah.

Verse 20 begins with a Hebrew word that is not translated in the NRSV but that the NIV translates as "now." This word, however, can also be translated as "on the other hand." The second precedent they cite is closer to the situation: it recounts what Jehoiakim, the current reigning king in the narrative, did when another prophet had delivered an oracle similar to Jeremiah's. In this case, the king sent his officials to Egypt, where the prophet had fled, in order to execute him and prohibit him from having a proper burial. This example threatens Jeremiah in two ways: it demonstrates the current king's policies toward prophets who speak against his interests, but, even more, since God had not punished Jehoiakim for executing another prophet with the same message, it implies this was the correct action. Therefore, if Uriah was a false prophet, then so is Jeremiah. The elders seem to acquiesce that this is a closer precedent.

Jeremiah has one ally in the crowd, Ahikam, who is a member of the Shaphan family who will support Jeremiah throughout the second half of the book. Recognizing that the second precedent puts Jeremiah at great risk, Ahikam somehow manages to save Jeremiah from immediate execution, although the text does not provide details for how this was done. Ahikam represents the minority position of those who believed Jeremiah. It demonstrates that although the passage states that "all of the people" opposed Jeremiah, clearly some believed him.

As a whole, the author has artfully crafted this story to convey important aspects of the traditions surrounding Jeremiah. In a compact space, the text illustrates the ways various groups within Jerusalem reacted to the prophetic oracles. These reactions span the expected gamut from explicit outrage to cautious trepidation to full support. Second, it characterizes Jeremiah as someone who staunchly carries out his mission, even if it would cost him his life, as v. 15 in particular expresses. Third, it depicts God as giving a stay of execution for the city, waiting over twenty years to carry out the punishment here decreed. In this way, it supports the book's view that God's punishment on the city was not, in fact, swift; God extends the offer of repentance, giving the people a whole generation (twenty years) to comply. Each element in the passage, then, serves a larger intertwined narrative purpose.

Serve Nebuchadnezzar Like a Dumb Ox, 27:1-15

The next story in this section of the book provides more evidence of why Jeremiah was so hated. The chapter commences with a brief description of a sign-act performed by Jeremiah; God orders him to strap on a yoke, like those used for beasts of burden. These yokes would have been quite large and heavy, making him a spectacle. The bulk of the chapter, however, focuses on the message this act symbolized: that God demands Judah to submit to Babylon.

While the story in the previous chapter was set at the beginning of the reign of Jehoiakim, some twenty years before the Babylonian siege, this oracle is set in a much different historical context: the beginning of the reign of Zedekiah. This would be soon after the first deportation of Judah's elite, which included King Jehoiakin (Jehoiakim's son) as well as the highest-ranking priests of the temple of Jerusalem and other leaders. It addresses the twin prongs of colonization: subservience of both the royalty (vv. 1-15) and the religious personnel of the temple (vv. 16-22). Jeremiah urges the people of Jerusalem to submit to both forms of Babylonian colonization.

Jeremiah's oracle begins by addressing the other vassal kings that neighbored Jerusalem (vv. 1-11). The oracle accuses them of listening to false prophets leading them to resist becoming Babylon's beasts of burden. Over and over again these verses equate acquiescence to Babylonian rule with the imposition of a yoke on their necks. It is a powerful visual symbol; every movement of the beasts serves the whims of their master. Jeremiah urges them to submit to this rule or risk total annihilation. In v. 12, he turns to Zedekiah with the exact same message: ignore those false prophets who urge resistance and submit Judah's neck to the master's control. The passage insinuates that, from the beginning of his reign, Zedekiah harbored fantasies of rebellion.

This message of submission to Babylon would make Jeremiah a social pariah. This is not the patriotic prophet declaring "Judah right or wrong" or even "Judah strong." His message of submission would be unwelcome in a city under siege, trying to maintain its existence and identity in the face of the unjust encroachment of the empirical forces of the Babylonians. The book never shows Jeremiah as backing off of this message, not even when the city experiences its final siege. In fact, the prophetic oracles cast that siege as the direct divine punishment for failing to fully submit to Babylonian rule throughout these turbulent years. It is obvious, then, why those running the city and urging policies of resistance and rebellion would have viewed such a message as treasonous. By placing these oracles directly after the depiction of the city's total opposition to Jeremiah, the book attempts to highlight the radical nature of Jeremiah's oracles.

Particularly poignant in this passage is Jeremiah's claim that for those nations that submit to Babylonian rule, their citizens would be allowed to live peacefully on their ancestral land (27:11). *What good is death?* the prophet cries. Just submit and live. These are the words of someone who sees all too clearly that Judah cannot stand against so large a foe. But what makes this passage different from contemporary debates about foreign politics is the way it engages religious viewpoints. While Jeremiah 27 might read like the ranting of a pro-Babylonian Judean, the oracle undercuts Babylon's claims of superiority by refusing to attribute their success to the potency of the Babylonian gods. Instead, it is Judah's God who controls Babylon. In a brilliant rhetorical move, the passage assigns the same subservient position to Nebuchadnezzar that he imposes on Judah, except that the Babylonian king is the servant or slave, not of a colonizing power, but of Israel's God. While it might sound like an honorific to call Nebuchadnezzar Yahweh's servant (v. 6), it is the same word used repeatedly throughout these verses to indicate a subservient status, like that of a slave. In this way, the text depicts submission to Nebuchadnezzar as submission to Yahweh.

Temple Treasures, 27:16-22

The final verses of the chapter pick up the focus on the religious aspect of colonization. While some scholars conclude that these verses were later additions to the chapter, they fit well in this present context by directly addressing religious elements. In Jeremiah 27:16-22 the focus shifts to how the priests in Jerusalem, followed by the people, reacted to the removal of sacred objects from the temple in the first deportation by the Babylonians. At first glance, their hope that the vessels would soon return might seem to be simple optimism, but in the ancient world the intertwining spheres of court and sanctuary make this hope rebellious. The Babylonians demonstrated their control of Jerusalem not only by the removal of the legitimate king, Jehoiakin, and his replacement with a vassal king, Zedekiah, but also through the removal of portable sacred objects from the national temple (see

2 Kgs 24:13), a practice quite common in the ancient world (Mayer 2002). When the Assyrians had conquered Babylon in 689 BCE, for example, they took the statue of Marduk, which was in Babylon's national temple, and set it up in the temple of their national god, Aššur, in a subservient position in order to symbolize that Marduk/Babylon now served Aššur/Assyria. The Babylonians (and others) employed this policy of removing people and items revered by the native population in part to keep people from rebelling against their rule, since rebellion would result in the execution of those exiled and the destruction of sacred objects.

No biblical text clearly states the exact objects the Babylonians took with them to Babylon. Biblical texts speak loudly by remaining silent on the fate of the ark of the covenant and its concomitant cherubim. Many biblical texts assert that the ark and the cherubim had formed Yahweh's throne and footstool in Solomon's temple, symbolizing that God was invisibly present above them. In 1 Kings 8:1-11, for example, God's glory, which represents the moment when the temple becomes Yahweh's dwelling, appears when priests install the ark and cherubim. Chronicles replicates this focus on the centrality of the ark, as does the description of the tabernacle in Exodus. Biblical historians ponder at what point the ark disappeared from the temple, since neither description of either deportation found in both Kings and Chronicles mentions its fate. Psalm 132 might reflect a tradition of its removal, although scholars disagree whether this psalm refers to its original placement in the first temple or the expectation of its return to the second temple (Laato 1992 and Patton 1995). Instead of the ark, 2 Kings 24:13 refers only to the golden vessels that the Babylonians destroyed. The books of Ezra and Nehemiah use the return of these golden vessels as a symbol of the second temple's continuity with the temple of Solomon (Ackroyd 1972). The Babylonians would have taken the vessels to represent their divinely ordained superiority over the land of Judah.

Once again, the text blames illegitimate prophets for providing false hopes. The only way the restoration of those vessels would have occurred would have been either through Judah's complete submission to Babylonian rule, a situation countered by the previous oracle, or by the defeat of Babylon. After all, the only way Babylon recovered the Marduk statue was by defeating Assyria. Jeremiah's oracle states that the only thing the people of Jerusalem could hope for is that the temple would remain standing and that nothing else would be removed. Verses 19-20 echo the description of the final fall of Jerusalem with the removal of the bronze pillars, golden sea, lampstands, and other temple treasures (2 Kgs 25:13-17). This echo of what really came to pass brands Jeremiah as a true prophet in contrast to the false prophets who predicted that all would be well and the city would prevail.

As in the first half of the chapter, the oracle's punch line in the final verse reveals that the oracle's aim is not merely to provide a description of the city's history. Its aim is theological: to depict God as the one in control of this whole horrible history. This final verse states that Yahweh will decree or appoint the time when the temple vessels will be returned, implying that it is the same Yahweh who decreed their removal, both in the first deportation of 597 and in the second deportation of 587. Judah's only hope remains in the sovereignty of the God they worship. Human rebellion will not save the vessels, nor will human effort return them; it will only happen when and if Yahweh decrees it. Once again, the prophet's ability to see this divine purpose isolates him from the rest of the city.

Portrait of a False Prophet, 28:1-17

Continuing with this section's focus on Jeremiah's opposition, the book moves to the story of a confrontation between Jeremiah and one of the prophets of Jerusalem whom Jeremiah has just accused of prophesying lies. As this text immediately follows Jeremiah's oracle of the yoke (27:1-15), Jeremiah remains in the temple precincts. There Hananiah, a prophet who seems to be known to the original audience, confronts him. The chapter depicts Hananiah as one of the prophets claiming that Yahweh has revealed to him that Judah would be rid of Babylonian rule within two years (vv. 2-4).

Jeremiah's reaction drips with his typical sarcasm. "Amen to that" he asserts, but in no way meaning that he views Hananiah as a true prophet. "From your mouth to God's ears," as the saying goes. Jeremiah points out, though, that prophets have never been sent with good news, as a quick perusal of the biblical prophetic books would confirm. He ends this speech as he did the one in chapter 26: history will prove who is right. Hananiah reacts violently, tearing the yoke off of Jeremiah's shoulders. This prophetic confrontation has taken place with priests and people as witnesses. Whether it should be read as a different version of the trial scene presented in chapter 26 or as a separate incident does not really matter. It is an additional narrative that illustrates Jeremiah's opposition.

The story ends with a rather gruesome prophetic sign. In a number of biblical texts, when people question a prophet's message, God gives a sign by which the veracity of the prophet can be tested. In 2 Kings 20:8-11, the sun moves backwards in order to validate Isaiah as a true prophet. Similarly, in 1 Samuel 10:1-8, Samuel gives Saul a complex sign that he shall in fact become the first king of Israel. In these two cases, the sign itself is not something threatening, just unusual occurrences that serve as a confirming omen. Here in Jeremiah 28, however, the sign is Hananiah's own death. Jeremiah tells him that although he has broken a wooden yoke, Babylon's divinely ordained imperial rule will be an iron one: unbreakable and heavy. In order to prove his point, Jeremiah quotes God's plan to kill Hananiah within a year of this confrontation. If vv. 12-16 take place at the same time as 1-11, Hananiah dies less than two months later, an omen that should convince the people that Jeremiah is the only true prophet.

An Incendiary Letter, 29:1-32

Jeremiah 29 paints a picture of those deported to Babylon in 597 in the same hues as the portraits of those remaining in the city in the previous three chapters. In the final scene of this collection, Jeremiah provokes those previously exiled with a letter that essentially tells them that they will not live to see their return to the city. The letter's message to settlers in Babylon depicts at least a three-generation exile; given that a generation lasted about twenty years, this three-generation sojourn approximates the prediction of a seventy-year exile found here in v. 10, repeated from 25:11-12.

The chapter is replete with parallels to earlier parts of Jeremiah. First, the social configuration of the exiles who are the recipients of the letter in v. 1 mirrors that of the city of Jerusalem. Jeremiah's letter addresses the elders accompanied by priests, prophets, and all the people, the same crowd that opposed Jeremiah in the temple in chapter 26. Second, Jeremiah accuses those left in Jerusalem of listening to false prophets, represented here by Shemaiah, a parallel to Hananiah in chapter 28. Third, one of the exiles, probably a former temple functionary, writes to the priests in Jerusalem, ordering them to arrest Jeremiah, just as the initial attempt to arrest Jeremiah in chapter 26 commenced with the priests and prophets of the temple. In a very economical way, this chapter portrays those exiled in Babylon as equally bad as those left in the city.

The chapter also has rhetorical hooks to both earlier and later material in the book. In addition to the reference to the seventy-year exile, 29:17 once again likens those remaining in Jerusalem to rotten figs (see ch. 24), while the reaction of those who see the city's destruction in v. 18 echoes a similar description in 19:8. The chapter also points forward; the brief reference to God's eventual restoration of the city in 29:10-14, which fits poorly in this chapter, anticipates the fuller descriptions of restoration in the next section of the book. The use of rhetorical hooks, a common scribal practice seen in Ezekiel as well, weaves together disparate parts of a longer book.

The details in this chapter result in a text that undercuts any attempt to conclude that those who were spared from directly experiencing the horrors of 586 were in some way more righteous than those left behind. But this chapter begs to be read from the perspective of the audiences of the final form of the book. Once again, the contemporary reader is reminded that the book did not reach its final form until after the fall of the city, after those characters who are trying to arrest Jeremiah had all been exiled, killed, or otherwise displaced from a city that lay in ruins. As the remaining leaders in the city, they would have been the ones exiled when the city fell, especially "the king who sits on the throne of David" (v. 16). This means that the exiles addressed by the character of Jeremiah in the book now include those who had tried to arrest him. Jeremiah's letter from the past now resonates across the decades to tell all the exiles, "Give up and settle into your new pathetic life as an exile."

The theme of the false prophets reaches its climax in this chapter (Osuji 2010), but this theme that has wound its way through chapters 26–29 does not primarily reflect a crisis about human authority. The chapters really address a profoundly foundational theological question that must have plagued the original audience: where was God when this happened? The book of Jeremiah maintains that God authored the disaster, but only after ample opportunity for the people to avert that fate. Prophets played an important role in times of imminent threat by providing appropriate warnings. The book of Ezekiel likens the false prophet to a watchman whose failure to warn the city if an enemy approaches makes him personally responsible for the resulting deaths (Ezek 3:16-21; 33:1-9). In this light, the false prophets of Jeremiah are not just delusional; they are criminally liable. The book firmly asserts that God had sent warning, but that the people had not recognized the true prophet when he appeared. It was not that God sent a lying spirit to lead the people astray so that they could be killed (1 Kgs 22) or so that they would not repent (Isa 6). Although earlier in Jeremiah God tells the prophet to cease interceding for them (7:16), here God wants the people to listen, wants them to repent. This message, which is put in the mouth of the true prophet, removes any blame from God for the city's disaster. The people had their chance, but they missed it. Even those already exiled, who should have recognized their own failures, continued in their false belief that they deserved God's rescue.

Jeremiah 26–29 uses the character of Jeremiah to punctuate some of the main themes of the book. While the narratives may have roots in the historical prophet's life, the author has arranged the material in a purposeful way to address the theological crisis resulting from the fall of Jerusalem: where was God as the city fell? These chapters depict Jeremiah as a true prophet who tried to warn the people, especially the elite, to change their ways, which placed him in mortal danger for pronouncing such messages. Although the chapters hint at supporters, as a whole they portray Jeremiah as a solitary and therefore courageous voice. While the portrayal raises the question of why people did not recognize him as the true prophet, it also presents Jeremiah's views as radical, demanding that people should act in a way that was not reasonable, and predicting a future that the community did not want to face. In this way, these narratives illustrate that following Yahweh's commands does not result in a happier life, more prosperity, or any kind of ease. For the survivors of the fall, at least, it simply means escaping with one's life and making the best of what is left to them.

Consolation and Restoration
Jeremiah 30–33

Against this backdrop of immense disaster and minuscule survival, the book of Jeremiah inserts two chapters full of stunning poetic depictions of restoration, followed by two prose stories that also end on notes of a future hope. They do not seem to fit well into their present context, although both the Hebrew and Greek versions of the book place these chapters here. There are, however, some indications that a later hand added them. For example, 31:29-40 seems to know the book of Ezekiel, thus suggesting a date in the late exilic period at the earliest. The content alone appears to undercut the messages of the rest of the book that disaster is comprehensive and unavoidable. Stylistically, chapters 30–31 interrupt the sequence of prose narratives in chapters 26–29 and 32–45 with poetic oracles, a kind of musical interlude, with a return to prose narrative in 32–33.

The book of Jeremiah sets off chapters 30–31 as a separate "book" or scroll that God commands Jeremiah to write (30:2). Scholars often refer to these chapters, then, as "The Book of Consolation." If chapters 30–31 did originate as an addition to the book, they perhaps reflect the fact that even ancient readers could only tolerate so much of the text's sweeping messages of wholesale destruction. Like a voice crying out in protest, the small poems in chapters 30–31 sing a counter-vision to that of a smoldering landscape strewn with corpses. The poems are clearly written to fit the context of Jeremiah; they pick up images from across the book in ways that tie the poems to their present setting. For example, they affirm that God's punishment was fierce and comprehensive. They also use images found in the earlier poems of destruction, such as the city's personification as a female and the widespread terror it experienced. Even more explicitly, 31:27-28 echoes the language of planting and uprooting found in the first chapter of the book.

These chapters also emphasize the restoration of the northern kingdom. After the reign of Solomon, the nation of Israel split into two independent monarchies: Judah in the south and Israel in the north. The Assyrians had destroyed the northern kingdom in 722 BCE, so when Jeremiah was alive, Judah was the sole representative of the larger Israel. When the Assyrians conquered Israel, they dispersed the elite of that population across their whole empire, a policy that they carried out with all conquered peoples. In addition, as with any war, there were a fair number of refugees, some of whom came to Judah, as well as Jews living in Egypt where many had gone as mercenary soldiers. Theoretically, there were Israelite families across the whole Fertile Crescent for centuries. I say "theoretically," however, because more than likely they had assimilated into the cultures of where they lived, probably intermarrying as a matter of course, so that in some parts of the area, a distinct group of "Israelites" probably no longer existed. Even so, the book of Jeremiah follows the prophetic tradition by imagining a future when all the tribes that made up the full people of Israel would be restored. This observation points to the fact that restoration visions are purely utopian, often containing elements that are impossible to achieve (O'Connor 2006).

Because the northern kingdom retained the name of "Israel," references to Israel in poetic and prophetic literature can be ambiguous. There are other clues in this material that "Israel" includes the north. The most obvious indication is that the poems depict God as desiring the return of *all* the tribes and families (see, e.g., 30:4; 31:1; 33:24-26). The nation of Judah consisted of primarily one tribe, so the use of "all" includes the rest of the Israelites. The references to people in the poems reinforce this comprehensive view. First, there are references to David in 30:9 and 33:14-26. While he was the founder of the monarchic dynasty that ruled in Judah, he was also one of only three kings whose kingdom included all twelve tribes and the first to rule them from the capital city of Jerusalem. References here to David then serve a dual function: to reaffirm that the ideal shape of the nation of Israel consists of twelve tribes ruled by one king and to maintain Jerusalem, the capital of the tribe of Judah, as the correct center of that rule.

The other names in these chapters, however, serve the same purpose. The traditions associated with these names can be found in the book of Genesis, a narrative that weaves together traditions of the various ancestral founders of the tribes of Israel. First, Jacob is mentioned eight times (30:7; 30:10 [bis], 18; 31:7, 11; 33:26 [bis]). In Genesis, Jacob is the father of all the founders of the twelve individual tribes. In Genesis 35:10, God changes his name to "Israel," designating him as the founder of the nation as a whole. References to Jacob in the prophetic literature, then, recall a nation of both north and south. The passages also talk about the restoration of "Ephraim" (31:6, 9, 18, 20), who was both one of Jacob's sons but, more significant here, also one of the most prominent of the northern tribes. The poems that depict mother and father weeping for a returning Ephraim (although here the father is God and the mother is the city) contain an impossible hope that the Ephraimites would return. The poems also personify the city as a woman in 31:15, but this time the city is Ramah in Benjamin and the woman is Rachel (Brown-Gutoff 1991). In Genesis 35:16-21, Rachel is the mother of Benjamin and the grandmother of the other two prominent tribes, Ephraim and Manasseh. This poem then attributes the same trauma and tragedy to the fall of Judah of the northern kingdom as for the south.

Chapters 32–33 function as another bridge between sections of the book of Jeremiah. In terms of content, they replicate the message of the Book of Consolation, but in terms of style they anticipate the prose narratives about Jeremiah's life that follow in chapters 34–45. This dual function explains why some scholars group these chapters with the Book of Consolation, while others place them with the prose narratives. They both relate events in Jeremiah's life that are set during the period of the final siege of Jerusalem, the dark days about which Jeremiah had prophesied. In both stories he speaks from jail, a setting that marks him as a true prophet to whom no one would listen. Both oracles express the inevitability of the sweeping disaster at the end of the siege, but set against this message of inescapable disaster, the prophet also intones images of a utopian future. Although these read to us today as messages of hope, within their narrative settings, they are messages of resistance to the reality of violent conquest (Davidson 2011a).

The placement of these four chapters raises interesting questions about their function in the book as a whole. Many Old Testament prophetic books, such as Amos and Ezekiel, move from oracles of condemnation to those of restoration. If these chapters were placed at the end of the book, then their purpose would be clearer: they would be providing hope and demonstrating that God does not desire the total annihilation of Israel. This placement would also give some purpose to the disaster, either as a short-term punishment for an egregious sin (see 31:29-30) or as a kind of trial or purification of the community. Yet the book of Jeremiah, in both the Hebrew and Greek versions, embeds these chapters a little past the halfway point. In the Hebrew version, instead of visions of restoration at the end of the book, Jeremiah 50 51 presents a revenge fantasy against Judah's destroyer. While the Greek version of the book ends with Jeremiah's consolation of Baruch found in 45:4-5 (E; Fretheim 2002, 25), for the readers of the Hebrew version, resolution does not come with a return to the land; it only comes with the destruction of their enemy.

In either arrangement, then, these chapters of restoration read like a fantasy or dream of an idyllic life. They remind the reader of Judah's corporate identity, even in the midst of their destruction. The poems paint pictures of communal identity, personified not only in the weeping mother (31:15-20) but also in the wounded collective body of 30:10-17 and the festive pilgrimage of 31:1-14. These are images that reinvigorate empathy for the victims of Babylonian aggression and, as a result, illustrate the human toll of colonial aggression. As such, they function as resistance literature to the overpowering reality of colonial expansion that led to their destruction (Davidson 2011a).

Comfort, Healing, and Restoration, 30:1-24

This section of the book begins with divine instructions to write out the subsequent oracles because they pertain to a future time. If they are written out, later generations will be able to return to the oracles of Jeremiah and confirm once more that he was a true prophet. This carries forward the characterization of Jeremiah as an ideal prophet (van der Toorn 2004). Scholars debate the date of the material, but the reference to the restoration of the Davidic monarchy in v. 9, something that failed to take hold, suggests that it was either written early in the Persian period when restoration was imminent or much later when hopes for an ideal Davidic messiah had taken hold.

This passage begins with the second of four references to the recording of Jeremiah's oracles in a "book," an anachronistic translation. Books were not invented until after the death of Christ. Perhaps the best translation for the term would be "text." These references to writing scattered throughout Jeremiah indicate the rise of writing as a medium for preserving Israelite traditions that began in the exilic period when Jews sought to preserve their traditions in the wake of the loss of self-rule.

The phrase "the days are coming" (v. 3) found scattered in Israelite prophecy indicates a distant, sometimes indeterminate future. It often introduces descriptions of a utopian future. Verse 3 sets the tone for these two chapters: it will be a time when God "will restore the fortunes" of both Israel and Judah, perhaps signaling a new exodus (Yates 2006), again a common motif in Israelite oracles of salvation. Although the Assyrians had destroyed the northern kingdom of Israel about 135 years previously and scattered the populace throughout the Assyrian empire, Israelite restoration texts hope for the return of all the descendants of the twelve tribes of Israel, united once again under a Davidic king. References to Jacob in vv. 7 and 10 reinforce this restoration of all twelve tribes, since Jacob, whose name was changed to Israel (Gen 32:28), is the father of the founders of the twelve tribes of Israel.

This first oracle (vv. 5-11) recognizes the reality of the disaster Judah had experienced. The text characterizes the time of travail as a period of terror

(v. 5) and likens the painful deaths of Judean warriors to women dying in childbirth (v. 6; Erbele-Küster 2006). But God promises to deliver them from these horrors by breaking the metaphorical yoke from off of their neck (v. 8), an image that echoes Jeremiah 27. Verses 10-11, which are not found in the Septuagint version of Jeremiah, reiterate these same themes in poetic form. God will gather together all twelve tribes, calm their trembling fear, and restore them to their land where God's justice will take hold.

The next oracle (vv. 12-17) again recognizes that this restoration will not erase the horrors of the siege. There will be scars. The author multiplies words for wounds, sickness, pain, and healing, creating a picture of a maimed survivor whom God ultimately heals (v. 17). The passage attributes these wounds to Judah's sins, which have left it without advocate (v. 13) or ally ("lover," v. 14). The tone of the passage briefly reverses in v. 16 with a term often translated as "therefore," which makes little sense in English. The language here is that of a legal sentencing, stating that God promises to destroy those who have destroyed Judah. As a result, even though the poem asserts that Judah's "wounds" were deserved, both those who had inflicted those wounds and those who did nothing to help Judah also deserve to be punished.

While this may not sound like a logical argument (and, note, it is not written as if it were), studies of both groups and individuals who experience deep trauma reveal that one predictable outcome of such trauma is the inability to make logical sense of what happened. The victim, for example, often cannot put events in sequential order, often cycling back over the trauma again and again (O'Connor 2011b). This idea that while, on the one hand, God brought Babylon as a punishment against Jerusalem yet, on the other hand, will destroy this attacker actually structures the Hebrew version of Jeremiah. In earlier chapters of the book, Jeremiah consistently depicts Babylon as sent by Yahweh, yet the book ends with poems describing Babylon's demise. The short oracle here in vv. 12-17 is a microcosm of the larger trajectory of the book.

The next verses, 18-22, elicit the outline of a restored Jerusalem, which is never named, sitting at the center of the twelve-tribe nation. The poem envisions the restoration of permanent buildings, including palaces. It begins with the statement that this is a city built on a hill, that is, on the heights of Jerusalem (v. 18). Such a concept was rather common in the ancient Near East, since temples were usually built either on a natural hill or on a raised platform. This reference to a city on the hill, then, focuses on Jerusalem as a sacred site. Although the temple is not specifically mentioned, the city functions as a holy city: ritual thanksgiving will go out from it (v. 19), and an assembly, which often means a religious assembly, will gather there (v. 20), drawing near to God's presence (v. 21). It will be a secure land with effective leadership (v. 21), centered on the true king, Yahweh (vv. 21-22). (Later, Puritans used the image of the "city on the hill," picked up in Matt 5:14, to describe their settlement in the Americas.)

Verses 23-24 do not fit well with either what precedes or what follows. These verses use storm language as an image of God's destructive power. Verse 24 seems to admit that the image makes little sense. "Some time later," it states, "you will understand." Is it promising destruction of Judah or further revenge against Judah's enemies? While the text does not make this clear, it does undercut any attempt to view the promises of Judah's restoration as somehow connoting a kind and approachable deity. This God can still destroy in an instant.

A Festive Pilgrimage, 31:1-14

The theme of the city as a sacred center continues into these next verses. The section begins with a reaffirmation of God's promise to restore all twelve tribes of Israel. The passage recognizes that the tribes of Israel have been scattered far and wide throughout the known world. It depicts the people as those who have survived the violence that killed many others (v. 2). Yet the poem asserts, all evidence to the contrary, that God has loved them "forever" (or "with an everlasting love" in the NRSV [v. 3]). While such a divine assertion may ring untrue given their experiences, these particular verses focus less on the actual experience of disaster and more on the abundant joy that will accompany Israel's restoration. While 30:19 hints at a festive mood, the festivities blossom in 31:4-14 with music, dancing, and songs of joy. These are coupled with images of harvest and agricultural bounty. While these images may reflect the celebration of harvest festivals or other such events, here they are attached to the return of the exiles. As the exiles return, all the nations will shout out with joy (vv. 6-7).

Keeping with the prevailing patterns in this section of the book, the text once again depicts the remnant as bearing the marks of their horrendous experience. The assembly that God leads back in vv. 8-14 includes those who suffer from permanent physical impairment (the blind and the lame of v. 8), as well as women and children, who re-symbolize the totality of Jerusalem's destruction. Verse 7 calls them the remnant that had been scattered throughout the Fertile Crescent by God (v. 10). They have languished or withered in exile (v. 12), mourning their losses (v. 13).

These images of a community permanently marked by the traumas they have undergone contrast with images of joyful restoration. The way back for the remnant is a smooth road along life-giving rivers (v. 9). They come laden with bountiful gifts for God: grain, wine, oil, and even cattle (v. 12). God is both father (v. 9) and shepherd (v. 10) to them. The whole community, from young to old, males and females, will rejoice together (v. 13). The passage ends with the image of the priests sated with the fat from the healthy sacrifices offered up in thanksgiving for all the goodness that God provides.

Although vv. 8-14 do not call this a pilgrimage, the images play with that motif. The people stream to their destination with offerings. Singing and dancing were part of these sacred processions (see, for example 2 Sam 6:1-5). The journey ends with the priests celebrating God's goodness. This image of the restoration of Judah engages liturgical language, highlighting the city's role as a site for mediating God's blessings. This last focus on God's beneficent presence contrasts with images of God's destructive effect on the city in earlier parts of the book.

A Mother Comforted, 31:15-20

The next cycle of restoration images picks up on the personification of the city as a female seen earlier in the book of Jeremiah. While Jeremiah 2, for example, portrayed the city as an adulterous wife, here the passage focuses on her as a mother to the citizens of the city. It sets up a nice pairing with the image of God as Ephraim's father in the previous section. The poem opens with the image of a mother weeping for her children. The text recognizes that the destruction of the whole nation of Israel not only included the fall of Jerusalem but also started much earlier with the destruction of the northern kingdom. These poems trace the slow demise of the nation, bit by bit, as the empires of Mesopotamia pick off tribe after tribe. The trauma of the fall of Jerusalem triggers the collective memory of the trauma of the fall of the north 135 years earlier (Albertz 2012).

While the end of v. 15 ("they exist no more") alludes to the impossibility of the restoration of the north, Yahweh's voice provides a counterimage: the return of all the tribes. The language of v. 16 tinges this hope of return with the fantasy of revenge. The line that the NRSV translates as "for there is reward for your work" can also read "because there will be payback for what this has cost you." The hopelessness of such a utopia contrasts with God's assertion of hope in v. 17. While this vision of the restoration of the north is an improbable fantasy, it should be noticed that the visions of the restoration of Judah, to which it is tied, also are now cast as beyond hope (Halvorson-Taylor 2012). In other words, the details in this poem reveal that the restoration visions are not plans for an imminent future, written as people return to the land. They are instead utopian visions that address a community that cannot even imagine realizing these dreams; only God can accomplish them. This feeling of impossibility would have worked in the immediate decades after the fall of the city, but studies of the literature of refugees and those experiencing collective trauma show that elaborate idealizations of the "homeland" are more indicative of the third generation in exile or later (Ahn 2011, 223–58; Najafizadeh 2013). Even after Jews had returned and restored the nation under Persian colonization, the disappointment over the shape of that new existence would have fed fantasies for the restoration of a kind of indigenous empire centered in Israel (Faust 2012, esp. 167–80).

This poem about the restoration of the north includes reflexes of the tragedy that it had suffered, while also attributing that suffering to its own sinfulness (vv. 18-19). Notably, the speaker of these verses is Ephraim, who reconfirms devotion to Yahweh. The earlier poems of this section cast Ephraim as a parallel to Judah. Here, though, the focus is not so much on the violent end of the nation but on the shame that military defeat attaches to those defeated. It may also be an oblique hint that, before Jerusalem fell, the people in the south had probably attributed the fall of the north to the fact that they were not the true Israel because they did not worship at Jerusalem. The fall of Jerusalem laid bare the lie in that interpretation: Judah is no more special than Israel.

The speaker changes in v. 20, the first time we hear the voice of Rachel. This one short verse resonates with maternal pathos. First, she presents a clear picture of who Ephraim is to her: her precious and delightful baby. Then she hints that she cannot get over his loss, talking about him again and again. The verse ends with her "belly" (or her uterus) yearning for him (translated as "I am deeply moved for him" in the NRSV), tying her love to this visceral response of a mother. The language opens up a brief glimpse into the pain of the mothers who had lost children in this war, literally giving them a voice. This loss of offspring would have been widespread among the audience. Certainly there was a high rate of childhood mortality in the ancient world, a rate that would have been higher for exiles, forced laborers, and the colonized. This circumstance means that this verse would have triggered a visceral reaction in its audience, even among those who did not directly lose children in the war. The loss of children in horrific ways, however, is also a common trope in the poetry describing the fall of Jerusalem. Lamentations, for example, depicts one of the great horrors of the siege as mothers having to eat their children in order to survive (4:10), while 2 Kings 6:25-32 contains the story of two women deciding which child to eat first. Mothers also lost adult children as these cities were destroyed through various atrocities. Verse

20, which gives voice to the maternal weeping that opens the poem, succinctly creates an audience that would empathize with the speaker. The fall of the northern kingdom was as brutal as that of the south, and the two nations shared the same fate as well as the same impossible fantasies of reversal.

A Compendium of Images of Restoration, 31:21-30

The second half of this chapter contains a number of shorter oracles of restoration, perhaps gathered here to create a small subsection in the book. These chapters include some of the texts of Jeremiah that have been most influential on Christianity. Yet these shorter oracles have the least ties to the rest of the book of Jeremiah. Because they are not placed in a prominent position, rhetorically they do not undercut or redirect the book's overall perspective on the sinfulness of the people and the veracity of Jeremiah alone.

It is not always clear how to divide up the verses in this section. For example, the Hebrew text puts 31:21-22 together as a unit, although in terms of content, they do not seem to fit well together. The first verse provides another image of God bringing Israel back. The road markers (NRSV) serve as metaphors for God's guidance as people return. It must be remembered that this verse is addressed to people who have lived outside the land of Israel for multiple generations, so they would probably have many reasons for not returning, especially since moving to Israel would mean leaving jobs, homes, and communities. This verse depicts God as smoothing out the transition. The next verse addresses a "faithless daughter," presumably a sinful Judah or Jerusalem, since Israel as a whole is usually personified in this section as a male (Ephraim or Jacob). The verse also reflects a later generation of the original exiles reluctant to go back to their ancestral land. Isaiah 40–55, which contains poems addressed to this same group, has similar exhortations that presume an audience hesitant to resettle.

Verse 22 ends with an image that must have resonated with the original audience but makes little sense to us today. The verse states that they should return because it is going to be like nothing they have seen before. The passage then gives an image of reversal: a woman encompassing (NRSV) or surrounding a warrior. It is not clear what this means. If it refers to a maternal hug or to sexual union, then it is not something new. Whatever the image is supposed to connote, it uses an image of gender reversal to represent a clear message (Bauer 1999a, 145; Carvalho 2013, 264–65). The return of those living in Diaspora will be an unexpected reversal, worth the journey.

The Hebrew version groups the next four verses together (vv. 23-26) as prose accounts using agricultural imagery (Leene 1992). The images in this section have dual meanings, so that they connote the restoration of both rural and urban areas. The blessing of the holy mountain in v. 23 refers to the restoration of sacred sites, especially Jerusalem since it refers to only one mountain. This blessing recalls the metaphor of the city on the hill in 30:18. The Lord also blesses the righteous "abode" (NRSV). The word translated as "abode" here actually invokes a pastoral image. It is used for places where domesticated animals, such as sheep or camels, are housed, as well as for shelters for shepherds (which might be in the same location). By designating this pastoral land as "righteous," the verse suggests that the land is innocent of the sins the people in the city have committed and, therefore, is not cursed. Archaeology confirms that outside the area in and around Jerusalem, the land of Israel suffered little devastation during the Babylonian advance (Zorn 2003; Becking 2009). The passage promises the restoration of the whole of Judah throughout this pastoral landscape, casting the restored as farmers and shepherds (v. 24). These starving, languishing families will eat their fill and be sated (v. 25).

The final verse refers to God awaking from slumber (v. 26). While most translations of this verse ascribe it to Jeremiah, there is nothing in the text that states he is the speaker. On the contrary, in this section of the book, the first-person speaker is God. Divine sleep is a common motif in the ancient Near East (Batto 1987). In the Mesopotamian creation epic, *Atrahasis*, the gods want to destroy the newly created humans because their noise keeps them awake. Many war poems that invoke the gods to come help in battle begin with a call to the deity to awake. This is seen in the Old Testament as well (Pss 7:6; 44:23; 59:5; Isa 51:9). This passage presumes this motif. Here God awakes to restore the people who are languishing and dying.

The next section, vv. 27-30, picks up on language found elsewhere. Verses 27-28 echo the images of planting and uprooting found in Jeremiah 1:10, but here they are explicitly applied to both Israel and Judah. This repeated language indicates that the restoration involves the switch from God's destructive actions (the first four verbs in 1:10) to those that are life-giving (the second two verbs in that verse). This echo of 1:10 introduces a reference to a proverb that must have been used as a popular explanation for why the exile lasted so long, since Ezekiel 18:2 quotes the same proverb. In both Jeremiah and Ezekiel, the text refutes the implications of the maxim, although with slightly different emphases (Hutton 2009). The proverb is used to state that the effects of the sins of an earlier generation unduly impact later generations. While this is quite true, it seems it was also being used by those in exile to say that they had been innocent of the sins that had led to the fall of Jerusalem; the city's fall was attributable to decisions made by earlier kings and leaders. The book of Kings represents this view, since it blames the fall of Jerusalem on the sins of Manasseh, a king who died fifty-five years before that fall (2 Kgs 21:9-16; 23:26).

Neither the book of Jeremiah nor Ezekiel lets the exiles off the hook. They both firmly assert that the sinful generation was the one that was exiled. While this may sound like a pessimistic view of history, it actually provides hope for later generations. If each generation suffers punishment for its own sins, then God can choose to reward the righteous behavior of the current generation (see the whole of Ezekiel 18 for a fuller discussion of this concept). The refutation of intergenerational punishment for sin takes hold in the Second Temple Period. It is one way that the retelling of the history of the monarchy in Chronicles differs from that in Kings; Chronicles depicts the reward or punishment of each king within his own lifetime.

God's New Covenant, 31:31-40

The longest oracle in this section comprises vv. 31-36, followed by a few random verses that again combine images of destruction and restoration. The discussion of the new covenant, which has several parallels with material in other biblical books, dominates the passage, however. The book of Jeremiah as a whole works on the presumption that adherence to God's commands would have saved the city. The book also imagines restoration in the same terms: a secure reinstatement depends on loyalty to God's covenant stipulations. The same idea is again found in the book of Ezekiel. Israel's past inability to remain obedient to God's laws and statutes makes the hope for an idyllic future foolish. Both books resolve the situation by imagining a metaphoric change of heart in the restored community. In the ancient world, the heart represented the will or the inner identity of the person. For Ezekiel, the new covenant will entail a heart transplant (Ezek 11:19; 36:26). In Jeremiah, the heart will be tattooed with God's laws, so internalized, in other words, that individuals will naturally act in conformity with God's plan for an ideal people. This fulfills the command in Deuteronomy 6:5 to love God with one's whole heart.

The passage in Jeremiah 31 likens the covenant to a marriage (31:32), a common motif in both Deuteronomy and the prophetic literature. It reengages the marriage metaphor found in chapters 2–3 (see, for example, Jer 3:1), another image that is prominent in Ezekiel (see chs. 16 and 23). It also associates covenant fidelity with peace and security as seen in v. 36. In this verse, the reference to Sabbath rest (translated as "cease" in the NRSV) echoes the discussion of the Sabbath in Jeremiah 17. Ezekiel 20 also uses the concept of the Sabbath as a way to represent the whole law. In other words, for both of these prophetic books, the covenant stipulations are not burdens to be born but gifts from God, such as rest and security.

Another resonance with Ezekiel appears in 31:37-40. These verses do not seem to form a whole coherent oracle, but they do echo some of more prominent images in the book of Ezekiel. First, the end of Ezekiel (chs. 40–48) contains an elaborate vision of a rebuilt Israel. In the vision, a heavenly being leads the prophet through this rebuilt land, measuring the spaces as they go. The verses in Jeremiah 31 include references to measuring. Verse 37 refers to the impossible idea of measuring the cosmos. Verse 38 asserts that the city will be rebuilt, with special mention of its gates; gates figure prominently in the description of the rebuilt temple and city in Ezekiel 40–48. A measuring line is then extended to measure the surrounding land in v. 39, just as the land is measured in Ezekiel 47–48. Finally, the last verse in Jeremiah 31 combines an image of a field strewn with corpses that will be restored and never again conquered (compare Ezek 37:1-2 as well as Ezek 39; Stavrakopoulou 2010, 120–22).

These parallels both within the book of Jeremiah and within the book of Ezekiel suggest that this section of Jeremiah was added to the book, perhaps during the period of the nation's restoration. While the superscriptions of both Jeremiah and Ezekiel place Ezekiel after Jeremiah, these sections of their respective books seem to suggest that they are both responding to the issues of return. While I would argue that the versions in Ezekiel precede those in Jeremiah (Patton 1999), in part because they are more fully explained there, it is interesting how the author of the final form of Jeremiah has woven the images into this new text so that they resonate with and interplay with other elements of the book, such as the image of planting or the concept of Sabbath rest. Even the covenant on the heart has a particular Jeremianic cast to it, with echoes from Deuteronomy. These additions, then, are not just clumsy insertions of other ideas but rather attempts by the author to connect other prophetic traditions with the living traditions associated with Jeremiah.

The Symbol of Ancestral Land, 32:1-44

A narrative tradition about an episode in Jeremiah's life follows on these poetic texts of restoration. The tales of the prophet that start here but blossom more fully in chapters 34–45, while appearing to be biographical information, are more properly read as narratives that use the prophet's character as a vehicle for conveying the theological themes associated with him. The prophetic tale is a common genre, found in the accounts of Elijah and Elisha in the books of Kings, in the story of Jonah included among the prophetic books, and in the narratives of the young Daniel in the book that bears his name.

This tradition of valuing prophetic lives and actions over the oracles that they spoke continues past the biblical period in texts like "The Lives of the Prophets" (see Hare 1985) and even into the Quran. In prophetic tales, the prophet is often an ideal figure who is courageous in the face of life-threatening opposition, countercultural in his singular actions, and/or powerful, even dangerous, in his ability to wield divine power (the notable exception being Jonah). In some respects, then, prophetic tales functioned in similar ways to the lives of the saints within Christian traditions, although prophetic tales do not usually contain the trope of the virtuous life.

When reading the tales associated with Jeremiah, the goal should be to recover the prophetic message that is symbolized through the tale itself. Characters within the narrative represent larger factions and reveal social tensions that the story seeks to address. The details, which are not preserved primarily to provide biographical information, contribute to this larger rhetorical goal of symbolizing a prophetic perspective on situations and events. For example, chapter 32 begins with Jeremiah under arrest and confined within some area of the palace courtyard. Jeremiah 37:11-16 describes the arrest of Jeremiah, there focusing on how those in power used his trips to Benjamin as an excuse to arrest him for treason. As the story is told in 32:3-5, however, the issue is Jeremiah's oracles against the monarchy, predicting the fall of the city and the capture of Zedekiah. In chapter 32, then, the issue is not Jeremiah's stance as a traitor but rather his claim to be a true prophet. While the political and prophetic are intertwined, chapter 32 chooses to focus on the latter element, while chapter 37 concentrates on whether his acts are treasonous.

The scene is set in a particular historical context: in the midst of the siege of Jerusalem. If it does refer to the same arrest as depicted in chapter 37, then the story takes place after the Egyptians have tried to rescue Judah by attacking the Babylonian troops, an attempt doomed to failure. Once the Egyptians lose, the city's fate is sealed, just as the *Titanic* was sunk the moment it hit the iceberg. The rest of the story recounts the slow death of a sinking ship. According to Jeremiah 37:11, Jeremiah's arrest occurs when the city still has hope; the Babylonian army has retreated, which would make Jeremiah's prediction of wholesale destruction seem at best silly and at worst unpatriotic. Chapter 32, however, opens with no note of reprieve; the Babylonian army is actively besieging the city, suggesting that this encounter with the king occurs sometime after the Egyptians withdraw, thus confirming Jeremiah's earlier predictions.

The passage opens with Zedekiah asking Jeremiah why he prophesies such negative things about him and the city; vv. 3-5 summarize the gist of the messages of doom that populate the bulk of chapters 2–29. Jeremiah's answer at first glance seems hardly to address the question posed. He does not say, as he said in earlier parts of the book, because you are evil, the people are evil, the religious establishment is evil, and you all deserve to die. In fact, once again, his answer is quite surprising. To be sure, it contains the notes of inescapable doom, but that message is surrounded by a countermelody that suggests an unexpected twist.

Instead of answering Zedekiah's question, Jeremiah tells a story of God telling him to buy some ancestral land. Ancient Israel had strict regulations about land ownership designed to keep land holdings in the hands of certain family groups. As God predicts in v. 7, Jeremiah's cousin offers to sell some land owned by their extended family to Jeremiah. Two terms are used for this land: first, it is inherited land, owned by right of kinship ("right of possession"), and, second, it was probably being used by others to pay off a debt ("right of redemption," v. 8; Domeris 2011). Given the fact that Jeremiah has predicted victory for the Babylonian invaders, it may be at first surprising that he decides to buy this land. If we as readers assume that chapter 16's notice that Jeremiah would not marry carries into this part of the book, then the chapter presents a man, imprisoned for treason, who cannot be executed as a false prophet if his predictions of disaster do not come true (in other words, who can only use the land if he is wrong and therefore executed), and who has no children to whom to bequeath the property. Buying or redeeming this land would be of no use to him or anyone else. The passage, however, is rather explicit in locating the acreage in Benjamin. We know from both archaeology (see, for example, Becking 2009) and Jeremiah 40 that Benjamin was relatively unscathed by the Babylonian army. The destruction happened primarily in and around Jerusalem. It could be that this purchase of land is meant to contrast the fate of Judah with that of other parts of Israel, which would serve to focus the guilt on the Jerusalem elite.

The passage itself, however, explains the purchase of land in a different way: here it functions as a sign-act, like Jeremiah's donning of dirty underwear (13:1-11) or a yoke (27:1-11). Before the explanation is given, the text slows down to describe the elaborate, formal, and public process Jeremiah must go through to purchase the land. This is not a rash decision but a deliberate act. Davidson (2011a) addresses the visibility of this sign-act. Verse 12 mentions a variety of witnesses to the signing of the deed, which is formally sealed as a matter of public record. The fact that those executing the transaction must come to the court where Jeremiah is confined highlights the odd nature of his decision, as if someone imprisoned for revolutionary acts today were to insist on conducting the ordinary legal business of someone who is free. The picture that the author lingers over up to v. 14 plays with striking contrasts.

The purpose of this purchase, however, begins to come into focus starting in God's speech in v. 15: "Houses, fields, and vineyards will again be bought in this land." Jeremiah responds with a long prayer (vv. 17-25) that contains many elements of formal address. While Jeremiah's speech utilizes a higher degree of formality in comparison with other Near Eastern and Israelite prayers, it does not resonate with how Jeremiah's speech has been characterized in earlier parts of the book. The laments in chapters 11–20, for example, contain no formal appeasement of God; in fact, there Jeremiah calls God a liar and seducer. In the prose accounts of his confrontations with the Jerusalem elite in 26–29, he is also rather caustic. The speech here projects a different persona for this main character. The prayer provides images of God's power through references both to creation and to Israel's history. In some ways, it looks like an individual lament, such as those found in the book of Psalms, which often start with an address to God (32:17a) and include a statement of trust (32:17b-23a) as well as a description of the problem (32:24). The prayer here differs from the psalms, however, in that it includes a description of the people's sins in v. 23b, something usually missing in the psalms, and includes neither a formal request nor a vow of praise. Instead, once the problem is described, God immediately responds (Fischer 2010).

God's response is correspondingly lengthy (vv. 27-44). It seems to be divided into three units: vv. 27-35, which review the circumstances that led up to the siege (here depicted as wholly God's actions); vv. 36-41, a description of God bringing back all of those exiled; and vv. 42-44, which paint a quick sketch of the restored nation. This brief outline demonstrates that the speech fleshes out the message of v. 15; yes, the city will be destroyed, but the destruction will not last forever (Brueggemann 1996).

The first section of God's speech focuses on idolatry as the cause for the city's fall (Fretheim 2004). The speech casts every segment of Judean society (royalty, religious leaders, and elite citizens; v. 32) as worshipers of the Canaanite god, Baal. Although references to Baal in the Hebrew Bible are ambiguous since "Baal" is a title and not a name, they are usually associated with the young storm god who is also a warrior. While chapter 44 will castigate the people in Egypt for worshiping the goddess titled the "Queen of Heaven," this text focuses on the pre-fall worship of local deities. It depicts the Judeans as carrying out rituals on their rooftops (perhaps in worship of a sun or astral deity; v. 29), turning their backs on God (perhaps a reference to a ritual act toward another deity; v. 33), and setting up sacred objects to represent those deities within the temple precincts (v. 34), all sins also outlined in Ezekiel 8.

This first speech ends with a reference to child sacrifice. The reference to "Molech" (32:35 NRSV) is unclear, even though it appears throughout the Hebrew Bible. Scholars debate whether it is the name of a deity (about whom there is no reference in any text outside the Bible) or if it is the name of the sacrifice itself. What is clear is that *molech* is always associated with child sacrifice. Child sacrifice was practiced in North Africa and the Levant by the Phoenicians (who also worshiped Baal) and probably Moab (see 2 Kgs 3:27). The Bible references child sacrifice as well. While the prophetic books condemn it, the Pentateuch recognizes God's right to take the firstborn. Exodus 22:29-30 is perhaps the clearest statement that the firstborn belongs to God. In most other laws in the Pentateuch, God accepts a substitute in place of sacrificing the child, either by sacrificing a lamb (Exod 13:13; 34:20), by dedicating certain people into permanent temple slavery (usually translated as "service," which masks that this service is not voluntary; Num 3:12, 41; 8:16-18), or by the donation of a specified amount of money (Num 3:46-50; 18:15-16). Ezekiel 20:25-26 also notes that Israel's divinely revealed laws included allowances for child sacrifice, but it explains those laws as "not good," meant to defile those who practiced them (Patton 1996). Apparently, then, there was a lively debate about the role and efficacy of child sacrifice throughout this region.

God seems to try again to explain the sign in vv. 36-41 and once again begins by affirming the sweeping destruction of Jerusalem (God's affirmation reflects the fact that this text speaks to a group whose collective identity is formed by this national tragedy). This speech echoes the images of return in chapters 30–31. God will actively gather them up from *all* the lands where they are scattered and will personally lead them back to their ancestral land (e.g., 30:10-11; 31:10-12). This return will include a change in heart, although here not a heart tattooed with the law but a heart that has only one purpose (31:33-34). The return also includes a new covenant (31:31-33) that will enable the Israelites to live securely in the land. The speech ends with a reversal of Deuteronomy 6:5; here it is God who will stay true to the covenant "with all my heart and all my soul" (32:41).

The final section of the divine speech in 32:42-44 paints a brief picture of the utopian world of restoration. First, it encompasses the whole land, from rural fields to urban environments (v. 44), reversing the desolation referred to in the previous verse. Second, it extends throughout the whole southern region of Judah, down into the Shephelah and Negeb (v. 44). While these three speeches contain echoes of the restoration images in chapters 30–31, however, the significant differences that they contain demonstrate that they are more than mere summaries or mimicries. For example, nowhere does God's speech make reference to the restoration of the northern kingdom. The text mentions neither Jacob nor Israel, and the restoration only extends north as far as Benjamin. This is clearly a restoration of the southern kingdom alone. Jeremiah's prayer also contradicts 31:29-30 when he states that God punishes later generations for the sins of earlier ones (32:18).

The question still remains, How is this report of a dialogue between God and the prophet a response to Zedekiah's question? Perhaps it is not, but the juxtaposition of the texts invites the audience to supply the connections. The most obvious contrast is between Zedekiah's claim that Jeremiah is predicting total destruction and Jeremiah's assertion that the nation as an entity will not be totally destroyed. Zedekiah's speech implies two interlocking charges: that Jeremiah is somehow complicit in the fall of the city (either by sowing doubt and rebellion among the people or by his prophetic pronouncements making the things he describes come true) and that Jeremiah is a traitor who acts on Babylon's behalf. Jeremiah's speech negates both assumptions. First, his vision asserts that the nation will not be destroyed, only this particular regime. And, if his prophetic pronouncements have the power to bring into reality what he speaks, then these speeches of restoration participate in the re-creation of the Judean state. Second, he places himself as part of the ideal reconstituted nation and not as part of the Babylonian power structures. What he envisions, then, is not the destruction of the nation but rather its radical reformation. In the words of a true revolutionary, he essentially says that this regime needs to be burned down so that another one can rise in its place. As with most revolutionaries, such speech clearly threatens the established power structures, so Zedekiah's reaction contributes to the characterization here of Jeremiah as a radical revolutionary.

The speech also serves to highlight the sinfulness of the indigenous powers in control when the city fell. By depicting God as hyperpowerful—able to create the very heavens and earth (32:17), defeat mighty armies (32:21), and control all human existence (32:19)—and then having this deity promise to restore the nation securely, even if that means changing the internal structure of the people so that they cannot sin, Jeremiah leaves no room to attribute the fall of Jerusalem to the strength of the Babylonian army or the power of their gods. The fall did not happen because Baal was angry or because the Israelites had not sacrificed enough of their children. It fell for one reason and one reason only: that particular group of people deserved it. Again, this rhetorical strategy shines a sharp light on Zedekiah as a failed leader, thus making his fear of Jeremiah reasonable.

This discussion, however, only addresses how the speeches approach political factors internal to Judah, in part because that is how the passage explicitly packages the story. Davidson points out, though, that given the fact that Babylonian aggression constituted violent colonization, the vision of restoration actually functions as resistance literature (2011a). He notes that vv. 1-15 preserve a distinctive indigenous identity, which is itself a resistance to colonizers who wish to erase or replace that identity. I would add that the divine speeches that follow, which attribute the destruction to Yahweh, take agency away from the colonizer who now serves only as God's puppet. Babylon does *not* have the final word in this story; Israel's God does. The passage, then, while ostensibly dealing with a rivalry between Zedekiah and Jeremiah, invisibly addresses questions of power, agency, and identity that arose under the pall of colonization. Therefore, while the story is set before the city fell, the content and structure of the story more clearly addresses communities under multigenerational colonized contexts, especially later generations who are told that, although the punishment may seem long, the utopian restoration will last "to the thousandth generation" (32:18 NRSV).

Contours of a Restored Nation, 33:1-26

The final chapter in this section of the book provides a broad outline of what a restored idyllic nation would look like. The chapter consists of a long vision of the future that God recites to the prophet. The setting of the scene continues from the previous chapter: Jeremiah under arrest at the palace, with the Babylonian army besieging the city. The passage paints a utopian picture that sweeps from the pasturelands, towns, and villages outside the city to Jerusalem with its final focus on the restoration of the Davidic monarchy. Like the previous presentations of the idyllic life, it includes references to the wholesale tragedy of the nation's collapse, which rhetorically highlight the complete reversal that serves as the main subject of this chapter. The reader should imagine the sound of siege works, taunts, and suffering as the background noise to the divine speech.

The passage begins with a short description of the complete devastation that would close this part of Israel's history. The brief reference to the corpse-filled city in v. 5 efficiently reminds the reader that no matter what might have been hoped for when the siege began, it would only end once the army breached the walls. The passage as a whole, however, does not linger over the violence. Instead it is concerned with the larger theological problem that the city's fall raised: where was Yahweh as the corpses were piling up? The passage tips its hand to this broader issue in v. 24: "Have you not seen what this people are saying: Here are the two tribes that Yahweh had chosen but has now rejected?" In other words, their conquerors claimed that Judah had lost because Yahweh had abandoned them. This passage answers the claim.

Like the other restoration passages in this section of the book, the restoration includes both the southern and northern kingdoms, especially highlighted in the reference to two families or tribes in v. 24 (see also vv. 7, 26). Unlike the earlier chapters, however, this vision keeps the restoration of Judah, and Jerusalem in particular, at the focal point of the reconstructed nation. This clearly looks for the reestablishment of the double pillars of Judean authority: a Davidic king and a temple priesthood. For Jeremiah 33, Israel revolves around a renewed Jerusalem, here renamed to signal a new beginning: "Yahweh is our righteousness" (v. 16 NRSV).

Although the chapter describes the political reorganization of Israel, the renaming of the city reminds the reader that the political configuration flows from how they think about God's relationship to the city's fall. Is this a god that can be relied on? The chapter answers this question in a number of ways. For example, it begins with an unusually long epithet for God. Throughout most of the book of Jeremiah, God either has no epithet or has the standard title of "Yahweh of the armies" (traditionally translated "LORD of hosts"; Rofé 1991). Verse 2, however, has a much longer epithet. In most English translations, such as the NRSV, Yahweh is identified as the one who formed the earth and established it. While this is a common motif in the ancient Near East, especially during the Persian period, the Hebrew text is deliciously ambiguous; the word for "earth" does not appear. The verse could just as easily be translated, "Thus says Yahweh, the one doing this; Yahweh, the one planning this, to establish this; Yahweh is his name." This more literal translation suggests that "this" refers to the destruction of the city: Yahweh planned it, executed it, and decreed it. I would argue that the double meaning of the verse is intentional. Both project a God in complete control, one whose power is unsurpassed, a meaning reinforced by the pronouncement of the divine name. The deliberate ambiguity then makes God's power even more apparent by drawing a clear parallel between God's power to create (the one who makes the earth) and the power to control history (the one behind these events).

The text keeps God's power at the forefront even in the description of the restoration. The oracle begins by stating that God will tell Jeremiah "great and hidden things" (v. 3 NRSV). As startling as it may be that God destroyed Judah, even more unexpected will be its restoration. After all, the book of Jeremiah depicts the destruction of Jerusalem as fully predicted: Jeremiah had been warning the people to repent or the city would be destroyed. God's note that the destruction followed on their sins here in 33:5 and 8 casts the fall of the city as the "business as usual" part of their history. It is the fact that God will reverse this that is news. Notably, too, in this chapter the restoration does not follow on any kind of repentance by the people. It is based solely and emphatically on God's eternal promises.

The author fills the chapter with hyperbole. The text presents both the images of destruction as well as their mirrored restorations in absolute terms, neither of which reflect historical realities. For example, 33:12-13 claims that wholesale destruction extended throughout the southern part of Judah, including the land of Benjamin. Later in chapter 40, it will be clear that Benjamin did not experience the same degree of destruction as did Judah. This oracle, however, does not intend to give an accurate account of damages but rather to paint a picture of the widespread change that followed on the Babylonian invasion. To be sure, this chapter is clearly told from the perspective of those who viewed the Davidic monarchy and the Jerusalem temple as central components of Israelite identity, so for them the loss of these institutions did mean a kind of annihilation of the "nation," even if only as a social entity. However, even for those whose daily lives may have changed little with the foreign invasion, such widespread colonization did mark a change in the economic and social fabric of Israelite identity. This oracle uses images of devastation to illustrate that change.

The images of devastation, however, serve additionally as a rhetorical foil against which restoration becomes an unanticipated reversal. This section combines various images of restoration, often using images found in other parts of Jeremiah, to present an ever-increasing picture of a world worth waiting for. The restoration commences with the city, first engaging a metaphor of healing (v. 6), seen already in 30:12-17, combined with images of purification in v. 8. Verse 9 depicts the people as trembling with fear, a motif usually associated with the city's demise, but here it is a reaction to "all the good" that God will do for them. Reversal is also at the center of vv. 10-11, where the sounds of wedding feasts described as ceasing in 16:9 are restored. Chapter 16 contrasts the sounds of wedding feasts with an image of unburied corpses (16:6), while in this chapter the mirth of both weddings and temple offerings replaces a land utterly devoid of any living creature, a picture that would conjure up a completely silent land (33:10-11).

The image of the wasteland also starts the vision of restoration in 33:12-16. In this section, the repopulation of the land starts in the pasturelands and villages of Judah. From a steppe devoid of animals to a field filled with sheep, the picture replaces devastation with plenty. The tableau includes the human realm with the brief reference to the shepherd counting the sheep as they pass by under hand (v. 13). The vision then returns to the city of

Jerusalem, insinuating that the farmers and herders can live in peace because the capital city will again be restored with a strong king on the throne (vv. 14-16).

These verses introduce the second major theme in this chapter: the restoration of the social structure of pre-fall Jerusalem. The city is configured as the seat of two important groups: the royal and priestly families. While most of the material in vv. 14-26 focuses on the restoration of the Davidic monarchy, v. 18 refers briefly to the Levitical priesthood. At first glance this may be a secondary addition to this chapter, but it does follow on the images of purification and offering in vv. 8 and 11. It also parallels other exilic and postexilic texts, such as Ezekiel, Chronicles, Zechariah, and Malachi, that evidence tension between priestly groups.

The bulk of the chapter stays clearly focused on the role of the Davidic monarchy, however. This section seems to combine four different oracles related to the restoration of the monarchy, each one introduced by a distinct opening formula (vv. 14, 17, 19, 23). They all contain stock images of royal exaltation, such as referring to the king as the "Branch" (v. 15; cf. Isa 4:2; 11:1; Ezek 19:10-14; Zech 3:8) who sits on the throne (v. 17; cf. Isa 9:7; 16:5; Zech 6:13) and executes justice (v. 15). His sons also sit on his throne, a clear reference to the establishment of a dynasty (vv. 17, 21-22, 26; see 2 Sam 7, Ps 132:11, and 1 Chr 17), and he is called God's servant (vv. 21, 22, 26; see also Ezek 34:23-24; 37:24-25). Like Ezekiel 34:25, Jeremiah 33:26 parallels David and Jacob.

While it is not surprising that the passage views God's covenant with David as a permanent covenant, what is striking is how it couples this with God's covenant with day and night (vv. 20, 25), a concept that links God's covenant to the creation of the world. Although no formal covenant is made between God and personified day/night in the Bible, in the covenant that follows the flood in Genesis 8:22, God promises that day and night will exist eternally. Jeremiah 31:35-37 also contains a short poem that links Yahweh's covenant with Israel to the "fixed order" of the created cosmos, much like Second Isaiah (Huffmon 1999; Fretheim 2002, 444–46). The hyperbolic statement is clearly contrary to fact: the Davidic line had been dethroned, and at no point was the reestablishment of dynastic succession secure. The exalted royal language, then, cannot serve as exaltation of a ruling king.

Most scholars would see this language as that of hope. Perhaps it represents the political ambitions of some group in exile or left in the land. Perhaps it is royal propaganda by the last remnants of the Davidic monarchy. Or maybe it is theological rhetoric of a fading priesthood whose livelihood depended on royal support. These are all certainly factors for consideration, but the text's comingling of tragedy and utopia suggests that the divine speech has little to do with practical agendas and much more to do with the role fantasy plays in oppressed situations. No matter whether the chapter was penned by a prisoner named Jeremiah sitting in a jail cell while the Babylonian army raged outside the city walls (a highly unlikely historical reconstruction) or by a scribe during the Persian period of Judah's restoration musing on how a perfect world would look to a prophet like Jeremiah (a far more likely scenario), the passage functions as resistance to the dominant culture of colonization that was the political reality of post-597 Judah. For this author, the only solution to global colonization was trust in a God whose rule superseded that of any human ruler. To sing of a day when the king would return, the cities would teem with people bringing their offerings, and the farmlands would resound with the sound of bleating was to deny the supposed benevolent rule of the Persian (or Babylonian) emperor whom they served with their toil, tribute, and taxes.

Tales of the Prophet
Jeremiah 34–45

These twelve chapters contain odd material for a prophetic collection. Rather than sharing oracles or speeches by the prophet, they relate stories from Jeremiah's life. They do not form a coherent whole, either through their arrangement or in terms of internal consistency. While most of the stories are set in the final years of Zedekiah and later, two of them (chs. 35–36) are dated to the reign of Jehoiakim, at least eighteen years earlier. As a result, they read more as a collection of tales about this prophetic figure (Seitz 1989a, 236–81). It may be that these stories developed after the oracles were collected, although it is also possible that they circulated independently, since in some ways they resemble the stories from the life of Elijah in the books of Kings or the late text, "The Lives of the Prophets" (Hare 1985).

While the stories do not form a comprehensive narrative arc, some of their images and themes repeat. First, in most of them, those in power control Jeremiah's fate. He spends much of this section of the book as a convicted criminal (chs. 37–40) on death row, or more properly in a death pit (ch. 38). In chapter 40, he is given the choice of overlord (Babylon or the Babylonian appointed governor Gedeliah), but the fact that he ends up going to Egypt against his will attests to his own lack of autonomy. To be sure, while chapter 43 does not depict him as enchained, the choice to emigrate is clearly not his. Like refugees throughout time, he is swept up in the effects of empire, just another nameless, faceless soul in this sad parade of humanity.

One major theme found throughout this section engages how those who survive colonization must negotiate issues of autonomy and constraint, as Davidson notes in his study of chapter 40 (2011a). In a similar vein, O'Connor presents Jeremiah as the ideal exile, and these stories may, in fact, reveal the impossibility of autonomy within the context of imperial imposition. Nebuzaradan's offer to reward what he views as Jeremiah's support of the Babylonians by bringing him to Babylon in safety mirrors those in Judah who viewed Jeremiah as a traitor. The text asserts that neither side ever truly understood why Jeremiah spoke as he did. For the final redactor, what looked like Jeremiah's traitorous allegiance to Babylon was actually radical adherence to God's plan.

A second recurring image in this section is that of the scroll. Although the recording of Jeremiah's oracles was already noted in 25:13 and 30:2, this section of the book frames the stories with two bookended episodes of Baruch's recording of his words. In chapter 36, a chapter dated quite early in Jeremiah's life, King Jehoiakim burns the scroll created by Baruch bit by bit. Chapter 45, essentially Jeremiah's final scene, returns to the textualization of Jeremiah's words, as Baruch once again records his words and stories.

All of these stories depict Jeremiah's confrontations with Judean political leaders. Jehoiakim is the protagonist in chapters 35–36, Zedekiah in 34 and 37–39, and Gedaliah in 40–41. Those in charge of the martial law that prevailed after the assassination of Gedeliah controlled Jeremiah's fate in chapters 42–45. In all of these contests, Jeremiah represents the unheeded voice of God speaking an ignored truth to a stubborn power. These final stories about Jeremiah, then, preserve and complete his characterization as a lone, marginalized voice that has permeated the book.

Along the way, Jeremiah has three allies: his scribe Baruch, whose character is barely fleshed out; the Babylonian military leader, Nebuzaradan; and Ebed-Melech, a foreigner and eunuch. None of these figures brings Jeremiah back into the center of Judean society. In fact, they help to further Jeremiah's identification with cultures on the margin of ancient Jerusalem. The marginalization also appears in the first two chapters of this section in which he stands up for the release of slaves and pronounces the fringe group, the Rechabites, as more righteous than the Judean elite. The stories as a whole, then, identify him with slaves, a nomadic tribe, the working class (scribes), traitors, and the unclean. Yet, the stories assert, it is just from this left of center stage that the trustworthy voice originates.

Chapter 45 seems to close off the book as a whole with its repetition of key phrases from chapter 1. In the Hebrew version of Jeremiah, which forms the basis for this commentary, this section of the book is followed by oracles against foreign nations, with the account of the fall of Jerusalem, found also in 2 Kings 25, closing the book. In the Greek version, those oracles against the nations are found much earlier in the book, just after 25:13a. In the Greek arrangement, then, this chapter does close off the book before the historical appendix. In both arrangements, however, Jeremiah ceases to be an active character in the book that bears his name. To be sure, the oracles against the nations are reported as his speeches, but the text provides no narrative context for these speeches, nor does Jeremiah participate in any dialogue. Jeremiah as a narrative character recedes after chapter 45.

Free the Slaves, 34:1-22

The text sets the first chapter in this narrative collection during the second siege of Jerusalem. The chapter seems to contain two oracles that blend into one another: vv. 1-6, which predict Zedekiah's survival of the fall of the city, and vv. 7-22 on the fate of the city's slaves. The backdrop of siege heightens the immediacy of both oracles.

The passage begins with a short oracle addressed to Zedekiah that affirms he will not be killed when the city falls. It is an odd oracle because it contains no overt condemnation of Zedekiah, unlike other parts of the book (see, for instance, 21:3-7; 24:8-10). In fact, the king seems to be granted an honorable burial. It may be that the book merely reflects historical facts, but still one could imagine a way to have rhetorically cast his fate in a more negative light. The notice in v. 7 that reports the fall of all fortified cities of Judah save two may be trying to do just that. Certainly it reveals the level of disaster that befell all of Judah during Zedekiah's reign.

The bulk of the chapter deals with the fate of indentured servants in the city. Unlike most of the book, which does not describe the catalysts for certain oracles, vv. 9-11 explain the situation Jeremiah addresses. Zedekiah had commanded people to release their debt slaves, but as the siege wore on, they reconscripted them. The detail in the description suggests that this was not a regular practice during sieges. In fact, one could imagine that the release of indentured servants would actually put the poor at more risk for starvation and serve the interests of the elite who could then reserve food supplies for their own families (Domeris 2007). This oracle does not seem to reflect the immediate realities of siege warfare.

Instead the passage refers to three distinct Israelite traditions: the exodus event, the laws governing debt slavery, and treaty rituals. God's speech opens in v. 13 with a reminder to the audience that they themselves had been freed from slavery by God. While this is a short notice, it depicts God on the side of those who are enslaved. The text immediately links this tradition to the divinely revealed law. While Sinai is not mentioned, the law described in v. 14 can be found in Exodus 21:2 and Deuteronomy 15:12. These slavery laws distinguish between two types of slaves: permanent and indentured slaves. Israelites could enslave fellow Israelite males to pay off debts, but only up to six years. This kept the debt ceiling lower, since it discouraged rich landowners from allowing debts to compound. Permanent slaves came from non-Israelite males (probably through wars; Lev 25:44), Israelite males who married and chose to stay with another slave (Exod 21:5-6), and, in Exodus 21:7, most female slaves (although see Deut 15:17). This latter regulation aimed to protect the women since the presumption was that men of the household could sleep with female slaves (see Exod 21:8-10). Therefore, a woman freed from slavery probably had little chance for marriage and therefore was vulnerable to poverty, assault, and early death. In this chapter, the speech makes explicit the command to release both male and female slaves, again ignoring the risk of such a decision for them. Instead, the law depicts the men of Jerusalem as evil because they violate not just the king's decree but also Yahweh's law.

The punishment for this transgression engages covenant treaty ceremonies. In fact, the whole chapter depicts both Zedekiah's decree (v. 10) and God's law (v. 13) as covenants or treaties. First, God uses the term for "emancipation" (v. 17; NRSV translates it as "release") ironically. Since the landowners have refused to emancipate their slaves, God will emancipate them. This ironic use casts the landowners as God's slaves. It also plays on their vulnerability: once freed, they will be vulnerable to the attacks of the Babylonians. This ironic twist, then, plays with the dual function of debt slavery in the ancient economy: it provided the rich a means to maintain their wealth, but it also afforded some protection for the enslaved.

Verses 18-19 refer obliquely to a covenant-ratifying ceremony in which the corpses of animals were split in two, and those making the covenant had to pass through the middle of the split corpses. In Genesis 15, God utilizes this ritual for a covenant with Abram. Hittite texts provide more information about this ritual. There, the splitting of the animals unleashes a curse against either party who might try to break the treaty. If someone does violate the treaty, they share the fate of these butchered animals. Jeremiah 34, then, depicts the butchering of the citizens of Jerusalem at the fall of the city as the realization of a curse invoked during the making of the covenant with God. Deuteronomy 28 contains blessings and curses for those who do and do not follow the law. Both Jeremiah 34:20 and Deuteronomy 28:26 include the lack of proper burial as one of the curses. "Their corpses will be food for the birds of the skies and the beasts of the land."

This oracle ends with God's promise to bring destruction to the city. Here Zedekiah shares the same fate as other leaders and the rest of the people, a portrayal that seems to contradict what was predicted in the first oracle. It should be noted, however, that the passage does not predict the leaders' deaths. Rather it notes their enslavement (taken to Babylon). In this sense, then, their fate is a kind of just deserts. Because they thought they were free to enslave others, their slave status to God was reinforced by their enslavement to the Babylonians. Although we do not know many details about the forced labor the Judean exiles experienced, there is some indication that they would have been used to keep the irrigation systems in Babylon in working order (Ahn 2011). The chapter probably reflects the traditions of enslavement to a foreign power as handed down to subsequent generations. The passage plays with multiple images of enslavement that would have resonated within a community whose immediate context included forced labor as a way both to indict the original generation it holds responsible for the city's fall and also to maintain that Yahweh is a God who cares for the fate of slaves.

Models of Obedience, 35:1-19

The next story is placed in an earlier period: during the days of Jehoiakim, that is, before either siege of Jerusalem. This chapter forms a self-contained story, although its details are rather odd. In one sense, it seems to report a sign-act, with Jeremiah acting out an oracle. The action described, however, reads as an unlikely set of events, and the use of the first-person narrative connotes that the text describes something that the people did not witness. In this narrative, Jeremiah claims to have tried to get a particular group of people, the Rechabites, who were known for vowing not to drink, to abandon their principles. They refuse to do so. Their refusal and staunch adherence to a human command becomes the foil to depict the Judeans' disobedience of God's commands as starkly evil.

Although today not much more is known about the Rechabites than is contained here, the original audience clearly needed no introduction to this group. The narrative depicts them as a semi-nomadic kinship group that observed strict rules of piety. As a group that adopted a kind of voluntary marginal status, they also stood outside the power structures of empire (Davidson 2013). The chapter stresses over and over that the commands they follow came from one of their ancestors, and not divinely revealed laws. Even so, the customs to which they adhere are particularly stringent. Wine was the primary drink in that part of the world, especially in light of the unreliability of safe drinking water. In addition, the fact that they voluntarily lived a nomadic existence also placed them at the margins of society.

The story, however, does not aim primarily to honor the Rechabites as much as to condemn the Israelites. The story of how Jeremiah tries to force them to drink, a wholly unsavory action, like trying to trick a vegetarian into eating meat, making a celibate priest watch pornography, or tempting a kosher Jew to eat a cheeseburger, is meant to highlight the firm resolve of this group to honor their vow of obedience to arbitrary and difficult practices (the story presumes the audience would view drinking wine and living in houses as desirable actions). From v. 14 on, however, the "I" who speaks is now Yahweh, who explains that the temptation of the Rechabites served to show the Jerusalemites how deserving of destruction they are in contrast. The Rechabites will live because they remained obedient to a human command, while the Judahites will be destroyed because they failed to obey God's commands.

The Authority of the Written Word, 36:1-32

For some odd reason, this chapter is my favorite one in the book. As a contemporary reader, I love the odd bits of detail the chapter contains. This narrative lingers over the storytelling, building suspense and painting a picture. Every time I think of the book of Jeremiah, I imagine a king with a fur-collared cloak huddled by a fire, laughing in evil delight as he cuts column after column off a long parchment scroll. I can see the pages curling up in the hot fire and his dirty-toothed grin as he thinks he has defeated that pesky prophet. (There is actually no evidence that he wore fur or had dirty teeth by the way.)

Why does the book pause so long over this scene? And why does it delight in recording the names of so many of the silent characters? Robert Carroll (1995) reads this as evidence that the book betrays some anxiety about whether oral or written messages were more permanent, more authoritative. In the preexilic period, when Israel was primarily an oral culture, writing supplemented the real creative medium: the oral performance. During the exile, since the social locations for oral performance had been destroyed, writing became more primary, first as a way to preserve older oral traditions and then as a means for conveying new ideas. This transition is seen more clearly in the book of Ezekiel where the length of the visions, for example, suggest their written origin. This circumstance contrasts with a book like Amos that reads much more like a collection of originally spoken oracles with few attempts to create a literarily cohesive text.

The book of Jeremiah is much more mixed. The first ten chapters of the book, for instance, have far more in common with Amos than they do with Ezekiel. But the accretion of narrative prose as the book progresses gives evidence to a growing literary element in its production. Although not the first mention of a scroll in Jeremiah, this chapter gives the clearest indication that the circulation of Jeremiah's oracles in written form was in some way noteworthy. In v. 17, the leaders ask how Baruch had come to have this written record, a question that seems silly to our modern ears but that reveals an awareness of a change in how prophetic oracles circulated.

The chapter keeps Jeremiah in prison or "confined" in some way, so the leaders may simply question how it was possible for Jeremiah to keep producing prophetic oracles since he was not able to preach them publicly. Most scholars view this chapter, as they do this whole section of prose material, as a later addition to the book, one that certainly reached its final form well after the fall of the city. This means that the original audience for the book would have been those who had also lost the original place where prophets proclaimed their messages (Römer 2000). The story then also addresses whether prophecy from Yahweh ceased with the fall of the city. This chapter views prophecy as still active, even if the prophets are imprisoned, confined, or banished.

At this time, there may have also been some nervousness about whether the scribes could be trusted to provide reliable access to the oracles of the prophets (Brummitt and Sherwood 2011). How would a community know if that scribe was trustworthy? Could they have missed something? Or, worse, could they have just made it all up? The chapter goes out of its way to depict Baruch as an extremely passive character. He adds nothing to Jeremiah's messages. In fact, the book of Jeremiah portrays scribes as positive figures, which suggests that the scribal community had a hand in collecting the Jeremiah traditions. Perhaps these scribes felt pride in being able to preserve the traditions. Notably, Jeremiah is not depicted as an elite member of society, so his oracles would likely not have been preserved by the elite, such as the royalty or the priesthood. The scribal classes may have resonated with this condemnation of the Judean leadership and so have preserved and enhanced the traditions associated with this prophetic figure. The traditions around his arrest and marginalization as a political activist and traitor seem especially associated with the positive view of the scribes. Whether they enhanced these traditions or simply preserved them, they give witness to a postexilic group that viewed the pre-fall government as wholly corrupt.

The names in the chapter suggest either that the author places them there to give a flair of credibility to the story (Grabbe 2006) or that the people named meant something to the original audience, just like the use of a specific date in v. 9. The characterization of the group called princes, or leaders, recalls the story of Jeremiah's arrest in chapter 26. While both accounts depict internal division concerning Jeremiah within the Jerusalem community, the leaders function as a rhetorical bridge between the evil king and the persecuted prophet.

Both stories place the issue of Jeremiah's authenticity at the fore. To these groups, this chapter adds the scribal family of Shaphan (Römer 2009). Baruch stands in the scribes' residence when he publicly reads the scroll

(v. 10), and he becomes the acting speaker who confronts the royal officials, including the king, in vv. 14-18. Baruch and Jeremiah hide together (v. 19), a detail that v. 26 attributes to divine agency, much like Elijah's concealment in 1 Kings 19. Here, however, the text has a different focus: the way that it asserts the continued delivery of Jeremiah's messages without the presence of either the prophet or the scribe testifies to the way texts outlast oral performances, even those by later disciples. Fretheim points out that the scroll is able to enter spaces where Jeremiah is barred, such as the royal court, again attesting to the superiority of the written message over the oral (2002, 502–506). This text thus elevates the scribal class, since not only does the king fail to have the last word but Jeremiah can also add to his oracles when he redictates the scroll, giving the scroll the final word. The scribes have won, and the text survives!

Jeremiah and Zedekiah, 37:1-21

This chapter contains two tales of the prophet, the first about his role in Egypt's attack on the Babylonian army and the second concerning a secret meeting between Jeremiah and the king. Both return to the siege of Jerusalem during the reign of Zedekiah, the same time frame with which the collection of these prophetic tales began. This would be at least ten years after the previous story. It is not clear why the editor did not arrange these narratives in chronological order (di Pede 2006), but it does demonstrate that this part of the book should not be read as the prophet's biography (Callaway 1999). In addition, the view of the kings continues to be inconsistent. In the second story, Zedekiah is more sympathetic, while other tales make him more culpable (Roncace 2005). These variations contribute to the impression that this section of the book results from a haphazard collection of tales that developed around the figure of Jeremiah.

The first story deals with an important turning point in the siege against Jerusalem. Although the books of Kings do not report this, Ezekiel 17:15 suggests that Zedekiah courted the Egyptians, while the texts here and in Jeremiah 34:21 refer to an Egyptian attack on the Babylonians during the siege of Jerusalem. Certainly Judah had turned to Egypt as an ally, not a surprising move since the Egyptians would also want to stop Nebuchadnezzar's advance.

While there is evidence that Pharaoh Psammetichus II had toured the Levant prior to Babylon's encroachment (Carvalho 2015, 197), it is not clear if it included a visit to Judah. Even so, Psammetichus would have had a vested interest in the fate of Judah, since its fall would mark Babylon's advance toward Egypt.

Verses 1-11 contain Jeremiah's prediction that the Egyptian attack would be unsuccessful. At the same time, it also depicts the hope of the citizens of Jerusalem that Egypt would be its savior. After all, the Egyptians would have had the only force strong enough to stop the Babylonians. When the Egyptians did attack the Babylonians, the siege would have to have been lifted for a time. This probably provides the framework for Jeremiah's journey to check on the family property in Benjamin in v. 12. Once Egypt lost, it was only a matter of time before Jerusalem fell. The city had no more hope.

The story of Jeremiah's arrest for treason serves as a bridge between the story of the Egyptian attack and the prophet's meeting with Zedekiah. Here the text brings to the fore the fact that Jeremiah's oracles constituted a threat to Judah's current government. Jeremiah 37:16 also tries to blend the tradition about Jeremiah's detention in a residence that has been converted to a type of jail with his confinement in a pit, seen in the next chapter. There was no true prison system in ancient Israel. Most crimes were punished through fines, restitution, servitude, or death. Detainment was used only as a temporary measure until a final solution could be determined. For prophets, this meant that they could be detained until events proved whether their predictions came true or not. If not, then they would be executed. In the case of Jeremiah, if events prove him wrong, the people of Jerusalem can execute him, but if the city does fall, then the Babylonians will probably kill him. This explains the significance of chapter 40 where the Babylonians try to reward him as a traitor who was on their side.

The final episode in this chapter has King Zedekiah secretly summoning Jeremiah. In this story, like the story of Saul's attempt to contact the spirit of Samuel (1 Sam 28), the king secretly believes in the prophet (or at least fears him), while ostensibly he opposes him. In both cases, the king hopes to get a positive message from God, and in both cases the meeting becomes an opportunity for the prophet to condemn the king face to face. Samuel predicts Saul's death on the battlefield, while Jeremiah tells of the king's capture by the Babylonians.

Although the story ends with Jeremiah once again detained, the king has guaranteed that he will be fed and provided for as long as possible. Even so, the brief note that he would have food as long as the food supply held out intones an ominous reminder to the audience that widespread starvation preceded the fall of the city. In fact, Lamentations 4:9-10 notes that those who died by the sword were better off than those who suffered the slow death of a starvation so pervasive that people turned to cannibalism. The final snapshot of Jeremiah in this chapter depicts a prisoner starving alongside those who have arrested him.

An Unexpected Ally, 38:1-13

The first half of chapter 38 tells a different story of Jeremiah's arrest than is found in other parts of the book. In this version, Jeremiah's opponents first throw him into a well and leave him to die in the mud at the bottom. This scene occurs before his detainment in a cell in the court of the guard in chapters 32–33, as well as 37:21. The text here contains a vibrant story with interesting physical details, which sets it apart from most prophetic tales. The story slows down to describe the mud encasing the prophet's feet and the rope that pulls him up, along with the rags used to protect his body from further harm.

Jeremiah only speaks once in this story: a short oracle that leads to his arrest. Yet the narrative does not focus on the original delivery of this oracle but on the officials' report of it to the king. The oracle predicts the downfall of Jerusalem using the triple trope of sword, famine, and pestilence but seems to encourage desertion ("Those who go out to the Chaldeans . . . will live," 38:2). If the story is set at the same time as the previous chapter, which seems to be the case, then Jeremiah would have been delivering oracles such as these while Egypt, Judah's ally, was trying to save the city. Jeremiah's oracle would have flown in the face of the international policy in place at the time.

An unexpected savior arrives for Jeremiah in the figure of Ebed-melech, described as both a eunuch and a Cushite—in other words, a servant or slave, and a foreigner. The narrative characterizes this outsider to the Jerusalem elite as nobler than the royal officials who have cast Jeremiah in the pit. The text describes them as wicked (v. 9), while Ebed-melech risks his standing for the sake of justice because he recognizes the cruelty of starvation. The soft cloth that protects the prophet's armpits, as three men from the royal court pull him from the cistern, symbolizes the extent of Ebed-melech's compassion. This level of humane treatment contrasts with the heartlessness of the Judean elite.

Although the story is ostensibly about the fate of Jeremiah, it also reveals the parallel between Jeremiah and the fate of the city's population. While Ebed-melech saves Jeremiah from starvation, God will not spare the people from the same fate. While the reader knows that Jeremiah will in fact survive the siege and live out his life in Egypt, a neighbor of Cush (Roncace 2005, 88), Ebed-Melech effectively spares his life here. In the process, though, the story makes clear the horror of starvation. Jeremiah, with his feet stuck in a muddy cistern, represents the inhabitants of the city. Both will starve by staying where they stand.

Although Ebed-melech is the main actor, the story highlights Zedekiah's reluctance to harm Jeremiah. Zedekiah is depicted as a weak king, afraid to confront his own officials. The cowardice of the king contrasts with the bravery of the slave. This reading of Zedekiah's character is certainly in line with the second half of the chapter. In this sense, then, every character symbolizes a different group. Zedekiah represents those who were afraid to do or say the right thing during the siege, Jeremiah symbolizes the righteous who were fated to starve because of the decisions of the wicked leaders, and Ebed-melech stands for those who tried to make a difference but were unable to completely counter the disastrous decisions of the elite.

A Secret Meeting with the King, 38:14-28

The second story in the chapter seems to pick up immediately where the previous one left off. In this story, Zedekiah meets with Jeremiah, probably seeking some kind of favorable oracle from Yahweh. In order to get an oracle that he can trust, however, the king has to listen to the message privately. If the treasonous message from Jeremiah had been heard publicly, the text assumes that there would have been cause to execute him. As the story plays out, Jeremiah does in fact deliver a treasonous oracle, telling Zedekiah that if he surrenders to the Babylonians, the city and his own family will be spared. While Zedekiah does not take this advice, he at least spares Jeremiah by keeping the oracle a secret. The reader should expect that what Jeremiah describes in vv. 22-23 foreshadows what will happen. This is certainly the case for v. 23, which matches the description of Zedekiah's fate in 2 Kings 25. The passage plays with irony as well: just as Jeremiah's feet had sunk in the mud of the cistern earlier in the chapter, here the women will use the same image to describe the betrayal of Zedekiah by his allies.

Secrecy is a major element of this story. Why relate a story of an event that no one knew about? It may have arisen as a way to fill in Jeremiah's public silence during the period of his arrest. This is the second nod the book gives in that direction; the first was in the replacement of Jeremiah with Baruch as the spokesperson or at least the recorder of oracles not preached publicly. Of course, an arrested prophet could not speak publicly, but these stories depict him as still actively involved in the events of the final years of the city. They also counter any vestigial tradition that he may in fact have been a Babylonian spy or supporter. These stories of his statements about surrendering explicitly occur in the context of calls to repentance. This attempt by the storyteller to make Jeremiah completely orthodox, even to the point of telling "secret stories," indicates how controversial the traditions of Jeremiah's stance were at the time. In addition, the stories deflect guilt away from the

Davidic monarch and place it more squarely on the shoulders of the royal officials. This allows for a continued hope in the restoration of the Davidic monarchy.

The Fall of the City of Jerusalem, 39:1-18

Chapter 39, another hinge chapter, connects two segments of the text by placing a bit of what will come next first, and then placing a bit of what preceded later in the chapter. The first half of the chapter, vv. 1-14, belongs with the material in chapter 40 and following, while vv. 15-18 fit better in chapter 38. Although we have seen this earlier in the book where the prose material starts to appear among the prophetic oracles, a closer parallel is found in Genesis 37–39. While Genesis 37 starts the Joseph cycle, chapter 38 interrupts that cycle to tell one last story of Jacob's family before returning to the Joseph narrative. The chapter here in Jeremiah does the same thing. It tells about the fall of the city and release of Jeremiah before doubling back to him in the court of the guard.

Before talking about vv. 1-14, then, it might be best to mention the end of the narrative of Ebed-Melech, which for modern readers seems to be displaced to the end of chapter 39. In Jeremiah 39:15-18, God rewards the servant for saving Jeremiah and simultaneously reaffirms the disastrous fate of the city. The language in 39:18 echoes Jeremiah's speech about those who would surrender to the Babylonians in 38:2, rhetorically confirming the veracity of Jeremiah's oracles. In addition, it shows that Jeremiah's fate, which will be described in more detail in chapter 40, was not unique to him but available to anyone who trusted Yahweh, even a foreign eunuch among the servant class.

Like a good movie that places a legendary figure in the midst of the retelling of a national event, 39:1-10 retells part of the story of the fall of the city found in 2 Kings 25, with an addendum that focuses on Jeremiah (vv. 11-14). The book of Jeremiah ends with a full repetition of 2 Kings 25, the account of Jerusalem's fall, but with no additional material about the fate of Jeremiah. The repetition of the narratives of the fall form a frame around the intervening prophetic material, signaling that this begins the final section of the book. The rhetorical effect of this particular bracketing casts the vivid shadow of the city's fall on all the material that it frames.

The first part of this chapter focuses on the actions of Zedekiah, who flees the city in cowardice much like a captain abandoning ship (vv. 1-7), building on his characterization as weak in the previous chapter. The account then briefly describes the fate of the city (vv. 8-9), adding the names of the Babylonian officials but leaving out the gory details that had been so vividly conveyed in Jeremiah's oracles. Does this mean the reader is supposed to hear this brief description and recall the horrors that had been described? Or does this part of the story seek to soften the characterization of the Babylonians by mentioning the burning of buildings and the forced migration of some of the people but neither the rape, mutilation, murder, starvation of the whole population (Lemos 2006), nor the desecration of the temple (Albertz 2002)? The fact that the description ends with the Babylonians saving the poorest people and giving them land and income (v. 10) suggests that this is all part of a strategy to distance the Babylonians from blame.

The softening continues in the description of the Babylonians' treatment of Jeremiah. This segment of the story begins with Nebuchadnezzar himself giving orders to spare Jeremiah, a highly unlikely reality. Again this detail suggests the strength of the tradition that Jeremiah supported the Babylonians. The story seems to go out of its way to depict the Babylonians as also being fooled into thinking he had been a traitor, since they are willing to reward him. This story line will not be resolved until the following chapter. Because the chapter ends with the story of God rewarding Ebed-Melech for saving Jeremiah, the chapter as a whole clearly attributes Jeremiah's survival to God's agency, and not as a reward for Jeremiah's treason or to the beneficence of the Babylonians.

The Fate of Gedaliah, 40:1–41:18

In the next two chapters, after describing how Jeremiah came to be among those associated with the Babylonian-appointed governor, Gedaliah (40:1-6), the focus turns to telling the story of the fate of this first colonial government (Vanderhooft 2003). Jeremiah appears nowhere in the story after v. 6. It begins a section of the book that relates the theology of the prophet to the post-fall realities of Judeans. While the book of Ezekiel sets the prophet Ezekiel among those exiled to Babylon, the book of Jeremiah uses the narrative settings of both the communities left in former Judah as well as the refugee community in Egypt as its backdrop.

In the first six verses, the Babylonian captain releases Jeremiah and gives him three choices for relocation: to go to Babylon but not as an exile, to stay with the group loyal to Gedaliah, or, in a statement meant to signal that Jeremiah was completely free to go where he wanted, Nebuzaradan states, "Or go anywhere that seems right from your point of view" (40:5). Jeremiah chooses the middle path: to stay with the Jews gathered around Gedaliah. This group would have been those designated in the previous chapter as "the poorest of the land" to whom the Babylonians had given property and protection. In other words, Jeremiah voluntarily remains identified with the marginalized

(Davidson 2011b). The narrative shows that Nebuzaradan's generosity is not a reward to Jeremiah but a recognition of the power and justice of the god for whom he had served as prophet. Thus the Babylonian captain himself notes that the people's sin caused the fall of the city (vv. 2-3).

Once Jeremiah is firmly situated within this particular group, the story then turns to a long description of the intrigue that eventually led to Gedaliah's assassination. The story begins pleasantly enough. Gedaliah, settled in Mizpah in Benjamin, an area that the archaeological record attests was relatively unscathed by the Babylonian advance (Betlyon 2003), rules over these formerly oppressed Judeans. This focus on the renewed fate of the powerless subtly serves to present God as just, since the harshest punishments seem to have been meted out on the elite whose actions and decisions were primarily to blame for the fall of the city.

Other Judeans, who may have had more resources in the pre-fall world, begin to gather around Gedaliah, including those who had been able to migrate to neighboring countries as refugees and those who led various militarized groups. The text portrays Gedaliah in a positive fashion; he welcomes all of these groups, provides them food, and offers them protection (Ben Zvi 2010). The story becomes ominous starting at 40:13, however, with the report that the Ammonite king has recruited one of the militarized leaders, Ishmael, to assassinate Gedaliah, presumably so that Ammon could take over the land (E. Peels 2009). Gedaliah's incredulity led to his death: he welcomed the very killer about whom he had been warned (40:16–41:3). His refusal to kill someone accused of being his enemy contrasts with Ishmael's deceit and slaughter of eighty pious worshipers (41:4-8), thus sparking a cycle of growing violence (41:9-18). This segment about such a turbulent time ends with those who had been loyal to Gedaliah planning to migrate to Egypt out of fear for their own safety.

Jeremiah Taken to Egypt, 42:1–43:7

The focus of the story now returns to Jeremiah as the audience understands the purpose of the narration of the previous events. The fearful leaders ask Jeremiah to intercede on their behalf and direct them as to their next steps. Their negotiations with Jeremiah are filled with pious and deferential language: "Whether it is good or bad, we will obey the voice of the LORD our God to whom we are sending you" (42:6 NRSV). They even wait a full ten days until Jeremiah receives an oracle (42:7). The story begins, then, with a rather positive portrayal of these leaders.

The rest of chapter 42 (vv. 9-22) recounts the details of an oracle that has a fairly simple message: stay in the land and do not migrate to Egypt. First the prophet addresses their fear that the Babylonians will retaliate against them. Jeremiah assures them that if they stay in the land, God will protect them and they will end up better off than before (vv. 11-12). The details of the previous chapters, however, have helped the audience identify with these leaders' fear, so the radical nature of Jeremiah's call for fortitude has more of an impact. The text also hints at the fact that the people may no longer trust God to act in ways that are beneficial for them. After all, this is the same God to whom Jeremiah attributed Jerusalem's destruction in the first place. This is also addressed in the text, when Yahweh, echoing the language of Jeremiah 1:10, expresses regret for or at least a cessation of that destruction (42:10; Biddle 2004).

Jeremiah next turns to the other possibility: that the leaders will insist on going to Egypt. The passage describes the benefits of such a decision: Egypt is not a war zone and there is plenty to eat. To counteract the attraction of such a decision, the oracle promises that this will not allow them to escape their current misfortune. Famine, violence, and disease will follow (42:13-17). From there the oracle ratchets up: every disaster that has fallen on the citizens of Jerusalem will come upon those who flee to Egypt (v. 18), and they will die by the trifecta of disaster: sword, famine, and pestilence (v. 22).

The speech is written in a Deuteronomistic style that also picks up language from other parts of the book (Stipp 2010b). The most obvious resonances in this speech are the descriptions of Jerusalem's fall. In addition, the oracle begins with a reference to four of the six verbs found in the summary of Jeremiah's oracles in 1:10. Here it says that if they remain where they are, God will build them up and plant them and will refrain from pulling them down or uprooting them. This language will be echoed one more time in chapter 45, pushing the book towards its ending.

Chapter 43 narrates the reaction of these leaders who had said that they would do anything that the LORD required of them. Apparently "anything" did not include staying where they were. The leaders accuse Jeremiah of acting in collaboration with the Babylonians, again reinforcing the perception that Jeremiah was a traitor until the end. This passage emphasizes their accusation by extending it for the first time to Baruch as well. As a result, the leaders not only proceed to migrate to the eastern edge of Egypt but also apparently force others, including Jeremiah and Baruch, to go with them. Thus by the middle of chapter 43, the text locates Jeremiah in the one place he never wished to go.

Oracles against the Refugees in Egypt, 43:8–44:30

The last set of narratives about oracles Jeremiah delivers while in Egypt makes up the final section of the book that has any substantive focus on the figure of the prophet. These oracles cast the refugee community as no better than the population of Jerusalem when the city fell. Their characteristic sin remains that of idolatry, and the speeches make explicit parallels between how they act in Egypt and how they had acted in Judah before the nation's fall. As the stories progress, the text depicts the people as increasingly obstinate and brazen in their sin, so that by the end of chapter 44, the women who are worshiping the Queen of Heaven, and who implicate their husbands in their behavior, insist that Judah had fallen because her worship had been stopped (Harding 2013). Although a contemporary reader might find their confidence in goddess worship interesting and perhaps exhilarating, clearly the author of this section of Jeremiah intends the audience to be horrified by their wicked behavior and attitudes.

The first oracle contained in this section predicts Nebuchadnezzar's defeat of Egypt (43:8-13). Jeremiah performs a sign-act, setting up the pedestal on which the Babylonian king would establish his throne. This prediction undercuts any notion of Egypt as a safe haven from war. The historical record does not clearly preserve how far Nebuchadnezzar did, in fact, progress into Egypt; while there are some records of his attacks in 568/7 BCE, he did not establish a permanent presence in the country (Stipp 2010). Even without those historical facts, clearly the author of the account in Jeremiah had more than just a vague familiarity with Egypt, from the geography of the land to some information about the religious practices. In addition, it is noteworthy that this material never mentions the exodus from Egypt, because the traditions preserved here focus fully on Egypt's relationship to Judah during the late monarchy and early exile, and not with the mythic tradition of Egypt in Israel's past found in other parts of Jeremiah (Barmash 2012).

The first half of chapter 44 makes the most explicit parallels between the behaviors of the Jewish community in Egypt and of the citizens of pre-fall Jerusalem. Verses 1-10 mention how the community sins by worshiping other gods, but the main focus of these verses and those immediately following (11-14) remains on the fate of those committing such idolatry. First, the speech points to the fate of Jerusalem, desolate and without inhabitants (v. 2). It states that God had sent prophets, clearly an allusion to Jeremiah's prophetic role in Egypt as its parallel (v. 4), but neither group heeded these prophets (v. 5). This provoked and, by extension, continues to provoke God's wrath (v. 6). Verses 7-10 expand the picture of the impact their decisions made on themselves and their families, while vv. 11-14 wholly adopt the descriptions of the fall of Jerusalem to predict the downfall of the community in Egypt.

The final vignette in this section describes the worship of the Queen of Heaven, primarily by women. Unlike most other general references to idolatry in the book, this one provides some intriguing details, suggesting that either this practice was not well known by the general audience or that the author makes a specific point with these details. Scholars today debate the identity of the goddess in this passage (see, for example, Hadley 2001). The speech by the women suggests it was a goddess who had been worshiped in Judah before the nation fell (McKane 1994). While that might suggest a Canaanite/Israelite goddess like Asherah, there is nothing to prevent it being an Egyptian goddess, especially in light of the fact that Egypt had been an ally of Judah during some of this history. The details in the text do reflect some of what is known archaeologically about goddess worship, including the use of stamped baked goods as offerings and the prominence of libations, seen, for instance, in Egyptian wall paintings. The women's speech offers an intriguing theological argument (vv. 16-19). They attribute the fall of Jerusalem to the cessation of goddess worship (Pohlmann 2002). There is scant archaeological evidence for the reduction of the worship of multiple gods from the time of Josiah on, to which this may refer. Arguing that the city fell because the goddess was angry at the cessation of her worship actually made good theological sense in the ancient world. It was much harder to argue that Yahweh was angry if the Judeans had kept up the required practices temple practices before the city's fall.

Jeremiah's counter-evidence is the continued desolation of Jerusalem (vv. 20-23). He notes that Jerusalem would have been restored by this time if the cessation of worship of the Queen of Heaven had led to the destruction of the city. The fact that Jerusalem remains desolate proves it was destroyed *because* of their worship of her. The passage ends with God's concluding speech marking the refugees in Egypt as deserving of destruction (vv. 24-30). Yahweh swears an oath to destroy this community (v. 26) except for a small remnant that will return to Judah and give witness to their deserving fate (vv. 28). The passage ends with a sign that what Jeremiah speaks will come to pass: the death of Pharaoh Hophra, which occurred in 570 BCE.

As a result, these final oracles undercut any claim that the Jewish community in Egypt was the remnant of the chosen people or the vehicle for the continuation of God's covenant with Israel (Sharp 2003). To be sure, language of covenant appears nowhere in these chapters. Some scholars conjecture that these prose narratives aimed to depict the Babylonian exiles as the faithful remnant of Israel since they characterize both those in the land who perpetrated violence in chapter 41 and those in Egypt who practiced idolatry negatively. Yet it must be noted that these chapters mention the Babylonian community nowhere except as a group that Jeremiah refuses to join. I see no positive portrayal of wholesale Jewish communities in these narratives. The only positive portrayals depict the three most marginalized and consistently misunderstood characters: Jeremiah, Baruch, and Ebed-Melech. This suggests that the point of view in this section of the book is quite negative, one that legitimates God's continued decimation of Jewish populations both at home and abroad.

Jeremiah's Scroll Comes to a Close, 45:1-5

The final chapter in this narrative section marks a clear closure to this section of the book, one of three apparent endings of Jeremiah (O'Connor 2011b, 115–23): this chapter ends the material centered on Jeremiah, chapter 51 ends the oracles of Jeremiah, and chapter 52 contains a historical narrative of the end of the period, which reads more like a historical appendix. Chapter 45 states that Jeremiah dictated these messages to Baruch as a replacement to the scroll burned in Jeremiah 36:32. While chapter 45 dates this dictation to 605 BCE (v. 1), the events narrated take place after that initial dictation. In some way this rhetorical device is a bit like the movie *The Princess Bride* in which the grandfather reading the story to his grandson frames the narrative. This passage conspicuously echoes the summary of God's charge to Jeremiah in 1:10. The repetition rhetorically frames the bulk of the book as a series of oracles, first orally pronounced and then written down, that bring about what they envision. While this makes sense for the prophetic oracles cast as direct speech, the prose narratives at first glance do not match this function. However, in the ancient world, writing had a kind of prophetic character that brought about what was predicted by the written word. Thus, even the written prose narratives in this section of the book are cast as prophetic oracles.

If a contemporary reader takes this rhetorical framing seriously, it suggests that the narratives should not be read as linear descriptions of historical events. They should be read as oracles in which the details become metaphors for an ominous threat. The historical inaccuracies of these texts become insignificant when the stories are read as oracular paintings of the world after the fall of the city, a world where wrong has not been righted and where the prophet remains a lone voice speaking against the dominant culture. The author reinforces this purpose of the narratives in 45:2-5, which focus now on the figure of Baruch. Here, Baruch replaces Jeremiah as the one whose fate deserves lamentation because of the harsh messages he must communicate. On the one hand, following Scalise, Baruch's ideal response to Jeremiah's messages contrasts with the incorrect response of Jehoiakim in 36:1-8 (2007). In addition, by merging the characters of Baruch and Jeremiah in this closing scene, the written version of the oracles completely replaces the oral pronouncements in terms of content, function, and effect.

In the end, then, neither Jeremiah nor Baruch represents a victor, or hero who is vindicated. Their chosen status is not a blessing. With the inclusion of Baruch, the passage ends by reminding the audience that Jeremiah represents all of those who dare to speak God's truth to a community that does not want to hear. He is one of those who sees the realities of the world through God's eyes, which in sum present the futility of any human effort except obedience to God's word delivered through the prophet. Jeremiah represents all of those who are fated to see the downfall of people after people, escaping only with their own lives and not with any comfort, reward, or restoration.

Oracles against Foreign Nations
Jeremiah 46–51

The final section in the Hebrew version of the book of Jeremiah is a series of oracles addressed to nations other than Judah, a series usually referred to as oracles against the nations, or OAN. Several prophetic books contain a similar collection, especially the larger collections of Isaiah (see chs. 13–23) and Ezekiel (chs. 25–32). Collections such as these are part of the literary stage of a book's production; the compiler gathers together oracles associated with these prophets that were addressed to other countries and places them as a distinct section of the book. While there is wide speculation about the origins of this type of oracle, what is clear is that each collection fits the style, theology, and vocabulary of the larger books in which they are found.

Their rhetorical function within the final form of a prophetic collection varies. The OAN that start the book of Amos, for instance, lead up to a scathing indictment of the northern kingdom of Israel. In the book of Ezekiel, they serve as a bridge between the oracles condemning Judah and those promising restoration. The two major recensions of the book of Jeremiah, the Greek and Hebrew versions, differ primarily in their placement of this material. In the Greek version, the one many scholars view as older, the oracles are placed immediately after 25:13, following a broad overview of God's future punishment of the Babylonians. This arrangement more closely parallels that of Ezekiel, since Jeremiah's oracles of restoration would then come after the judgments on Israel's enemies.

The Hebrew version of the book is more difficult to explain, mainly because it is unlike the arrangements found in other prophetic books. Such a difficulty, however, may signal that this arrangement is the older one, since it would not make much sense to have moved the oracles to the end of the book if they had originally been placed at chapter 25. This discussion, though, presupposes that one of the versions of the book of Jeremiah is the "correct" and chronologically original one and the other is a corruption. It is more likely that the collections simply developed differently among different

Jewish groups, perhaps among groups living in different parts of the ancient world in the Diaspora.

The placement of the OAN in the Hebrew version makes them function as a note of hope. God's sweeping and unrelenting judgment of Judah that permeates the book of Jeremiah is not the final word. God's judgment extends throughout the whole cosmos. As Fretheim points out, while most of the judgments in this section are negative, some are positive as well (2002, 575–80). In this sense, this section of the book completes the mission given to Jeremiah in chapter 1 to become a prophet to the nations (1:5, 10) with oracles that contain both judgment and restoration. The placement of these oracles at the end of the book, then, completes the bracket around the book formed by chapter 1's call of Jeremiah with the final words of the prophet that extend to the nations surrounding Judah.

While the arrangement of the OAN in both Amos and Ezekiel have a clear pattern (Amos's are arranged geographically, while Ezekiel's follow a sevenfold pattern), the final arrangement of Jeremiah's oracles is less clear. While the oracles may follow a chronological order, the section is bookended by long oracles against the two major superpowers at the time: Egypt (ch. 46) and Babylon (chs. 50–51). In between, the prophet addresses Philistia (ch. 47) and Moab (ch. 48), followed by a chapter with quick indictments of Ammon, Edom, Damascus, Kedar (Arabia), and Elam. Surprisingly, the material against Moab is the longest and most detailed of this interior material.

The oracles against Babylon, however, are clearly the climax of this section of the book. The images in the poetry are vibrant, vehement, and unrelenting. Kalmanofsky likens them to revenge fantasies expressed by a colonized subject (2015). While some scholars find it inconsistent that a book that has been generally pro-Babylonian should end with such a sweeping curse of Babylon, for this reader, the logic makes perfect sense. As the preceding chapters have shown, one of the rhetorical aims of the prose material is to contrast the assumption of the characters in the book that Jeremiah was a traitor and puppet for the Babylonians with the book's perspective that all along he spoke for God, who used the Babylonians to punish Judah. By making the prophet's final words powerful poetic condemnations of Babylon, the rhetoric depicts the prophet as hating the Babylonians as vigorously as any survivor of the fall. In fact, it sets him apart again as an ideal figure who does not cooperate with the colonizers after the city's fall but ends up in Egypt cursing Judah's enemy (Pyper 2015).

Egypt's Ambiguous Fate, 46:1-28

Chapter 46 contains at least three parts: two oracles addressed to Egypt (vv. 1-12 and 13-26) followed by an oracle of restoration for Israel (vv. 27-28). The first oracle against Egypt is dated to the Battle of Carchemish in 605, which marked the clear ascendancy of Babylon over the Levant. The battle, primarily between Egypt and Babylon on the northern Euphrates, was a turning point in the balance of power between these two enemies. The second oracle addresses the final battle between Egypt and Babylon during the lifetime of Jeremiah: Babylon's attack on the land of Egypt itself after the Babylonians had destroyed Judah. According to the oracle against Egypt in Ezekiel, this happened sometime after 571 (Ezek 29:17). It is not clear how thoroughly Babylon succeeded in invading Egypt, although the evidence indicates that Egypt did not experience a wholesale defeat at this time. This suggests that the oracles in Jeremiah and Ezekiel predicting a total Babylonian victory were composed at some date earlier than the actual conclusion of the Babylonian advance.

As is typical in the OAN, Jeremiah's poetry engages the cultural, mythic, and religious images that the Israelites associated with Egypt (Galvin 2011, 118–63). It should be noted that, as a rule, oracles against Egypt reflect the book's contemporaneous political position and do not make reference to the exodus or any other earlier biblical traditions about Egypt. These oracles, then, do not engage Israel's characterization of Egypt as a mythic enemy but rather address the complexities of Judah's actual interactions with Egypt during the monarchy and after the exile, at which times there was a significant Jewish population settled around the Nile.

The first oracle resembles the style and language of the oracles against Judah in the first ten chapters of the book. It has a classic poetic form with short verses that create a kind of staccato breathlessness as it presents images of battle. The poem focuses on the beginning and end of the battle: the preparation of the troops and then their rout in defeat. It uses the image of the two rivers, the Nile and the Euphrates, as a unifying metaphor. These sources of fresh water literally fed the economy that supported the great war machines. The poetry depicts Egypt as a flood washing over the battlefield and then turning back. The poem itself never mentions Babylon; the only peoples it mentions besides the Egyptians are their African allies. But the poem repeatedly refers to the site of battle: the northern Euphrates River, clearly linking the poem to the defeat at Carchemish.

The poem resonates with other material in Jeremiah, especially chapter 8. Both chapters contain images of cavalry (8:16; 46:4, 9). Both make reference to a balm from Gilead (46:11, compare 8:22) that is ineffective in bringing healing. In both cases, the result of the battle is terror (8:15; 46:5). In chapter 8, the Babylonian cavalry devour the land, while in 46:10, their swords devour the Egyptians. The main difference between chapters 8 and 46 is the object of defeat: Judah versus Egypt. Perhaps this poem intentionally parallels the fate of Egypt with that of Judah, since Judah's defeat was in part due to Egypt's weakness.

The oracle ends by centering on the shame of Egypt's defeat. The passage couples the language of shame with the personification of Egypt as a female. In fact, the poem uses the same epithet for Egypt, "virgin daughter," used for Israel in other parts of the book (14:17; 18:13; 31:4, 21). In Jeremiah 2–3 the personification of the city as a promiscuous woman casts its defeat as shameful (2:36; 3:25). This poem's wording engages the parallel found elsewhere in Jeremiah that defeat of male warriors turns them into women to their own shame.

Scholars debate the date of the next oracle (vv. 13-24). Although the prose introduction dates it to an attack by Nebuchadnezzar, there is no clear date given for the attack. While it could refer to Nebuchadnezzar's pursuit of Egypt after the battle of Carchemish, the warning of Jeremiah in chapter 44 and the oracle of restoration at the end of 46 suggest a date after the migration of refugees from the fall of Jerusalem. Notably, however, neither oracle makes reference to Judah or a Diaspora community.

This second oracle again predicts a similar fate for Egypt as that experienced by Judah. Babylon will invade the land, attack the fortified cities, and exile the inhabitants. The oracle also begins with a call to arms in defense against a devouring sword (v. 14). The oracle repeats the image of warriors grappling and collapsing together (v. 16; see v. 12) and continues the personification of Egypt as female (most obviously seen in English in vv. 19 and 24, but also in the use of female pronouns to refer to Egypt throughout the passage). While v. 16 suggests that the battle takes place outside of Egypt, perhaps signaling that vv. 13-16 should be read as a separate oracle, vv. 19-24 describe the collapse of cities in the northern part of Egypt.

Animal imagery permeates these verses, mirroring the prominence of animals in Egyptian iconography. Snake imagery in Egyptian art represented a wide variety of deities and motifs. For example, the uraeus serpent that was part of the Pharaonic headdress symbolized royalty, while the sun god battled the serpent Apophis every night to re-create the world anew each day (Carvalho 2015, esp. 213–14). The retreat of the royal army here in Jeremiah 46 is likened to a snake slithering away.

Bovine imagery also permeates the passage, even more in the Greek version than in the Hebrew. Egypt is likened to a young heifer, and those doing business there are young calves (vv. 20-21). Hathor was a prominent bovine goddess, representing fertility within the Egyptian religious system, who often wore a uraeus serpent along with a sun disk between her horns. This passage then personifies Egypt as a Hathor figure, a personification that also matches the references to Egypt as female. The Greek version extends the bovine imagery in v. 15 with mention of the Apis bull. This singular male bovine, mummified at its death, was associated with the cult of Ptah in Memphis, a city mentioned in vv. 14 and 19. Herodotus states that the Persian king, Cambyses, committed a sacrilege by killing the Apis bull, for which he was cursed (Fretheim 2002, 584). If the Greek version of Jeremiah represents a later tradition, it may have added the reference to the Apis bull in this chapter to reflect the Persian period incident.

A prose explanation of the passage follows the poetic oracle (vv. 25-26). It states that the disaster that will befall Egypt is a punishment from Yahweh meted out not only to the people but also to their sun god, Amun. While the poems have attributed Egypt's disasters to the workings of Yahweh (see vv. 10, 15; Goldingay 2007), only here do they explicitly mention the sinfulness of Egypt. Again, as a result, Egypt's fate parallels that of Judah: God, who wills Nebuchadnezzar to destroy it and exile its citizens, will also eventually restore the country (v. 26).

This promise of restoration to Egypt seems to prompt the final oracle in this chapter: a short oracle of restoration addressed to the whole nation of Israel. Here then, Egypt's fate becomes the model on which Judah can base its hopes. These final verses (27-28) focus on the restoration of all twelve tribes of Israel, most explicitly by referring to the nation as "Jacob." Like the other restoration oracles in Jeremiah, this passage does not negate the punishment or disaster of the fall of the city; it characterizes that fall as a "just" punishment (v. 28 NRSV). But that punishment will not be God's final word on Judah, just like the punishment of Egypt. God will restore both countries, but this time in a manner so that Judah will never have to fear again (v. 27).

Oracle against Philistia, 47:1-7

This short chapter contains a single oracle against the Philistines. It has only a general date, but it is for an event that is unclear. Nebuchadnezzar attacked Ashkelon in 604, but this oracle is dated after an attack by Egypt. The oracle itself offers no specific details that would help place it. It describes military defeat, again ascribed to Yahweh's actions. It mentions that with this defeat,

Tyre and Sidon would lose their last ally (v. 4), which suggests a setting after the fall of Jerusalem either before or during Babylon's long siege of Tyre.

The passage describes the military defeat as a flood that pours into and through the land, destroying everything in its wake. The poet could be using imagery associated with tsunamis, which would have been a reality in this coastal region. While Philistia had been an enemy of Israel during the early monarchy, at this point in history, it was a peaceful neighbor. The oracle, then, seems to have less to do with castigating Judah's enemies and more to do with presenting the Babylonian advance as an attack led by the Israelite divine warrior, Yahweh. Given the focus, this oracle would fit better with the five short oracles in chapter 49 than it does here between the longer oracles against Egypt and Moab.

A Long-winded Diatribe against Moab, 48:1-47

The next chapter is odd in many respects. While Moab was certainly not a friendly ally to Judah, most biblical texts that reflect on this period, such as Isaiah and Psalm 137, depict Edom as the traitorous neighbor who turned against its natural ally, Judah. To be sure, many Pentateuchal texts warn the Israelites about being attracted to Moabite women and culture, a theme found in other texts as well, such as the book of Ruth, but the level of vitriol found in this poem is not expected in a text from this time. The chapter is almost twice as long as the one against Egypt, presenting a rhetorically mounting hatred first against Egypt and then Moab, culminating in the cursing of Babylon.

The structure of the chapter is not clear. It is probably made up of several different oracles, but the text contains few indications of breaks. The chapter provides no dates, unlike chapters 46–47. The general meaning of the oracles is clear enough—the destruction of Moab—but the text gives no indication whether this refers to a Babylonian attack or some later event. Verse 11 suggests that, from the perspective of the author, Moab had a more peaceful history than many of the other countries in the area. Is this a hint, then, that the Babylonians did not, in fact, defeat Moab?

The poems also assume a great deal of knowledge about Moabite geography, culture, and history—knowledge that has not survived into the contemporary period. While Josephus states that the Babylonians conquered Moab (Fretheim 2002, 595), no contemporary evidence corroborates that conclusion. The Old Testament consistently identifies the national god of the Moabites as Chemosh (Num 21:29; Judg 11:24; 1 Kgs 11:7, 33; 2 Kgs 23:13), a fact confirmed by Moabite inscriptions, but not much is known about this deity. Many of the oracles against Moab, such as those in Amos

2:1-3; Zephaniah 2:8-11; Isaiah 15–16; and Ezekiel 25:8-11, characterize Moab as prideful or boastful, a charge found here in Jeremiah. This characterization may imply that Moab had not suffered the same calamities as Judah, since it presumes the Moabites survived to taunt the defeated Israelites.

The first nine verses of the chapter describe the complete destruction of Moab, using terms for destruction and annihilation seen in Jeremiah's description of the fall of Judah. The oracle, then, envisions Moab experiencing the same defeat as Jerusalem. Sharp notes that these parallels between the fates of Moab and Judah are not accidental; they reflect a postexilic audience's anxiety about being the outsider in the Diaspora (2015). Another poetic oracle seems to be contained in and around vv. 16-20, but whether it begins before v. 16 or ends after v. 20 is unclear. This section again describes the collapse of Moab. The image of refugees fleeing down a highway in v. 19 captures the panic. This section focuses on the shame Moab would feel at losing its former ascendancy in the region. The poetic verses in vv. 28-35 also refer to the former pride of Moab, depicting its destruction as just deserts for its hubris. The final verses, vv. 40-46, tell the story from God's perspective: the raptor who sweeps in to destroy them (v. 40), the hunter who lays traps for them (vv. 43-44), and the enemy who burns and scalps its victims (v. 45).

Various materials link these poetic sections, some in prose, some intertwining prose and poetry. Some of these fragments are quite colorful. Verse 10, for example, curses those who do not attack the Moabites, depicting them as opposing God's work. Verse 25 uses the image of a broken arm (the arm being a symbol of strength) and a broken horn (a metaphor of high rank) to describe the fall of a personified Moab. Verses 37-39 contain flashes of mourning: from shaved heads to sackcloth to lamenting. Two motifs reoccur in these passages. One involves references to wine, perhaps reflecting a main crop of the Moabites. The poem, which first likens Moab to wine that has aged well in v. 11, depicts God pouring the people out and breaking the jars that held them. Verses 32-33 portray Moab as a luxuriant vine that God destroys. In vv. 26-27 Moab staggers and falls from its own consumption of wine.

The second motif engages the sounds that accompany destruction. These sounds include cries (vv. 3, 31), weeping (vv. 5, 32), mourning (vv. 17, 31, 39), wailing (v. 20), laughing (vv. 26-27, 39), shouts (v. 33), speech (v. 34), moaning (v. 36), lamentations (v. 38), and even silence (v. 2). In place of visual images of destruction, then, these poems use aural metaphors. Like the oracle against Egypt, this one ends with a brief promise of restoration (v. 47), which seems out of place and may be a later addition. It does little to redirect the overall sense of devastation that permeates the rest of this long chapter.

Devastation Far and Wide, 49:1-39

While the divisions of chapter 48 remain difficult to determine, chapter 49 contains more clearly differentiated sections. This chapter consists of oracles against five nations: three that border Judah—Ammon (vv. 1-6), Edom (7-22), and Damascus (23-27)—followed by Kedar in the Arabian Peninsula (vv. 28-33) and Elam, which is east of Babylon (vv. 34-39). Only the last two oracles contain dates. Only the oracles to Ammon and Elam anticipate restoration.

The poet levels the first oracle against Ammon (vv. 1-6). According to the book of Genesis, Ammon and Moab descended from Abraham's younger relative, Lot, a story meant to describe the close cultural ties among these peoples. The borders between these various nations were continually in flux. Sometimes a particular city or territory would belong to the Israelites, while at other times it would be Ammonite. This was especially the case with Ammon, where the border was not a large body of water like the Dead Sea. This oracle then focuses on the transitional character of the border between Ammon and the northern tribes of Israel. The oracle also reflects this same border instability in the reference to Heshbon in v. 3, a Moabite city in chapter 48. The Old Testament identifies the Ammonite national god as Milcom (2 Sam 12:30; 1 Kgs 11:5, 33; 2 Kgs 23:13), again a deity we know little about. Throughout the Old Testament, the biblical authors link the fates of Ammon and Moab, so it is not surprising that this oracle links the future restorations of both Moab and Ammon.

The longest oracle in this section castigates Edom (vv. 7-22). Edom serves as an object of Israelite wrath in other exilic literature. The verses here probably contain bits of separate oracles, some of which are repeated in other places both within Jeremiah (compare 49:18-21 with 50:40, 44-46) and outside of Jeremiah (Jer 49:9, 14-16 compared with Obad 1-4; see Graybill 2015, 134), but like the long passage addressed to Moab, this section does not preserve clear divisions between originally separate units. Verses 8 and 10 refer to Edom by the name of their ancestor "Esau," whom the book of Genesis depicts as the older brother of Jacob, the ancestor of the nation of Israel. Again, the use of a family structure in Genesis was a way for the Israelites to express how much they had in common with the Edomites. The opening poetic verses, then, stress the interconnection of Judah and Edom.

The section further implies this interconnection through the place names mentioned. While these verses do not name a national Edomite deity, they do contain two references to Teman, a region in Edom that Habakkuk 3:3 states Yahweh comes from. In addition, the passage mentions the city of

Bozrah that Isaiah 34:6 and 63:1 depict as a battleground for Yahweh. These raise the possibility that the Edomites worshiped Yahweh, although they probably worshiped other gods as well, thus forming a religious connection between Edom and Israel.

Like the oracles against Moab, these verses depict a total destruction of Edom, using repeated images of destruction (Graybill 2015). Even if gleaners leave produce on the vine or thieves leave goods in a house, God will leave nothing for the Edomites even in their hiding places (vv. 9-10). Like Moab, this in part punishes them for their pride (v. 16); they become an object of derision in the eyes of the international community (vv. 13, 15, 17, 20). The passage likens defeat to drinking a cup (v. 12), perhaps equating loss with drunkenness but more probably a reference to the cup of wrath seen in Jeremiah 25:15 (H. Peels 2007). This section portrays God's defeat of both Moab and Edom as an attack by an eagle (48:40; 49:22), with the defeated warriors likened to women in labor (48:41; 49:22).

The next oracle against Damascus (vv. 23-27) also uses the image of women in labor (49:24). This short oracle predicts the urban ruin of Syria with references to town squares, city walls, and strongholds (vv. 26-27). This contrasts with the oracle against the region of Kedar (vv. 28-34) that reflects the destruction of a seminomadic group. The inhabitants of Kedar live in tents (v. 29) and have herds of sheep, camels, and cattle (vv. 29, 32). The editor of the OAN may have added the oracles against Kedar and Elam (vv. 34-38) to an original set of oracles against Judah's neighbors. Unlike the other oracles, the text introduces these last two oracles with an historical context. The oracle explicitly links Kedar to the military advances of Nebuchadnezzar (vv. 28, 30) while the editor dates the oracle against Elam, the least specific of any of Jeremiah's OAN, to the beginning of the reign of Zedekiah (E. Peels 2000). While the oracle attributes Elam's demise to enemies summoned from around the globe, the section abruptly ends with a promise of restoration (v. 39).

Revenge Would Be Sweet, 50:1-46

The most vitriolic language in Jeremiah's OAN is saved for these final two chapters that predict God's wrath against the Babylonians. The first set of oracles against Babylon vacillates between oracles that condemn Judah's destroyer and those promising Israel restoration. This alternating pattern embodies the notion that Israel's restoration would not be complete without Babylon's demise. These predictions of Babylon's demise reinforce the theme by reusing language describing the fall of Jerusalem, especially found in chapters 2–6 (Hill 1999a).

On the one hand, this level of vitriol is understandable, since Babylon had so brutally destroyed Jerusalem. But the book of Jeremiah as a whole has depicted Babylon as Yahweh's instrument of punishment to whom Jeremiah had counseled Judah to submit. The book of Ezekiel, which does not have as positive a portrayal of the Babylonians, does not contain any oracles against that nation, so clearly the book of Jeremiah did not have to have this particular section. What is remarkable, then, is that Jeremiah contains oracles against Babylon that are also clearly the culmination of this book's OAN, which is obvious by their use of similar motifs of description found earlier in the book to describe Judah's fall (Carroll 1986, 814–17; Kessler 2003).

The Persians, who came from the east and not from the north, eventually destroyed the Babylonians, but the fact that this takeover was not as violent as the one predicted in these two chapters suggests to some scholars that the oracles were written prior to 538 (Kessler 2003, 206). As in many OAN, the composer uses hyperbolic language and imagery. Judah will satisfy its desire for vengeance after Babylon's complete destruction. This heightened language, which may reflect the feelings of those who had experienced devastation, also lends itself to later reuse, as Babylon becomes a kind of paradigmatic enemy, much like Nazis in our day. Audiences feel satisfaction with the multiple acts of violence against Babylonians and Nazis, since they represent evil incarnate.

On the whole, this chapter focuses on the fate of Babylon, but it intersperses that with three sections focused on the fate of the Israelites (vv. 4-7, 17-20, 33-34). While this chapter probably represents the combination of originally distinct oracles against Babylon, the text does not provide explicit transitions from one to another (Bellis 1999). The passages contain stock images of war (sword, fire, siege works, etc.), with the images bleeding into each other. Rhetorically the material communicates a wholesale pronouncement of judgment against Babylon.

Most of the descriptions of military defeat replicate the same poetic structure seen in the descriptions of Jerusalem's demise in the first part of the book, and they echo many of the same images (Thelle 2015). For example, the poems liken defeat to death in childbirth, an image found in other parts of Jeremiah (see, for example, 4:31; 6:24; 13:21; 22:23; 30:6; 49:22, 24; 50:43). Other parts of the poems are more direct, however. Verses 10-11 depict Babylon as spoil or plunder. Weapons, such as swords (v. 16 and five times in vv. 35-37), bows (vv. 14, 29, 42), arrows (vv. 9, 14), spears (v. 42), and horses (vv. 37, 42), figure prominently. The audience catches glimpses of those fleeing (vv. 16 and 28) as the enemy smashes idols (v. 2) and empties out the treasuries (vv. 25, 37), all elements of the fortified city's collapse (vv.

15, 30). Three places in the chapter (vv. 3, 9, 41) refer to Babylon's enemy as simply coming from the "north," a designation that seems to have no particular enemy in mind. It reflects a stock Israelite phrase for a devastating enemy who historically traveled on the main north-south routes to Jerusalem; the once-literal phrase takes on a metaphoric meaning (Amesz 2004). This mythic enemy, coupled with the hyperbolic images of Babylon's destruction, pushes the poems beyond descriptions of actual events and places them on a more cosmic plane. Whether the ambiguity of the foe and lack of historical referent evidence an early date for these poems (i.e., before Babylon was defeated in a less grandiose way by the Persians) or that these are late poems reflecting apocalyptic literature remains a matter of debate among scholars.

The poems explicitly and repeatedly depict Yahweh as the deity behind the promised collapse of this superpower (Pyper 2015). Verses 15b and 28 attribute the fall of Babylon to God's vengeance against the nation that had destroyed Jerusalem, while vv. 15a and 29 depict this fall as just deserts on an aggressive military machine. The oracles characterize Yahweh as angry (vv. 13, 25) and vengeful (vv. 15, 28). This depiction counters any notion that Yahweh favored Babylon. This final compiler emphasizes this message through the placement of three passages promising restoration for Israel that interrupt the narration of Babylon's annihilation. These interruptions explicitly link the downfall of Babylon with the restoration of Israel. All three focus on the restoration of both the northern and southern kingdoms, and all three depict this as a restoration of those exiled to Mesopotamia, without including refugees in Egypt or those who remained in the land. The first two engage pastoral images. They had been a flock devoured by the enemy (vv. 6-7), but God will settle them on their own pastureland (v. 19). The LORD will also forgive their sin (v. 20), a notice that contrasts with the assertion of Babylonian's sin in v. 14. The final collection juxtaposes a depiction of God as a lion that attacks Babylon in vv. 44-46 with that of a shepherd who wards off the lions (vv. 17-19).

Pile It On, 51:1-58

Revenge permeates chapter 51. This very long poem of fifty-eight verses constitutes a veritable tribute to revenge (Kalmanofsky 2015). Images of Babylon's military defeat crash up against each other, without sequence or historical referent. The poet punctuates these scenes with God's declaration that this is payback (vv. 6, 10, 11, 24, 36, 47, 49, 52, 56)! The metaphors of destruction once again form a rich tapestry of what looks to be war memorial but in reality is more revenge fantasy. As in chapter 50, much of the imagery in this section stems directly from the experiences of military defeat. Troops, cavalry, weapons, and slaughter permeate the passage. But in this chapter, the poet often pairs these images with metaphoric representations. Perhaps one of the more colorful images is that of Nebuchadnezzar as a great monster who has devoured the city of Jerusalem (v. 34; note the ironic reversal in v. 44 where Yahweh will force Babylon's main deity, Bel, to vomit out what has been swallowed). Other metaphors come from all walks of life. Babylon's mythic enemy will thresh and winnow the nation like grain (vv. 2, 33). The poem symbolizes the attacking troops with a swarm of locusts (vv. 14, 27) and later a flood (v. 55). It calls Babylon a "destroying mountain" that melts like a volcano (v. 25 NRSV); at its demise the earth will tremble and quake (v. 29). The enemy will trod the feminized city of Babylon down like a threshing floor (v. 33). While these metaphors of military defeat can be found in other military poetry, the overall effect conveys still one more picture of wholesale destruction.

In addition to these images, the chapter contains three references to drunkenness (51:7, 39, 57), similar to the oracles against Moab. Verse 7 refers to Yahweh's use of Babylon as a divine weapon, the result of which makes the nations rage or go mad. Building on the image of the cup of wrath (25:15), here the poet notes that Babylon had brought the downfall of many nations. Again the compiler or poet uses a notion of just deserts: v. 39, repeated in v. 57, has God punishing Babylon by making them so drunk that they sleep an "eternal sleep." While v. 7 includes a specific reference to wine, vv. 39 and 57 keep the nature of the drink ambiguous, leaving open the possibility it may refer to some kind of poison, liquid drug, or narcotic (McKane 1980).

God is a warrior deity who both controls the weather like a storm god (vv. 1, 16) and creates the world (vv. 15, 19). Verses 20-24 form a particularly vibrant poem of revenge, where the repetition of the phrase "with you I smash . . ." (NRSV) resounds like the metaphoric club of v. 20, addressed to some unnamed enemy who will smash the Babylonian empire to pieces at the instigation of Yahweh. The poem uses twinned targets: either natural pairs (horse and chariot; v. 21) or hendiadys (young and old; v. 22). The poem as a whole provides a collage of some of the most important social institutions of Babylonian culture. The political system brackets the poem: the army, citizens, ranchers, and farmers. While it is not an exhaustive list of social groups, the overall effect of the poem conveys the destruction of the whole empire. In the most explicit expressions of revenge in the chapter, v. 24 gives voice to the divine motivation for this destruction: to repay Babylon for what it did to Zion, echoing 51:11, which depicts the divine violence as "vengeance for the temple."

Jeremiah's Remote Symbolic Act, 51:59-64

The chapter ends with a unique presentation of the recording of this particular set of oracles. In these verses, Jeremiah writes these oracles against Babylon on a single scroll, at least six years before the city of Jerusalem fell. He gives the scroll to a royal official whose genealogy designates him as Baruch's brother. He tells him that when he goes to Babylon with Zedekiah, presumably when Jerusalem falls, he should throw the scroll into the Euphrates, thus unleashing the prophetic words inscribed on it. This scene reinforces the idea that writing itself could be part of the prophetic enactment of an oracle. It also hints at the possibility that these oracles against foreign nations were used in public acts, usually with a native population, to curse a national enemy. This scene also describes a third reference in the book to a scroll of Jeremiah's oracles (30:1 and 36:1 are Jeremiah's scroll; 36:32 and 45:2 refer to Baruch's copy; and the one here contains only the oracles against Babylon).

The prose notice cements the characterization of Jeremiah as a faithful Yahwist, devoted to the fate of Israel throughout his life. By setting the scene during a time of relative peace between Zedekiah and Babylon, it finalizes the book's refutation of Jeremiah as a traitor; it depicts him as a foe of Babylon throughout his life. This final arrangement of the book as a whole demonstrates that the compiler intends that the oracles against Babylon should be read or heard intertextually. While Jeremiah warns the city of its fall before the Babylonian armies have reached Jerusalem's gates, he also simultaneously curses Babylon by writing out these oracles for their future realization. As Jeremiah urges Judah to surrender during the siege of the city, the audience of the book's final form should hear echoes of his vision of Babylon as God's war club and cup of wrath, a distant song of God's vengeance against those assaulting them. As they sit in exile in Babylon, or in a refugee camp in Egypt, they might ironically recall the book's ending that expresses their own desires for vengeance (Hill 1999a). As they return to Judah under Persian authority, a poor settlement with no glorious return and Babylon still limping along, they would sing these same songs turning the historical Babylon into a trope for the mythic enemy, since the poems so clearly express the desire for revenge.

A Historical Epilogue

Jeremiah 52

The book of Jeremiah could have ended happily with the notice of the prophetic act that unleashes God's vengeance against the Babylonians (Brueggemann 2006, 86–98). It does not. Instead the collection ends by repeating, with a few variations, the final chapters of 2 Kings 24:18–25:30, which describe the fall of Jerusalem to the Babylonians. The account details the attack on the city, the breach of the walls, some of the significant plunder, and the fate of some of Jerusalem's leaders. Taking center stage in this tragic tableau is Zedekiah witnessing the execution of his sons, just before the Babylonians blind him (52:9-11). No matter what other purpose this chapter serves in Jeremiah, it first and foremost reminds the reader that the fall of the city casts a pall over the whole book.

The compiler of the book of Isaiah also placed material from 2 Kings into the final collection of the prophetic oracles. Just like here, these chapters in Isaiah provide the historical background for the prophet's work, borrowed directly from the books of Kings. And just like Jeremiah, that background was one of grave military threat, although for Isaiah it was the siege of Jerusalem by the Assyrians. There are significant and I would say meaningful differences between the two compilations, however. First, Isaiah figures as a character in those historical accounts, so they clearly form part of the tradition of that particular biblical prophet. Jeremiah, however, never appears in the books of Kings, nor does the final redactor add him to this chapter. Second, the Assyrian siege was unsuccessful; Jerusalem did not fall to them. This contrasts with the fall of the city to the Babylonians. In this way, the redactor of Jeremiah parallels the message of Jeremiah 7 and 26 where he admonishes the people to look to Shiloh to know that they are not immune from destruction. By using the same editorial technique of inserting historical information here with the exact opposite result, the final book undercuts the message of the book of Isaiah that God would defend the city.

Last, the absence of Jeremiah speaks loudly. While the kings heeded Isaiah's warnings, the book of Jeremiah has consistently portrayed Jeremiah as rejected by the royal group. He has been literally silenced by this point in the city's history, and his silencing alone explains the devastation of the city. By including the story of the fall of the city without Jeremiah's presence, then, the book paints the final brush stroke countering claims that Jeremiah was a false prophet. The city did not fall because Jeremiah failed to intercede to God (see ch. 15) or because he delivered false oracles (ch. 20). It fell because he had been silenced. Zedekiah's blindness now serves both a literal and metaphoric function: it leads directly to the exile and deaths of Jerusalem's next generation.

Works Cited

Ackroyd, Peter R. 1972. "The Temple Vessels: A Continuity Theme." In *Studies in the Religion of Ancient Israel*, ed. H. Ringgren et al., 166–81. VTSup 23. Leiden: Brill.

Aejmelaeus, Anneli. 2002. "Jeremiah at the Turning-Point of History: The function of Jer. XXV 1-14 in the Book of Jeremiah." *VT* 52:459–82.

Ahn, John J. 2011. *Exile as Forced Migrations: A Sociological, Literary, and Theological Approach on the Displacement and Resettlement of the Southern Kingdom of Judah*. BZAW 417. Berlin/New York: de Gruyter.

Albertz, Rainer. 2002. "Die Zerstörung des Jerusalemer Tempels 587 v. Chr.: Historische Einordnung und religionspolitische Bedeutung." In *Zerstörungen des Jerusalemer Tempels: Geschehen-Wahrnehmung-Bewältigung*, ed. J. Hahn, 23–39. WUNT 147. Tübingen: Mohr Siebeck.

———. 2012. "More and Less than a Myth: Reality and Significance of Exile for the Political, Social, and Religious History of Judah." In *By the Irrigation Canals of Babylon: Approaches to the Study of Exile*, ed. J. J. Ahn and J. Middlemas, 20–33. LHBOTS 526. London: T&T Clark.

Amesz, J. G. 2004. "A God of Vengeance? Comparing YHWH's Dealings with Judah and Babylon in the Book of Jeremiah." In *Reading the Book of Jeremiah: A Search for Coherence*, ed. M. Kessler, 99–116. Winona Lake IN: Eisenbrauns.

Auld, Graeme. 2009. "Jeremiah-Manasseh-Samuel: Significant Triangle? Or Vicious Circle?" In *Prophecy in the Book of Jeremiah*, ed. H. Barstad and R. G. Katz, 1–9. BZAW 388. Berlin/New York: de Gruyter.

Barmash, Pamela. 2012. "Reimagining Exile through the Lens of the Exodus: Turning Points in Israelite History and Texts." In *By the Irrigation Canals of Babylon: Approaches to the Study of Exile*, ed. J. J. Ahn and J. Middlemas, 93–106. LHBOTS 526. London: T&T Clark.

Batto, Bernard F. 1987. "The Sleeping God: An Ancient Near Eastern Motif of Divine Sovereignty." *Bib* 68:153–77.

Bauer, Angela. 1999a. *Gender in the Book of Jeremiah: A Feminist-Literary Reading*. Studies in Biblical Literature 5. New York: Peter Lang.

———. 1999b. "Dressed to Be Killed: Jeremiah 4.29-31 as an Example for the Functions of Female Imagery in Jeremiah." In *Troubling Jeremiah*, ed. A. R. P. Diamond, K. M. O'Connor, and L. Stulman, 293–305. JSOTSup 260. Sheffield: Sheffield Academic.

———. 2002. "Death, Grief, Agony, and a New Creation: Re-reading Gender in Jeremiah after September 11." *Word and World* 22:378–86.

Baumann, Gerlinde. 2002. "Jeremia, die Weisen und die Weisheit: Eine Untersuchung von Jer 9,22f." *ZAW* 114:59–79.

———. 2003. *Love and Violence: Marriage as Metaphor for the Relationship between YHWH and Israel in the Prophetic Books*. Collegeville: Michael Glazier/Liturgical.

Becking, Bob. 2004. "Jeremiah 44: A Dispute on History and Religion." In *Religious Polemics in Context: Papers Presented to the Second Conference of the Leiden Institute for the Study of Religion (LISOR) Held at Leiden, 27-28 April 2000*, ed. T. L Hettema and A. van der Kooij, 255–64. Assen: Van Gorcum.

———. 2009. "In Babylon: The Exile as Historical (Re)Construction." In *From Babylon to Eternity: The Exile Remembered and Constructed in Text and Tradition*, ed. B. Becking, et al., 4–33. Bible World. London/Oakville CT: Equinox.

Bellis, Alice Ogden. 1999. "Poetic Structure and Intertextual Logic in Jeremiah 50." In *Troubling Jeremiah*, ed. A. R. P. Diamond, K. M. O'Connor, and L. Stulman, 179–99. JSOTSup 260. Sheffield: Sheffield Academic.

———. 2011. "Assaulting the Empire: A Refugee Community's Language of Hope." In *Jeremiah (Dis)Placed: New Directions in Writing/Reading Jeremiah*, ed. A. R. P. Diamond and L. Stulman, 219–34. LHBOTS 529. New York/London: T&T Clark.

Betlyon, John W. 2003. "Neo-Babylonian Military Operations Other than War in Judah and Jerusalem." In *Judah and the Judeans in the Neo-Babylonian Period*, ed. O. Lipschits and J. Blenkinsopp, 263–83. Winona Lake IN: Eisenbrauns.

Biddle, Mark E. 1990. *A Redaction History of Jeremiah 2:1-4:2*. ATANT 77. Zürich: Theologischer Verlag.

———. 1996. *Polyphony and Symphony in Prophetic Literature: Rereading Jeremiah 7-20*. Studies in Old Testament Interpretation 2. Macon GA: Mercer University Press.

———. 2004. "Contingency, God, and the Babylonians: Jeremiah on the Complexity of Repentance." *RevExpo* 101:247–66.

Boadt, Lawrence. 2007. "Do Jeremiah and Ezekiel Share a Common View of the Exile?" In *Uprooting and Planting: Essays on Jeremiah for Leslie Allen*, ed. J. Goldingay, 14–31. LHBOTS 459. London/New York: T&T Clark. 14–31.

Boda, Mark J. 2001. "From Complaint to Contrition: Peering through the Liturgical Window of Jer 14,1-15,4." *ZAW* 113:186–97.

———. 2014. "'Uttering Precious Rather than Worthless Words': Divine Patience and Impatience with Lament in Isaiah and Jeremiah." In *Why?... How Long? Studies on Voice(s) of Lamentation Rooted in Biblical Hebrew Poetry*, ed. L. S. Flesher, C. J. Dempsey, and M. J. Boda, 83–99. LHBOTS 552. London/New York: T&T Clark.

Boer, Roland. 2013. "Spermatic Spluttering Pens: Concerning the Construction and Breakdown of Prophetic Masculinity." In *Prophets Male and Female: Gender and Prophecy in the Hebrew Bible, the Eastern Mediterranean, and the Ancient Near East*, ed. J. Stökl and C. L. Carvalho, 215–35. AIIL 15. Atlanta: Society of Biblical Literature.

Brenner, Athalya, and Fokkelien van Dijk-Hemmes. 1993. *On Gendering Texts: Female and Male Voices in the Hebrew Bible*. BibInt 1. Leiden/New York/Köln: Brill.

Bright, John. 1965. *Jeremiah: A New Translation with Introduction and Commentary*. AB 21. New York: Doubleday.

Brown-Gutoff, Susan E. 1991. "The Voice of Rachel in Jeremiah 31: A Calling to 'Something New.'" *USQR* 45:177–90.

Brueggemann, Walter. 1996. "A 'Characteristic' Reflection on What Comes Next (Jeremiah 32.16-44)." In *Prophets and Paradigms: Essays in Honor of Gene M. Tucker*, ed. S. B. Reid, 16–32. JSOTSup 229. Sheffield: Sheffield Academic.

———. 2006. *Like Fire in the Bones: Listening for the Prophetic Word in Jeremiah*. Minneapolis: Fortress.

Brummitt, Mark. 2006. "Of Broken Pots and Dirty Laundry: The Jeremiah Lehstücke." *The Bible and Critical Theory* 2/1, pp 3.1–3.10. DOI: 10.2104/bct.v2i1.72.

———. 2011. "Troubling Utopias: Possible Worlds and Possible Voices in the Book of Jeremiah." In *Jeremiah (Dis)Placed: New Directions in Writing/Reading Jeremiah*, ed. A. R. P. Diamond and L. Stulman, 175–89. LHBOTS 529. New York/London: T&T Clark.

———. 2013. "The Sublime Art of Prophetic Seeing: Aesthetics and the Word in the Book of Jeremiah." In *Beauty and the Bible: Toward a Hermeneutics of Biblical Aesthetics*, ed. R. J. Bautch and J.-F. Racine, 23–30. SemieaSt 73. Atlanta: SBL.

Brummitt, Mark, and Yvonne Sherwood. 2011. "The Fear of Loss Inherent in Writing: Jeremiah 36 as the Story of a Self-Conscious Scroll." In *Jeremiah (Dis)Placed: New Directions in Writing/Reading Jeremiah*, ed. A. R. P. Diamond and L Stulman, 47–66. LHBOTS 529. New York/London: T&T Clark.

Callaway, Mary Chilton. 1999. "Black Fire on White Fire: Historical Context and Literary Subtext in Jeremiah 37-38." In *Troubling Jeremiah*, ed. A. R. P. Diamond, K. M. O'Connor, and L. Stulman, 171–78. JSOTSup 260. Sheffield: Sheffield Academic.

———. 2004 "The Lamenting Prophet and the Modern Self: On the Origins of Contemporary Readings of Jeremiah." In *Inspired Speech: Prophecy in the Ancient Near East. Essays in Honour of Herbert B. Huffmon*, ed. J. Kaltner and L. Stulman, 48-62. JSOTSup 378. New York/London: T&T Clark.

Carroll, Robert P. 1986. *Jeremiah*. OTL. Philadelphia: Westminster.

———. 1995. "Manuscripts Don't Burn-Inscribing Prophetic Tradition: Reflections on Jeremiah 36." In *Synchronic or Diachronic? A Debate on Method in Old Testament Exegesis*, ed. J. D. de Moor, 39–51. OTS 34. Leiden: Brill.

Carter, Charles E. 2003. "Ideology and Archaeology in the Neo-Babylonian Period: Excavating Text and Tell." In *Judah and the Judeans in the Neo-Babylonian Period*, ed. O. Lipschits and J. Blenkinsopp, 301–22. Winona Lake IN: Eisenbrauns.

Carvalho, Corrine L. 2013. "Sex and the Single Prophet: Marital Status and Gender in Jeremiah and Ezekiel." In *Prophets Male and Female: Gender and Prophecy in the Hebrew Bible, the Eastern Mediterranean, and the Ancient Near East*, ed. J. Stökl and C. L. Carvalho, 237–67. AIIL 15. Atlanta: Society of Biblical Literature.

———. 2015. "A Serpent in the Nile: Egypt in the Book of Ezekiel." In *Concerning the Nations: Essays on the Oracles against the Nations in Isaiah, Jeremiah and Ezekiel*, ed. E. K. Holt, H. C. P. Kim, and A. Mein, 195–220. LHBOTS 612. London: Bloomsbury.

Carvalho, Corrine. *See also* Patton, Corrine.

Childs, Brevard S. 1979. *Introduction to the Old Testament as Scripture*. Philadelphia: Fortress.

Claassens, L. Juliana. 2013. "'Like a Woman in Labor': Gender, Postcolonial, Queer, and Trauma Perspectives on the Book of Jeremiah." In *Prophecy and Power: Jeremiah in Feminist and Postcolonial Perspective*, ed. C. M. Maier and C. J. Sharp, 117–32. LHBOTS 577. London: Bloomsbury.

Clements, Ronald E. 1996. "The Deuteronomic Law of Centralisation and the Catastrophe of 587 B.C.E." In *After the Exile: Essays in Honour of Rex Mason*, ed. J. Barton and D. J. Reimer. Macon GA: Mercer University Press.

Curtis, A. H. W. and T. Römer, eds. 1997. *The Book of Jeremiah and Its Reception/Le livre de Jérémie et sa reception.* BETL 128. Leuven: Leuven University Press.

Davidson, Steed Vernyl. 2011a. *Empire and Exile: Postcolonial Readings of the Book of Jeremiah.* LHBOTS 542. London: T&T Clark.

———. 2011b. "Chosen Marginality as Resistance in Jeremiah 40:1-6." In *Jeremiah (Dis)Placed: New Directions in Writing/Reading Jeremiah,* ed. A. R. P. Diamond and L. Stulman, 150–61. LHBOTS 529. New York/London: T&T Clark.

———. 2013. "'Exoticizing the Otter': The Curious Case of the Rechabites in Jeremiah 35." In *Prophecy and Power: Jeremiah in Feminist and Postcolonial Perspective,* ed. C. M. Maier and C. J. Sharp, 189–207. LHBOTS 577. London: Bloomsbury.

Davies, Philip R. 2000. "'Pen of Iron, Point of Diamond' (Jer 17:1): Prophecy as Writing." In *Writings and Speech in Israelite and Ancient Near Eastern Prophecy,* ed. E. Ben Zvi and M. H. Floyd, 65–81. SBLSymS 10. Atlanta: SBL.

DeJong, M. J. 2011. "Why Jeremiah Is Not Among the Prophets: An Analysis of the Terms נביא and נביאים in the Book of Jeremiah." *JSOT* 35:483–510.

Diamond, A. R. 1987. *The Confessions of Jeremiah in Context: Scenes of Prophetic Drama.* JSOTSup 45. Sheffield: JSOT.

Diamond, A. R. P., and Kathleen M. O'Connor. 1996. "Unfaithful Passions: Coding Women Coding Men in Jeremiah 2–3 (4:2)." *BibInt* 4:288–310.

Domeris, William R. 1999. "When Metaphor Becomes Myth: A Socio-Linguistic Reading of Jeremiah." In *Troubling Jeremiah,* ed. A. R. P. Diamond, K. M. O'Connor, and L. Stulman, 244–62. JSOTSup 260. Sheffield: Sheffield Academic.

———. 2007. "Jeremiah and the Poor." In *Uprooting and Planting: Essays on Jeremiah for Leslie Allen,* ed. J. Goldingay, 45–58. LHBOTS 459. London/New York: T&T Clark.

———. 2011. "The Land Claim of Jeremiah: Was Max Weber Right?" In *Jeremiah (Dis)Placed: New Directions in Writing/Reading Jeremiah,* ed. A. R. P. Diamond and L. Stulman, 136–49. LHBOTS 529. New York/London: T&T Clark.

Dubach, Manuel. 2009. *Trunkenheit im Alten Testament: Begrifflichkeit-Zeugnisse-Wertung.* BWANT 184. Stuttgart: Kohlhammer.

Dubbink, Joep. 2004. "Getting Closer to Jeremiah: The Word of Yhwh and the Literary-Theological Person of a Prophet." In *Reading the Book of Jeremiah: A Search for Coherence,* ed. M. Kessler, 25–39. Winona Lake IN: Eisenbrauns.

Duhm, Bernhard. 1901. *Das Buch Jeremia.* Tübingen: Mohr-Siebeck.

Erbele-Küster, Dorothea. 2006. "'Kann den ein Männliches gebären?' (Jer 30,6): Noch einmal *Gender Trouble* im Alten Testament." In *"Du hast mich aus meiner Mutter Leib gezogen": Beiträge zur Geburt im Alten Testament,* ed. D. Dieckmann and D. Erbele-Küster, 39–54. Biblisch-theologische Studien 75. Neukirchen-Vluyn: Neukirchener.

Faust, Avraham. 2012. *Judah in the Neo-Babylonian Period: The Archaeology of Desolation.* SBLABS 18. Atlanta: SBL.

Fischer, Georg. 2010. "Gebete als hermeneutischer Schlüssel zu biblischen Büchern—am Beispiel von Jeremia." In *Congress Volume Lujbljana 2007,* ed. A. Lemaire, 219–37. VTSup 133. Leiden/Boston: Brill.

Foreman, Benjamin A. 2011. *Animal Metaphors and the People of Israel in the Book of Jeremiah.* FRLANT 238. Göttingen: Vandenhoeck & Ruprecht.

Fretheim, Terence E. 2002. *Jeremiah.* SHBC. Macon GA: Smyth & Helwys.

———. 2004. "Is Anything Too Hard for God? (Jeremiah 32:27)." *CBQ* 66:231–36.

Friebel, Kelvin G. 1999. *Jeremiah's and Ezekiel's Sign-Acts: Rhetorical Nonverbal Communication.* JSOTSup 283. Sheffield: Sheffield Academic.

Friedman, Richard Elliott. 1987. *Who Wrote the Bible?* New York: Harper & Row.

Galvin, Garrett. 2011. *Egypt as a Place of Refuge.* FAT, 2nd series, 51. Tübingen: Mohr Siebeck.

Goldingay, John. 2007. "Jeremiah and the Superpower." In *Uprooting and Planting: Essays on Jeremiah for Leslie Allen,* ed. J. Goldingay, 59–77. LHBOTS 459. London/New York: T&T Clark.

Grabbe, Lester L. 2006. "'The Lying Pen of the Scribes'? Jeremiah and History." In *Essays on Ancient Israel in its Near Eastern Context: A Tribute to Nadav Na'aman*, ed. Y. Amit et al. 189–204. Winona Lake IN: Eisenbrauns.

Green, Barbara. 2012. "Cognitive Linguistics and the 'Idolatry-Is-Adultery' Metaphor of Jeremiah 2–3." In *Daughter Zion: Her Portrait, Her Response*, ed. M. J. Boda and C. J. Dempsey, 11–38. AIIL 13. Atlanta: SBL.

———. 2013. *Jeremiah and God's Plans of Well-Being*. Studies on Personalities of the Old Testament. Columbia: University of South Carolina Press.

Hadley, Judith M. 2001. "The Queen of Heaven—Who Is She?" In *Prophets and Daniel*, ed. A. Brenner, 30–51. Feminist Companion to the Bible, 2nd series, 8. Sheffield: Sheffield Academic.

Halvorson-Taylor, Martien A. 2012. "'There Is No One!': The Redaction of Exile in Jeremiah's Book of Consolation (31:15-22)." In *By the Irrigation Canals of Babylon: Approaches to the Study of Exile*, ed. J. J. Ahn and J. Middlemas, 107–22. LHBOTS 526. London: T&T Clark.

Harding, James E. 2013. "The Silent Goddess and the Gendering of Divine Speech in Jeremiah 44." In *Prophecy and Power: Jeremiah in Feminist and Postcolonial Perspective*, ed. C. M. Maier and C. J. Sharp, 208–23. LHBOTS 577. London: Bloomsbury.

Hare, Douglas R. A. 1985. "The Lives the Prophets (First Century A.D.)." In *The Old Testament Pseudepigrapha*, vol. 2, ed. J. H. Charlesworth, 379–400. ABRL. New York: Doubleday.

Hayes, Katherine M. 2006. "When None Repents, Earth Laments: The Chorus of Lament in Jeremiah and Joel." In *Seeking the Favor of God, Volume I: The Origins of Penitential Prayer in Second Temple Judaism*, ed. M. J. Boda, D. K. Falk, and R. A. Werline, 119–43. SBLEJL 21. Atlanta: SBL.

Henderson, Joseph M. 2007. "Jeremiah 2-10 as a Unified Literary Composition: Evidence of Dramatic Portrayal and Narrative Progression." In *Uprooting and Planting: Essays on Jeremiah for Leslie Allen*, ed. J. Goldingay, 116–52. LHBOTS 459. London/New York: T&T Clark.

Hill, John. 1999a. *Friend or Foe? The Figure of Babylon in the Book of Jeremiah MT*. BibInt 40. Leiden: Brill.

———. 1999b. "The Construction of Time in Jeremiah 25 (MT)." In *Troubling Jeremiah*, ed. A. R. P. Diamond, K. M. O'Connor, and L. Stulman, 146–59. JSOTSup 260. Sheffield: Sheffield Academic.

———. 2007. "The Book of Jeremiah (MT) and Its Early Second Temple Background." In *Uprooting and Planting: Essays on Jeremiah for Leslie Allen*, ed. J. Goldingay, 153–71. LHBOTS 459. London/New York: T&T Clark.

Holladay, Willliam L. 1976. "The Covenant with the Patriarchs Overturned: Jeremiah's Intention in 'Terror on Every Side' (Jer 20:1-6)." *JBL* 91:305–20.

———. 1986. *Jeremiah I: A Commentary on the Book of the Prophet Jeremiah, Chapters 1-25*. Hermeneia. Philadelphia: Fortress.

———. 1989. *Jeremiah II: A Commentary on the Book of the Prophet Jeremiah, Chapters 26-52*. Hermeneia. Philadelphia: Fortress.

Holt, Else K. 2007. "Word of Jeremiah—Word of God: Structures of Authority in the Book of Jeremiah." In *Uprooting and Planting: Essays on Jeremiah for Leslie Allen*, ed. J. Goldingay, 172–89. LHBOTS 459. London/New York: T&T Clark.

———. 2011. "King Nebuchadrezzar of Babylon, My Servant, and the Cup of Wrath: Jeremiah's Fantasies and the Hope of Vengeance." In *Jeremiah (Dis)Placed: New Directions in Writing/Reading Jeremiah*, ed. A. R. P. Diamond and L. Stulman, 209–18. LHBOTS 529. New York/London: T&T Clark.

———. 2013. "'The Stain of Your Guilt Is Still Before Me' (Jeremiah 2:22): (Feminist) Approaches to Jeremiah 2 and the Problem of Normativity." In *Prophecy and Power: Jeremiah in Feminist and Postcolonial Perspective*, ed. C. M. Maier and C. J. Sharp, 101–16. LHBOTS 577. London: Bloomsbury.

Huffmon, Herbert B. 1999. "The Impossible: God's Words of Assurance in Jer 31:35-37." In *On the Way to Nineveh: Studies in Honor of George M. Landes*, ed. S. L. Cook and S. C. Winter, 172–86. ASOR 4. Atlanta: Scholars Press.

———. 2012. "The Exclusivity of Divine Communication in Ancient Israel: False Prophecy in the Hebrew Bible and the Ancient Near East." In *Mediating Between Heaven and Earth: Communication with the Divine in the Ancient Near East*, ed. C. L. Crouch, J. Stökl, and A. E. Zernecke, 67–81. LHBOTS 566. London/New York: T&T Clark.

Hutton, Rodney R. 2009. "Are the Parents Still Eating Sour Grapes? Jeremiah's Use of the *māšal* in Contrast to Ezekiel." *CBQ* 71:275–85.

Janzen, J. Gerald. 1973. *Studies in the Text of Jeremiah*. HSM 6. Cambridge: HUP.

Jindo, Job Y. 2010. *Biblical Metaphor Reconsidered: A Cognitive Approach to Poetic Prophecy in Jeremiah 1-24*. HSM 64. Winona Lake IN: Eisenbrauns.

Job, John Brian. 2006. *Jeremiah's Kings: A Study of the Monarchy in Jeremiah*. SOTSMS. Aldershot/Burlington VT: Ashgate.

Johnston, Philip S. 2010. "'Now You See Me, Now You Don't!': Jeremiah and God." In *Prophecy and Prophets in Ancient Israel: Proceedings of the Oxford Old Testament Seminar*, ed. J. Day, 290–308. LHBOTS 531. New York/London: T&T Clark.

Joo, Samantha. 2006. *Provocation and Punishment: The Anger of God in the Book of Jeremiah and Deuteronomistic Theology*. BZAW 361. New York/Berlin: de Gruyter.

Kalmanofsky, Amy. 2008. *Terror All Around: The Rhetoric of Horror in the Book of Jeremiah*. LHBOTS 390. New York/London: T&T Clark.

———. 2011. "The Dangerous Sisters of Jeremiah and Ezekiel." *JBL* 130:299–312.

———. 2015. "'As She Did, Do to Her!': Jeremiah's OAN as Revenge Fantasies." In *Concerning the Nations: Essays on the Oracles against the Nations in Isaiah, Jeremiah and Ezekiel*, ed. E. K. Holt, H. C. P. Kim, and A. Mein, 109–27. LHBOTS 612. London: Bloomsbury.

Kelle, Brad E., Frank Ritchel Ames, and Jacob L. Wright, eds. 2014. *Warfare, Ritual, and Symbol in Biblical and Modern Contexts*. AIIL 18. Atlanta: SBL.

Kessler, Martin. 1997. "Jeremiah 25,1-29: Text and Context, A Synchronic Study." *ZAW* 109:44–70.

———. 1999. "The Function of Chapters 25 and 50-51 in the Book of Jeremiah." In *Troubling Jeremiah*, ed. A. R. P. Diamond, K. M. O'Connor and L. Stulman, 64–72. JSOTSup 260. Sheffield: Sheffield Academic.

———. 2003. *Battle of the Gods: The God of Israel Versus Marduk of Babylon: A Literary/Theological Interpretation of Jeremiah 50-51*. SSN 42. Assen: Van Gorcum.

Kugel, James L. 1981. *The Idea of Biblical Poetry: Parallelism and Its History*. New Haven: Yale University Press.

Laato, Antti. 1992. "Psalm 132 and the Development of the Jerusalemite/Israelite Royal Ideology." *CBQ* 54:49–66.

Lee, Nancy C. 2002. *The Singers of Lamentations: Cities under Siege, from Ur to Jerusalem to Sarajevo*. BibInt 60. Leiden/Boston/Köln: Brill.

———. 2007. "Prophet and Singer in the Fray." In *Uprooting and Planting: Essays on Jeremiah for Leslie Allen*, ed. J. Goldingay, 190–209. LHBOTS 459. London/New York: T&T Clark.

Leene, Hendrik. 1992. "Jeremiah 31,23-26 and the Redaction of the Book of Comfort." *ZAW* 104:349–64.

Lemos, T. M. 2006. "Shame and Mutilation of Enemies in the Hebrew Bible." *JBL* 125:225–41.

Lipschits, Oded. 2003. "Demographic Changes in Judah between the Seventh and the Fifth Centuries BCE." In *Judah and the Judeans in the Neo-Babylonian Period*, ed. O. Lipschits and J. Blenkinsopp, 323–76. Winona Lake IN: Eisenbrauns.

Low, Katherine. 2011. "Implications Surrounding Girding the Loins in Light of Gender, Body, and Power." *JSOT* 36:3–30.

Lundberg, Marilyn J. 2007. "The *Mis-Pi* Rituals and Incantations and Jeremiah 10:1-16." In *Uprooting and Planting: Essays on Jeremiah for Leslie Allen*, ed. J. Goldingay, 210–27. LHBOTS 459. London/New York: T&T Clark.

Lundbom, Jack R. 1995. "Jeremiah 15,15-21 and the Call of Jeremiah." *SJOT* 9:143–55.

———. 1999. *Jeremiah 1-20: A New Translation with Introduction and Commentary*. AB 21a. New York: Doubleday.

Macwilliam, Stuart. 2013. "The Prophet and His Patsy: Gender Performativity in Jeremiah." In *Prophecy and Power: Jeremiah in Feminist and Postcolonial Perspective*, ed. C. M. Maier and C. J. Sharp, 173–88. LHBOTS 577. London: Bloomsbury.

Maier, Christl M. 2013. "God's Cruelty and Jeremiah's Treason: Jeremiah 21:1-10 in Postcolonial Perspective." In *Prophecy and Power: Jeremiah in Feminist and Postcolonial Perspective*, ed. C. M. Maier and C. J. Sharp, 133–49. LHBOTS 577. London: Bloomsbury.

Maier, Christl, and Ernst Michael Dörrfuß. 1999. "'Um mit ihnen zu sitzen, zu essen und zu trinken': Am 6,7; Jer 16,5 und die Bedeutung vom *marze^{a}ḥ*." *ZAW* 111:45–57.

Mayer, Walter. 2002. "Die Zerstörung des Jerusalemer Tempels 587 v. Chr. im Kontext der Praxis von Heiligtumszerstörungen im antiken Vorderen Orient." In *Zerstörungen des Jerusalemer Tempels: Geschehen-Wahrnehmung-Bewältigung*, ed. J. Hahn, 1–22. WUNT 147. Tübingen: Mohr Siebeck.

McKane, William. 1980. "Poison, Trial by Ordeal and the Cup of Wrath." *VT* 30:474–92.

———. 1986 and 1996. *A Critical and Exegetical Commentary on Jeremiah*. 2 vols. ICC. Edinburgh: T&T Clark

———. 1994. "Worship of the Queen of Heaven (Jer 44)." In *Wer ist wie du, Herr, unter den Göttern: Studien zur Theologie und Religionsgeschichte Israels für Otto Kaiser zum 70. Geburtstag*, ed. I. Kottsieper and O. Kaiser, 318–24. Göttingen: Vandenhoeck & Ruprecht.

Mein, Andrew. 2007. "Profitable and Unprofitable Shepherds: Economic and Theological Perspectives on Ezekiel 34." *JSOT* 31:493–504.

Miller, Patrick D. 2001. "The Book of Jeremiah: Introduction, Commentary, and Reflections." In *The New Interpreter's Bible*, vol. 6, ed. L. E. Keck et al., 553–926. Nashville: Abingdon.

Mowinckel, Sigmund. 1914. *Zur Komposition des Buches Jeremia*. Kristiania: J. Dybwad.

Murphy, Kelly J. 2014. "Jeremiah." In *Fortress Commentary on the Bible: The Old Testament and Apocrypha*, ed. G. A. Yee, H. R. Page, and M. J. M. Coomber, 725–66. Minneapolis: Fortress.

Najafizadeh, Mehrangiz. 2013. "Ethnic Conflict and Forced Displacement: Narratives of Azeri IDP and Refugee Women from the Nagorno-Karabakh War." *Journal of International Women's Studies* 14:161–83.

Niessen, Christina. 2004. "Schuld, Strafe und Geschlecht: Die Auswirkungen der Genderkonstruktionen auf Schuldzuweisungen und Gerichtsankündigungen in Jer 23, 9-32 und Jer 13, 20-27." *BZ* 48:86–96.

Nissinen, Martti. 1998. *Homoeroticism in the Biblical World: A Historical Perspective.* Minneapolis: Fortress.

———. 2003. "Fear Not: A Study on an Ancient Near Eastern Phrase." In *The Changing Face of Form Criticism for the Twenty-First Century*, ed. M. A. Sweeney and E. Ben Zvi, 122–61. Grand Rapids MI/Cambridge UK: Eerdmans.

———. 2010a. "Biblical Prophecy from a Near Eastern Perspective: The Cases of Kingship and Divine Possession." In *Congress Volume Lujbljana 2007*, ed. A. Lemaire, 441–68. VTSup 133. Leiden/Boston: Brill.

———. 2010b. "Comparing Prophetic Sources: Principles and a Test Case." In *Prophecy and Prophets in Ancient Israel: Proceedings of the Oxford Old Testament Seminar*, ed. J. Day, 3–24. LHBOTS 531. New York/London: T&T Clark.

O'Connor, Kathleen M. 1988. *The Confessions of Jeremiah: Their Interpretation and Role in Chapters 1-25.* SBLDS 94. Atlanta: Scholars.

———. 1999. "The Tears of God and Divine Character in Jeremiah 2-9." In *Troubling Jeremiah*, ed. A. R. P. Diamond, K. M. O'Connor and L. Stulman, 387–401. JSOTSup 260. Sheffield: Sheffield Academic.

———. 2006. "Jeremiah's Two Visions of the Future." In *Utopia and Dystopia in Prophetic Literature*, ed. E. Ben Zvi, 86–104. Publications of the Finnish Exegetical Society 92. Göttingen: Vandenhoeck & Ruprecht.

———. 2007. "The Book of Jeremiah: Reconstructing Community after Disaster." In *Character Ethics and the Old Testament: Moral Dimensions of Scripture*, ed. M. Daniel Carroll R. and J. E. Lapsley, 81–92. Louisville/London: Westminster John Knox.

———. 2011a. "Terror All Around: Confusion as Meaning Making." In *Jeremiah (Dis)Placed: New Directions in Writing/Reading Jeremiah*, ed. A. R. P. Diamond and L. Stulman, 67–79. LHBOTS 529. New York/London: T&T Clark.

———. 2011b. *Jeremiah: Pain and Promise*. Minneapolis: Fortress.

Osuji, Anthony Chinedu. 2010. *Where Is the Truth? Narrative Exegesis and the Question of True and False Prophecy in Jer 26-29 (MT)*. BETL 214. Leuven/Paris/Walpole MA: Peeters.

Overholt, Thomas W. 1979. "Jeremiah 2 and the Problem of 'Audience Reaction.'" *CBQ* 41:262–73.

———. 1989. *Channels of Prophecy: The Social Dynamics of Prophetic Activity*. Minneapolis: Fortress.

Parker, Simon B. 2003. "Graves, Caves and Refugees: An Essay in Microhistory." *JSOT* 27:259–88.

Parker, Tom. 2007. "Ebed-Melech as Exemplar." In *Uprooting and Planting: Essays on Jeremiah for Leslie Allen*, ed. J. Goldingay, 253–59. LHBOTS 459. London/New York: T&T Clark.

Patton, Corrine. 1995. "Psalm 132: A Methodological Inquiry." *CBQ* 57:643–54.

———. 1996. "'I Myself Gave Them Laws that Were Not Good': Ezekiel 20 and the Exodus Taditions." *JSOT* 69:73–90.

———. 1999. "Pan-Deuteronomism and the Book of Ezekiel." In *Those Elusive Deuteronomists: The Phenomenon of Pan-Deuteronomism*, ed. L. S. Schearing and S. L. McKenzie, 200–215. JSOTSup 268. Sheffield: Sheffield Academic

———. 2004. "Layers of Meaning: Priesthood in Jeremiah MT." In *The Priests in the Prophets: The Portrayal of Priests, Prophets and Other Religious Specialists in the Latter Prophets*, ed. L. L. Grabbe and A. O. Bellis, 149–76. JSOTSup 408. London/New York: T&T Clark.

Patton, Corrine. *See also* Carvalho, Corrine L.

Pearce, Laurie E. 2011. "'Judean': A Special Status in Neo-Babylonian and Achaemenid Babylonia?" In *Judah and the Judeans in the Achaemenid Period: Negotiating Identity in an International Context*, ed. O. Lipschits, G. N. Knoppers, and M. Oeming, 267–77. Winona Lake IN: Eisenbrauns.

di Pede, Elena. 2006. "Jéremie et les rois de Juda, Sédécias et Joaqim." *VT* 56:452–69.

Peels, Eric. 2000. "God's Throne in Elam: The Historical Background and Literary Context of Jeremiah 49:34-39." In *Past, Present, Future: The Deuteronomistic History and the Prophets*, ed. J. C. de Moor and H F. van Rooy, 216–29. OtSt 44. Leiden/Boston/Köln: Brill.

———. 2009. "The Assassination of Gedaliah (Jer. 40:7-41:18)." In *Exile and Suffering: A Selection of Papers Read at the 50th Anniversary Meeting of the Old Testament Society of South Africa OTWSA/OTSSA Pretoria August 2007*, ed. B. Becking and D. Human, 83–103. OtSt 50. Leiden/Boston: Brill.

Peels, H. G. L. 2007. "'You Shall Certainly Drink!': The Place and Significance of the Oracles Against the Nations in the Book of Jeremiah." *EuroJTh* 16:81–91.

Perdue, Leo G. 2007. "Baruch among the Sages." In *Uprooting and Planting: Essays on Jeremiah for Leslie Allen*, ed. J. Goldingay, 260–90. LHBOTS 459. London/New York: T&T Clark.

Person, Raymond F., Jr. 1999. "A Rolling Corpus and Oral Tradition: A Not-So-Literate Solution to a Highly Literate Problem." In *Troubling Jeremiah*, ed. A. R. P. Diamond, K. M. O'Connor, and L. Stulman, 263–71. JSOTSup 260. Sheffield: Sheffield Academic.

Pham, Xuan Huong Thi. 1999. *Mourning in the Ancient Near East and the Hebrew Bible*. JSOTSup 302. Sheffield: Sheffield Academic.

Pilarski, Ahida Calerón. 2014. "A Study of the References to בת־עמי in Jeremiah 8:18-9:2(3): A Gendered Lamentation." In *Why? . . . How Long? Studies on Voice(s) of Lamentation Rooted in Biblical Hebrew Poetry*, ed. L. S. Flesher, C. J. Dempsey and M. J. Boda, 20–35. LHBOTS 552. London/New York: Bloomsbury/T&T Clark.

Plant, R. J. R. 2008. *Good Figs, Bad Figs: Judicial Differentiation in the Book of Jeremiah*. LHBOTS 483. New York/London: T&T Clark.

Pohlmann, Karl-Friedrich. 2002. "Religion in der Krise-Krise einer Religion: Die Zerstörung des Jerusalemer Tempels 587 v. Chr." In *Zerstörungen des Jerusalemer Tempels: Geschehen-Wahrnehmung-Bewältigung*, ed. J. Hahn, 40–60. WUNT 147. Tübingen: Mohr Siebeck.

Pyper, Hugh S. 2015. "Postcolonialism and Propaganda in Jeremiah's Oracles against the Nations." In *Concerning the Nations: Essays on the Oracles against the Nations in Isaiah, Jeremiah and Ezekiel*, ed. E. K. Holt, H. C. P. Kim, and A. Mein, 145–57. LHBOTS 612. London: Bloomsbury.

Raz, Yosefa. 2013. "Jeremiah 'Before the Womb': On Fathers, Sons, and the Telos of Redaction in Jeremiah 1." In *Prophecy and Power: Jeremiah in Feminist and Postcolonial Perspective*, ed. C. M. Maier and C. J. Sharp, 86–100. LHBOTS 577. London: Bloomsbury.

Rofé, Alexander. 1991. "The Name YHWH ṢĔBĀ'ÔT and the Shorter Recension of Jeremiah." In *Prophetie und geschichtliche Wirklichkeit im alten Israel: Festschrift für Siegfried Herrmann zum 65. Geburtstag*, ed. R. Liwak and S. Wagner, 307–16. Stuttgart/Berlin/Köln: Kohlhammer.

Rom-Shiloni, Dalit. 2013. *Exclusive Inclusivity: Identity Conflicts between the Exiles and the People Who Remained (6th-5th Centuries BCE)*. LHBOTS 543. London/New York: T&T Clark.

Römer, Thomas. 2000. "Is There a Deuteronomistic Redaction in the Book of Jeremiah?" In *Israel Constructs Its History: Deuteronomistic Historiography in Recent Research*, ed. A. de Pury, T. Römer, and J.-D. Macchi, 399–421. JSOTSup 306. Sheffield: Sheffield Academic.

———. 2009. "The Formation of the Book of Jeremiah as a Supplement to the So-Called Deuteronomistic History." In *The Production of Prophecy: Constructing Prophecy and Prophets in Yehud*, ed. D. V. Edelman and E. Ben Zvi, 168–83. Bible World. London/Oakville: Equinox.

Roncace, Mark. 2005. *Jeremiah, Zedekiah, and the Fall of Jerusalem*. LHBOTS 423. New York/London: T&T Clark.

Scalise, Pamela. J. 2007. "Baruch as First Reader: Baruch's Lament in the Structure of the Book of Jeremiah." In *Uprooting and Planting: Essays on Jeremiah for Leslie Allen*, ed. J. Goldingay, 291–307. LHBOTS 459. London/New York: T&T Clark.

Schaper, Joachim. 2005. "Exilic and Post-Exilic Prophecy and the Orality/Literacy Problem." *VT* 55:324–42.

Seitz, Christopher R. 1989a. *Theology in Conflict: Reactions to the Exile in the Book of Jeremiah.* BZAW 176. Berlin/New York: de Gruyter.

———. 1989b. "The Prophet Moses and the Canonical Shape of Jeremiah." *ZAW* 101:3–27.

Sharp, Carolyn. 2003. *Prophecy and Ideology in Jeremiah: Struggles for Authority in Deutero-Jeremianic Prose.* OTS. London/New York: T&T Clark.

———. 2015. "Embodying Moab: The Figuring of Moab in Jeremiah 48 as Reinscription of the Judean Body." In *Concerning the Nations: Essays on the Oracles against the Nations in Isaiah, Jeremiah and Ezekiel,* ed. E. K. Holt, H. C. P. Kim, and A. Mein, 95–108. LHBOTS 612. London: Bloomsbury.

Shields, Mary. 1995. "Circumcision of the Prostitute: Gender, Sexuality, and the Call to Repentance in Jeremiah 3:1-4:4." *BibInt* 3:61–74.

Smelick, Klaas A. D. 2004. "An Approach to the Book of Jeremiah." In *Reading the Book of Jeremiah: A Search for Coherence,* ed. M. Kessler, 1–11. Winona Lake IN: Eisenbrauns.

Smith, Mark S. 2004. *The Memoirs of God: History, Memory, and the Experience of the Divine in Ancient Israel.* Minneapolis: Fortress.

Stavrakopoulou, Francesca. 2010. *Land of Our Fathers: The Roles of Ancestor Veneration in Biblical Land Claims.* LHBOTS 473. London/New York: T&T Clark.

Stipp, Hermann-Josef. 1996. "Zedekiah in the Book of Jeremiah: On the Formation of a Biblical Character." *CBQ* 58:627–48.

———. 2010a. "Das judäische und das babylonische Jeremiabuch." In *Congress Volume Lujbljana 2007,* ed. A. Lemaire, 239–64. VTSup 133. Leiden/Boston: Brill.

———. 2010b. "The Concept of the Empty Land in Jeremiah 37-43." In *The Concept of Exile in Ancient Israel and Its Historical Contexts,* ed. E. Ben Zvi and C. Levin, 103–54. BZAW 404. Berlin/New York: de Gruyter.

Stone, Ken. 2007. "'You Seduced Me, You Overpowered Me, and You Prevailed': Religious Experience and Homoerotic Sadomasochism in Jeremiah." In *Patriarchs, Prophets and Other Villains*, ed. L. Isherwood, 101–109. Gender, Theology and Spirituality 3. London: Equinox.

Strawn, Brent A. 2005. "Jeremiah's In/Effective Plea: Another Look at נער in Jeremiah I 6." *VT* 55:366–77.

Stulman, Louis. 1986. *The Prose Sermons of the Book of Jeremiah: A Redescription of the Correspondences with the Deuteronomistic Literature in the Light of Recent Text-Critical Research.* SBLDS 83. Atlanta: Scholars.

———. 2004a. "Jeremiah as a Polyphonic Response to Suffering." In *Inspired Speech: Prophecy in the Ancient Near East. Essays in Honour of Herbert B. Huffmon*, ed. J. Kaltner and L. Stulman, 302–18. JSOTSup 378. New York/London: T&T Clark.

———. 2004b. "Jeremiah the Prophet: Astride Two Worlds." In *Reading the Book of Jeremiah: A Search for Coherence*, ed. M. Kessler, 41–56. Winona Lake IN: Eisenbrauns.

———. 2005. *Jeremiah*. AOTC. Nashville: Abingdon.

Thelle, Rannfrid I. 2009. "Jeremiah MT: Reflections of a Discourse on Prophecy in the Persian Period." In *The Production of Prophecy: Constructing Prophecy and Prophets in Yehud*, ed. D. V. Edelman and E. Ben Zvi, 184–207. Bible World. Oakville: Equinox.

———. 2015. "Babylon as Judah's *Doppelgänger*: The Identity of Opposites in the Book of Jeremiah (MT)." In *Concerning the Nations: Essays on the Oracles against the Nations in Isaiah, Jeremiah and Ezekiel*, ed. E. K. Holt, H. C. P. Kim, and A. Mein, 77–94. LHBOTS 612. London: Bloomsbury.

Thiel, Winfried. 1981. *Das deuteronomistische Redaktion von Jeremia 26-45.* WMANT 52. Neukirchen-Vluyn: Neukirchener Verlag.

van der Toorn, Karel. 1988a. "Echoes of Judaean Necromancy in Isaiah 28, 7-22." *ZAW* 100:199–217.

———. 1988b. "Ordeal Procedures in the Psalms and the Passover Meal." *VT* 38:427–45.

———. 2004. "From the Mouth of the Prophet: The Literary Fixation of Jeremiah's Prophecies in the Context of the Ancient Near East." In *Inspired Speech: Prophecy in the Ancient Near East. Essays in Honour of Herbert B. Huffmon*, ed. J. Kaltner and L. Stulman, 191–202. JSOTSup 378. New York/London: T&T Clark.

Tov, Emanuel. 1981. "Some Aspects of the Textual and Literary History of the Book of Jeremiah." In *Le livre de Jérémie: Le prophète et son milieu, les oracles et leur transmission*, ed. P.-M. Bogaert, 145–67. BETL 54. Leuven: Peeters/Leuven University Press.

Uehlinger, Christoph. 2015. "Virtual Vision vs. Actual Show: Strategies of Visualization in the Book of Ezekiel." *WO* 45:62–84.

Vanderhooft, David. 2003. "Babylonian Strategies of Imperial Control in the West: Royal Practice and Rhetoric." In *Judah and the Judeans in the Neo-Babylonian Period*, ed. O. Lipschits and J. Blenkinsopp, 235–62. Winona Lake IN: Eisenbrauns.

Varughese, Alex. 2004. "The Royal Family in the Jeremiah Tradition." In *Inspired Speech: Prophecy in the Ancient Near East. Essays in Honour of Herbert B. Huffmon*, ed. J. Kaltner and L. Stulman, 319–28. JSOTSup 378. New York/London: T&T Clark.

Viviano, Pauline. 2002. "Characterizing Jeremiah." *WW* 22:361–68.

Watson, Wilfred G. E. 1981. "Symmetry of Stanza in Jeremiah 2,2b-3." *JSOT* 19:107–10.

Westbrook, Raymond. 2007. "The Trial of Jeremiah." In *Reading the Law: Studies in Honour of Gordon J. Wenham*, ed. J. G. McConville and K. Möller, 95–107. LHBOTS 461. New York/London: T&T Clark.

Wilson, Robert R. 1999. "Poetry and Prose in the Book of Jeremiah." In *Ki Baruch Hu: Ancient Near Eastern, Biblical, and Judaic Studies in Honor of Baruch A. Levine*, ed. R. Chazan, W. W. Hallo and L. H. Schiffman, 413–27. Winona Lake IN: Eisenbrauns.

———. 2012a. "Forced Migration and the Formation of Prophetic Literature." In *By the Irrigation Canals of Babylon: Approaches to the Study of Exile*, ed. J. J. Ahn and J. Middlemas, 125–38. LHBOTS 526. London: T&T Clark.

———. 2012b. "The Persian Period and the Shaping of Prophetic Literature." In *Focusing Biblical Studies: The Crucial Nature of the Persian and Hellenistic Periods; Essays in Honor of Douglas A. Knight*, ed. J. L. Berquist and A. Hunt, 107–20. LHBOTS 544. New York/London: T&T Clark.

Yates, Gary E. 2005. "Narrative Parallelism and the 'Jehoiakim Frame': A Reading Strategy for Jeremiah 26-45." *JETS* 48:263–81.

———. 2006. "New Exodus and No Exodus in Jeremiah 26-45: Promise and Warning to the Exiles in Babylon." *TynBul* 57:1–22.

———. 2010. "Jeremiah's Message of Judgment and Hope for God's Unfaithful 'Wife.'" *BSac* 167:144–65.

Zorn, Jeffrey R. 2003. "Tell en-Naṣbeh and the Problem of the Material Culture of the Sixth Century." In *Judah and the Judeans in the Neo-Babylonian Period*, ed. O. Lipschits and J. Blenkinsopp, 413–47. Winona Lake IN: Eisenbrauns.

Zvi, Ehud Ben. 2003. "The Prophetic Book: A Key Form of Prophetic Literature." In *The Changing Face of Form Criticism for the Twenty-First Century*, ed. M. A. Sweeney and E. Ben Zvi, 276–97. Grand Rapids/Cambridge UK: Eerdmans.

———. 2009a. "Towards an Integrative Study of the Production of Authoritative Books in Ancient Israel." In *The Production of Prophecy: Constructing Prophecy and Prophets in Yehud*, ed. D. V. Edelman and E. Ben Zvi, 15–28. Bible World. London/Oakville: Equinox.

———. 2009b. "The Concept of Prophetic Books and Its Historical Setting." In *The Production of Prophecy: Constructing Prophecy and Prophets in Yehud*, ed. D. V. Edelman and E. Ben Zvi, 73–95. Bible World. London/Oakville: Equinox.

———. 2010. "The Voice and Role of Counterfactual Memory in the Construction of Exile and Return: Considering Jeremiah 40:7-12." In *The Concept of Exile in Ancient Israel and Its Historical Contexts*, ed. E. Ben Zvi and C. Levin, 169–88. BZAW 404. Berlin/New York: de Gruyter.

Other available titles from

Reading the Old Testament

Reading Deuteronomy
A Literary and Theological Commentary
Stephen L. Cook

A lost treasure for large segments of the modern world, the book of Deuteronomy powerfully repays contemporary readers' attention. It represents Scripture pulsing with immediacy, offering gripping discourses that yank readers out of the doldrums and back to Mount Horeb and an encounter with divine Word issuing forth from blazing fire. God's presence and Word in Deuteronomy stir deep longing for God and move readers to a place of intimacy with divine otherness, holism, and will for person-centered community. The consistently theological interpretation reveals the centrality of Deuteronomy for faith and powerfully counters critical accusations about violence, intolerance, and polytheism in the book.

978-1-57312-757-8 286 pages/pb **$32.00**

Reading Joshua
A Historical-Critical/Archaeological Commentary
John C. H. Laughlin

Using the best of current historical-critical studies by mainstream biblical scholars, and the most recent archaeological discoveries and theorizing, Laughlin questions both the historicity of the stories presented in the book as well as the basic theological ideology presented through these stories: namely that Yahweh ordered the indiscriminate butchery of the Canaanites.

978-1-57312-836-0 274 pages/pb **$32.00**

To order call **1-800-747-3016** or visit **www.helwys.com**

Reading Judges
A Literary and Theological Commentary

Mark E. Biddle

Reading the Old Testament book of Judges presents a number of significant challenges related to social contexts, historical settings, and literary characteristics. Acknowledging and examining these difficulties provides a point of entry into the world of Judges and promises to enrich the reading experience.

978-1-57312-631-1 240 pages/pb **$32.00**

Reading Samuel
A Literary and Theological Commentary

Johanna W. H. van Wijk-Bos

Interpreted masterfully by pre-eminent Old Testament scholar Johanna W. H. van Wijk-Bos, the story of Samuel touches on a vast array of subjects that comprise the rich fabric of human life. The reader gains an inside look at royal intrigue, military campaigns, occult practices and the significance of religious objects of veneration.

978-1-57312-607-6 256 pages/pb **$32.00**

Reading Job
A Literary and Theological Commentary

James L. Crenshaw

At issue in the Book of Job is a question with which most all of us struggle at some point in life, "Why do bad things happen to good people?" James Crenshaw has devoted his life to studying the disturbing matter of theodicy—divine justice—that troubles many people of faith.

978-1-57312-574-1 192 pages/pb **$32.00**

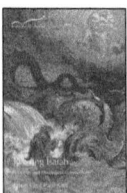

Reading Isaiah
A Literary and Theological Commentary

Hyun Chul Paul Kim

In this commentary, Hyun Chul Paul Kim brings together innovative interpretive approaches and the proposals of various scholars to interpret the book of Isaiah in light of the ancient literature/culture, intertextual allusions/correlations, and socio-historical contexts of the empires. While closely exegeting key issues of each chapter, the commentary also explores interpretive relevance and significance between ancient texts and the modern world.

978-1-57312-925-1 352 pages/pb **$34.00**

To order call **1-800-747-3016** or visit **www.helwys.com**

Reading Ezekiel
A Literary and Theological Commentary
Marvin A. Sweeney

In this volume, biblical scholar Marvin A. Sweeney considers one of the most interesting and compelling books of the Hebrew Bible. Ezekiel is simultaneously one of the Bible's most difficult and perplexing books as it presents the visions and oracles of Ezekiel, a Judean priest and prophet exiled to Babylonia in the sixth century BCE.   978-1-57312-658-8 264 pages/pb **$32.00**

Reading Hosea–Micah
A Literary and Theological Commentary
Terence E. Fretheim

In this volume, Terence E. Fretheim explores themes of indictment, judgment, and salvation in Hosea–Micah. The indictment against the people of God especially involves issues of idolatry, as well as abuse of the poor and needy.   978-1-57312-687-8 224 pages/pb **$32.00**

Reading Nahum–Malachi
A Literary and Theological Commentary
Steven Tuell

Nahum–Malachi, the last six books of the Christian Old Testament, span the period from the end of the Assyrian empire in the 7th century BCE to the fall of the Neo-Babylonian Empire and the emergence of Persia in the 5th century BCE. But these books also have a collective identity as the latter half of the Book of the Twelve—the ancient Jewish and Christian designation for the so-called "minor" prophets. This commentary maintains a balance between reading each of these six books in its own historical and social setting and considering the interrelationships and canonical functions of these books within the Book of the Twelve as a whole.

978-1-57312-848-3 304 pages/pb **$33.00**

To order call **1-800-747-3016** or visit **www.helwys.com**

THE SMYTH & HELWYS BIBLE COMMENTARY

Far too many Bible commentaries fall short of bridging the gap between insights of biblical scholars and the needs of students of Scripture. In an unprecedented way, the *Smyth & Helwys Bible Commentary* is visually stimulating, user-friendly, and written to make available quality Bible study in an accessible format.

Using a revolutionary format, the *Smyth & Helwys Bible Commentary* offers a wealth of visual information. Each volume includes artwork from across the centuries, photography, archaeological artifacts, maps, and much more.

View additional sample pages and find out more about hyperlinks online.

www.helwys.com/commentary

THIS SERIES WILL MAKE AN ENORMOUS IMPACT ON THE LIFE AND FAITH OF THE CHURCH.

Walter Brueggemann, author of *1 & 2 Kings*

The *Smyth & Helwys Bible Commentary* includes "commentary" and "connections" information within each chapter. The "commentary" provides an analysis of the passage, consisting of interpretation of the passage, its language, history, and literary form, and discussion of pertinent theological issues. "Connections" offers application of analytical insight for (1) teaching of the passages, including suggested approaches for instruction and additional resources for further study, and (2) preaching based on the passage, including suggested approaches, themes, and resources. Most Bible commentaries are limited to providing only "commentary," without the helpful "connections" included in this series.

Additional Features

- CD-ROM with powerful search & research tools
- Unique hyperlink format offers additional information
- Includes maps, photographs, and other illustrations relevant for understanding the context or significance of the text
- Quality craftsmanship in printing and binding
- Distinctive sidebars/special interest boxes printed in color
- Footnotes that offer full documentation

OLD TESTAMENT
GENERAL EDITOR

Samuel E. Balentine
Union Presbyterian Seminary
Richmond, Virginia

PROJECT EDITOR

R. Scott Nash
Mercer University
Macon, Georgia

NEW TESTAMENT
GENERAL EDITOR

R. Alan Culpepper
McAfee School of Theology
Mercer University
Atlanta, Georgia

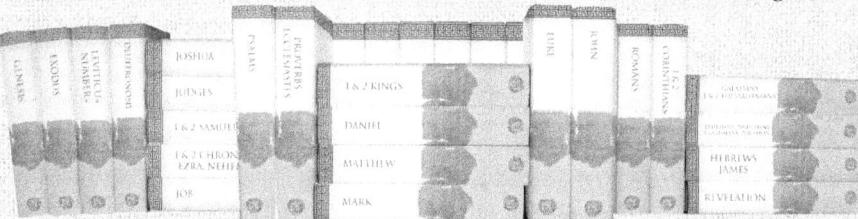

Choose our **Standing Order Plan** and receive a **25% discount** on every volume. To sign up or for more information call **800-747-3016** or visit **www.helwys.com/commentary**

www.ingramcontent.com/pod-product-compliance
Lightning Source LLC
Chambersburg PA
CBHW061941220426
43662CB00012B/1986